# THE INSURGENT ARCHIPELAGO

JOHN MACKINLAY

# The Insurgent Archipelago

*From Mao to bin Laden*

HURST AND COMPANY, LONDON

First published in the United Kingdom in 2009 by
C. Hurst & Co. (Publishers) Ltd.,
41 Great Russell Street, London, WC1B 3PL
© John Mackinlay 2009
All rights reserved
Printed in India

A Cataloguing-in-Publication data record for this book
is available from the British Library.

ISBN
978-1-84904-012-9 *hardback*
978-1-84904-013-6 *paperback*

www.hurstpub.co.uk

# CONTENTS

*Acknowledgements*                                                    vii

Introduction                                                            1

## PART I MAOISM

Introduction                                                            9
1. Mao the Prototype                                                   15
2. Evolution                                                           27
3. Gaps in Our Knowledge                                               43
4. The Chronology of Neglect                                           61

## PART II POST-MAOISM

Introduction                                                           77
5. Multiple Populations and Mass Communications                        81
6. The Migration Factor                                                99
7. The Virtual Battlefield                                            123
8. Post-Maoism                                                        143

## PART III RESPONDING TO POST-MAOISM

Introduction                                                          163
 9. The Expeditionary Approach                                        171
10. The Domestic Approach                                             197
11. The Insurgent Archipelago                                         221

*Notes*                                                               237
*Bibliography*                                                        267
*Index*                                                               279

# ACKNOWLEDGEMENTS

Very many colleagues have helped me to produce this book. I especially thank my publisher Michael Dwyer who remained undaunted by several elastic deadlines, and the British Academy for their generous research grant. I also wish to thank my post-graduate assistants from the Department of War Studies at Kings College London: Joshua Huminski, Will Hartley, Eric Randolph, Rudra Chaudhuri, Ryan Evans and Adam Stahl. Their energetic efforts kept the project moving ahead and individually they were essential to the detailed research and production and final editing of the book.

I also need to thank many individuals whose formal interviews, informal conversations and correspondence provided the ideas and much of the substance of the book. They range from officers and soldiers in the battalions I encountered in the field, Generals commanding international forces, senior civil servants in Whitehall, British domiciled Muslims and officials from several non government organisations. Some are named and some wished to remain anonymous. I wish to thank them all for the precious time that they gave me, for their hospitality in some wild places and for their inspiring ideas.

# INTRODUCTION

I joined 6th Gurkha Rifles in November 1964. To a newcomer they were a dauntingly close community, just a few British officers and several hundred men who had been through two campaigns together. They had enjoyed a tremendous continuity of experience, and no Gurkha soldier ever wanted to leave before he was pensionable. On parade or mounting the quarter guard in their long, starched shorts and dark puttees every rifleman wore the campaign ribbons for the Malaya Emergency and North Borneo, signifying years of active service.

In 1964 our regiment was quintessentially a counter-insurgent force of the post-colonial era. Gurkha battalions seldom left the Far Eastern Land Forces Command and over a period of a decade they learned their tactics and survival skills in the forests of Southeast Asia. By the 1960s the practicalities of countering insurgency had infused every regiment. The Gurkha way of doing things ran through our battalions from top to bottom, through each rifle company and the logistic support platoons, it was imbued in the rig and colour of our vehicles, even the food we ate and the time it took to cook it. Counter-insurgency cropped up everywhere, in every discussion, in every set of orders and in the personality of each unit.

Although the campaigns in Malaya and North Borneo were different, the Maoist adversary in both cases followed a tough, labour-intensive approach towards the organisation and conduct of their insurgency. Their tactics required them to move over long distances through the rainforest to meet and subvert their target populations. Our response reflected the Maoist imperative: we understood the importance of gaining popular support and securing a foothold in sympathetic communities. In Malaysia, we saw ourselves restoring a

1

monopoly of violence into the hands of the government and during the long tropical evenings we theorised about the phase we had reached in the Maoist interpretation of people's war. Our tactics also reflected a political process: the campaign was politically led, and each week our commanding officer flew in to district headquarters to attend the Security Executive Committee meeting, chaired by our Malaysian district officer, his civil administrators and the local police. Their efforts were essentially political and our job was to win and then maintain a level of security that allowed them to restore their writ and win the support of the population.

Twenty years later I left the army and became a research academic. By the early 1990s the UN Security Council had begun to deploy international forces in quick succession to complex emergencies in Asia and sub-Saharan Africa. For most NATO and former Warsaw Pact armies, peacekeeping now took priority and learning the techniques of peace support dominated their training programmes. During that chaotic decade my research took me to many international operations where my status as a UN researcher and my contacts with former colleagues in the British Army, who were by now commanding their own battalions and brigades, gave me exceptional access.

In 1996, after the Dayton Agreement had been signed, 60,000 NATO troops were engaged on what was described as a peace support mission to guarantee the political settlement in former Yugoslavia. By this time many British and US junior commanders had had time to reflect on the Bosnian operation and in particular on their own part in the restoration process. Although in those days I did not see myself as being on a journey through the evolutionary stages of insurgency, I was amazed to hear from the British battalions a well as the divisional staff, a conviction that what they were doing was in effect restoring a monopoly of violence, and that the techniques that had been most successful in this respect were the same counter-insurgent procedures that had been used in the past but which had officially been set aside in favour of peacekeeping.

Up to 1996 very few doctrine writers or conflict analysts had convincingly linked the counter-insurgent experience of Southeast Asia with Northern Ireland and the peace support operations in the Balkans and sub-Saharan Africa. So it was extraordinary to now be faced with this connection, which was a spontaneous reaction made with the irresistible conviction of soldiers at the forward edge of the operation. Their casual assertions seemed to challenge fashionable thinking that these operations had evolved from the foundations of peacekeeping. If these professionals on the ground were right, and their job was indeed to restore a monopoly of violence, then this raised some interesting questions. Were these so-called peace support operations in fact better explained by an evolutionary understanding of insurgency? Was it right to go on thinking of insurgency as irrelevant to complex humanitarian emergencies, as an inert technique, something that was immutable and was therefore only useful to a few particularly disaffected and underdeveloped societies? The evidence of the practitioners at the frontlines of 1990s emergencies was that the art of insurgency was something more animated and versatile, something that evolved and adapted itself with the societies from which it arose and therefore in its most modern form hard to associate with its previous manifestations. Instead of dismissing insurgency as a static concept, should we not have understood it as something that was rapidly evolving and could be utilised in any society, even post-industrial societies such as the NATO states? And if this was a possibility, instead of constantly putting aside the knowledge that we had gained about insurgency in favour of developing new and fashionable doctrines for peace-building, peace support, countering super-terrorism and so forth, was it not more sensible to husband our existing knowledge, to build on it and be more alive to the notion that insurgent energy could take on many forms and arise in any society?

After the events of 11 September 2001, these constantly unasked questions about the centrality of insurgency in the context of the twenty-first century took on greater significance. The US-led coalitions to Afghanistan and Iraq had been cobbled together under the emotional pressure of 9/11 and NATO partners had largely accepted the operational premise of the US strategy for countering terrorism. But disappointingly the US strategy writers had described the adversary as a unique terrorist organisation and once again the word "insurgency" was notably missing from the discussion. Just as the complex emergencies had been explained as unique, so too were al-Qaeda and its franchised off-shoots. The techniques of the globalised terrorists were portrayed as historically disembodied, a unique development that could only be defeated by an equally unique, historically disembodied counter strategy, in this case a Global War on Terror—a one-off phenomenon calling for a one-off response.

Fortunately the scale of the US counter-terrorist commitment attracted a stampede of critical analysis, led almost entirely by a bright new generation of counter-insurgency thinkers based in the US, who successfully challenged the counter-terrorist approach taken by the Bush administration. However, the focus of their writing was largely tactical, relating to the particularities of Iraq, Afghanistan and radical Islamist activism and failed properly to acknowledge that twenty-first century adversaries, just like the twenty-first century societies they sprang from, were infinitely more complicated than the territorially limited violence in Iraq and Afghanistan. Beyond these theatres an archipelago of supporters was spreading and evolving, like a flu epidemic, and dealing with the tactical minutiae of Anbar province and Helmand failed to address the true heartlands of the insurgent threat.

Here, the military compulsion to define the threat in one, tightly worded sentence could go dangerously wrong, for this was a threat that evolved rapidly. Its technique was to generate insurgent energy from a disaffected society, and this meant that it altered at the same speed as the social structures of its host, able to adapt far too swiftly to be fenced into the military's neat definitions. What it required was an evolving list of characteristics, of which only some would apply at any given moment.

We might therefore recognise a contemporary insurgency by the following descriptions. First, it is essentially a political process. While it is true that Maoist people's war theory depicted organised armed forces with heavy weapons and logistic trains attacking, defending and manoeuvring, this came in the later parts of his three-stage process, by which point the insurgent phase was over and it had become a civil war not an insurgency. Harnessing the insurgent energy of a disaffected society was more significantly described in the first of Mao's stages. It involved political activism, infiltration, propaganda, subversion and the selective use of terror and assassination. It was not a form of warfare, therefore not a method for laying siege nor an instrument for making foreign conquests and certainly not the exclusive intellectual territory of Clausewitzian theorists and military doctrine writers. It is politics. Second, the techniques of an insurgency evolve with the societies from which it arises. Since the Cold War the pace of social change has accelerated dramatically, not just in the rich, secure nations of the northern hemisphere, but also in developing countries as they have become gripped by global change. Just as the structures of these societies have altered out of all recognition, so it is possible that an insurgency arising from them can take on unforeseen characteristics. Furthermore, if the communications revolution has given birth to global communities and global movements, so too can it herald a form of insurgent energy that is de-territorialised and globally connected. Third, organising an insurgency is an act of desperation, a course of action only taken when all other avenues of advance have been blocked. It is the option of the weaker side whose towering political ambitions are not matched with the commensurate power to translate them into reality. Fourth, and most importantly, an insurgency has to involve the population; its energy, its ability to sustain itself and to continuously replace and regenerate its losses, arises from popular support. Violent political activists who achieve these effects entirely through terrorism and have no method or structures to organise popular support are probably no more than a terrorist gang: unsustainable, vulnerable to decapitation and therefore lying outside the concept which distinguishes insurgencies.

The proposition of this book is that, in the context of a world beset by a huge and destabilising rich-poor divide, the leaders of the wealthiest and most powerful nations habitually fail to understand the continuing relevance of insurgency. For a great many of the world's disadvantaged it is the most direct way to express outrage, gain recognition and improve their circumstances. But political violence is not only the expedient of the very poor; it is also used by communities that are comparatively comfortable, but who nevertheless see themselves as excluded from or discriminated against by a more powerful host society. To understand how these feelings manifest themselves, how they evolve through violence, and how they can be harnessed and exploited in order to create a political movement is central to an understanding of the twenty-first century security environment.

Insurgency has utility for an array of different populations. Its techniques cannot have a rocklike permanence; they must evolve in order to reflect the nature and the development of the populations which seek to use them. An insurgency in an intensely traditional society will be similarly traditional, but in a contemporary society that is loosely structured, the use of political violence is more impulsive, organic, less defined by territory and consequently less recognisable as an insurgency. The insurgent's art is to take advantage of an environment to exploit a society's aspirations and the way it exists. The counter operation organised by the state needs to be as socially astute as the insurgent's. To win back the population the state needs to have a political idea, a strategy that overwhelms the insurgent manifesto. Just as important, at the operational level, it needs to have a counter-insurgent instrument that can engage the contemporary characteristics of the adversary.

The war against terror has been conducted on two separate planes. The US and its allies have engaged on a traditional plane, guided by a wishful aspiration that their globalised adversary needed sanctuaries in order to continue its activism and was organised in vertical structures and controlled by top-down management systems. However their military expeditions, robust language and kinetic security measures have not engaged the sources of the dissident energy which launched the attacks on Madrid, Nairobi, New York, London, Washington and other cities. The communities which are the heartlands of the insurgent energy, the energy that has attacked our cities and our populations, live and act on a different plane. They stretch around the world in an archipelago of individuals, cells and communities; they have no territory, they exist in isolated but interconnected groups that are horizontally related rather than vertically ordered, and their shared sense of outrage is regenerated by the exertions of the media and the visibility of the campaign. In these wispy, informal patterns, without territory and without formal command structures they are not easily touched by the kinetic blows of a formal military campaign.

Looking ahead, several developments may derail this strangely separated campaign and the split-level relationship between the globalised insurgents and the US-led counter-insurgency. On the military plane the US and its NATO allies may have reached a decisive point in their relationship. In 2009 the new US administration was determined to increase its expeditionary commitment to Afghanistan. The

Europeans' superficial enthusiasm for this proposal is increasingly undermined by their different geography and security imperatives. There is in Europe a growing realisation, backed by polling results and local activism, that their military participation in US expeditions angers their own Muslim minorities and becomes the recruiting sergeant for future waves of disaffection. Even without this threat, participating in US military expeditions is politically risky, financially costly and in overseas theatres has seldom achieved a form of success that is relevant to European security. It is increasingly likely that the next person to detonate himself or herself in the rush hour traffic of a European city will be native to the country they are targeting, and almost certainly not an activist sent from Iraq or Afghanistan. Prioritising the objectives in a European nation's strategy to prevent that detonation must set the immediate domestic need above a more tenuous expeditionary obligation. It is palpably unsound for Europeans to send military units overseas before securing their own homeland populations, particularly if the military expedition increases domestic insecurity in other ways. Whereas the overseas and the domestic are still proclaimed to be mutually supportive in US thinking, in European security logic the diminishing public support for expeditionary forces makes this an increasingly problematic option.

Meanwhile, in some European states domestic efforts to counter terrorism are beginning to assume the architecture of counter-insurgency operations. The British counter-terrorist campaign led by the Home Office and the police has vastly increased in size and scope to include key ministries, departments, regional administrations, local government and a multitude of local NGOs. Despite its limited success in countering radical activism, its unwieldy structures and the absence of rigour in the design and direction of the campaign, the British domestic operation is—in evolutionary terms—hugely significant and may turn out to be a prototype for the next generation of counter-insurgency operations. Although the architects of this operation would strenuously deny any attempt to describe it as a counter-insurgency campaign, by combining powerfully supported political and social objectives with a kinetic counter-terrorist operation, that is precisely the sort of campaign in which they are engaged. Although the British continue to send military contingents to support their

NATO obligations and their US ally, their domestic operation—CONTEST—is much more effectively targeted to engage their home-grown problems with radicalisation and jihadist activism.

At the operational level CONTEST is beginning to resemble its adversary. It has become a sprawling network of loosely federated parts that includes government officials, Internet interceptors staring at their screens, fiercely independent Muslim NGOs working locally in the streets and the black suited counter-terrorist squads. There are no overt military participants and the elements of the campaign cannot be reduced to an organisation chart that could demonstrate a top-down style of command. In substance and appearance Operation CONTEST is a thousand times removed from the British campaign in the Malaysian jungles. Nevertheless, the two are related, and explaining the evolutionary threads that connect them is the subject of this book.

# PART I

# MAOISM

## INTRODUCTION

To rise up, to spring up, to surge as in the waters of the Nile or to soar as in Horace's poetry, and then more prosaically when used by the Roman staff officer, to rise up in insurrection. Long before the twenty-first century, insurgency was a tricky word, which had to be used carefully and with precision. Like terrorism, it was not a neutral word. Depending on who you were, insurgency conveyed different messages. To Maoists it meant genesis, freedom and a fresh start to a new political era; countering it was therefore repressive, the actions of despots, torturers and colonial regimes. But to the US and the rich, safe European nations that comprised NATO, insurgency was something that had for more than a century threatened their commerce, their possessions and their security; and for some European armies, countering it has been their *raison d'etre*, their burden and their constant intellectual challenge.

In the prevailing era of international conflict more and more violence is explained by the concept of insurgency. However as we use the word more freely it grows less and less precise, for at the heart of every modern insurgency we increasingly find social, political, economic and environmental factors that exist in the same space and alter the nature of what would otherwise be a purely military campaign.

Countering insurgency therefore has many dimensions and requires the beleaguered government to tackle poverty, protect its population, and encourage economic revival as well as the restoration of security. These very different concerns all emanate from this increasingly multipurpose word—insurgency.

Whereas most nations have grown from the crucible of war, a minority have a significant and sustained experience of living with insurgency.[1] Very few of our political leaders and key communicators understand the principles that govern insurgency. They use the word carelessly and blunt its meaning without understanding its significance. They proclaim wars "against terror" and denounce as terrorists organisations which have the characteristics of a fully developed insurgency.[2] This failure of definition is exacerbated by the rapid evolution of different forms of insurgency that has followed in the wake of Mao, and what turned out to be the first modern insurgency.

Insurgency changes at the same speed as the society from which it arises. During the twentieth century, technology, society and the nature of the state began to change at greater and greater speed. By the twenty-first century the world had passed into yet another security era in which the great powers were more likely to find themselves engaged in containing the consequences of insurgency rather than conventional war fighting. Furthermore, by this time it was probable that an insurgency, which successfully challenged our rich, safe societies and also grew from within them, was certain to exploit their novel characteristics. It would therefore be very different from the traditional insurgencies of the previous century.

The purpose of Part I of this book is to provide an introduction, or a doctrinal stepping off point, for the central proposition of the book. It describes how, in response to societal changes, insurgency rapidly evolved from its Maoist version into several different forms by the 1990s. It also argues that towards the end of the twentieth century, pre-eminent counter-insurgent armies in NATO failed to see or to understand what were probably the harbingers of the current security era.

These four chapters explain why the West's long experience of insurgency and counter-insurgency must provide a perspective from which to understand the prevailing security era. But they also argue that there are serious caveats in this approach, that our Western perspective is flawed and our narrative of the last forty years of insurgency has some crucially important gaps, and that there is a danger that we expect too much from our institutional memory. We have been surprised by global insurgency because during the 1990s Western counter-insurgency doctrine was moving backwards at a time when the harbingers of global insurgency were already active, incubating around us undisturbed, unchallenged and conceptually beyond our experience or interest.

Beginning with the Maoist prototype, Part I explains the evolutionary process by which Mao's concept of people's war developed into contemporary global jihad, with the narrative emphasising the Western experience. It argues that since insurgencies reflect their environment, the Maoist prototype was bound to change with the rapid improvement of transport, communications and commercial techniques. It explains how insurgents continuously exploited this changing environment, including the growing size of populations, urbanisation, and more recently the migration and establishment of communities in different regions. As populations grew and became concentrated into urban spaces, so insurgents adapted with them. Populations continued to be the primary resource of the insurgent, and therefore the techniques of subversion had to evolve from the crude tactics of guerrilla warfare in the empty wilderness to the exploitation of communications and the mobilisation of populations which lay in the concrete jungles of the city.

During this evolutionary period, Western colonial powers and the US had distinct experiences and their surviving doctrines are nationally idiosyncratic. There never has been an international model for countering insurgency, and among NATO nations only the British had a continuous experience which ran from the 1850s to the present.[3] However, this asset was to some extent diminished by the British reluctance to reduce their knowledge to a doctrine. Nevertheless, over the last one hundred years the British handbooks which did emerge show how operational concepts were evolving. They were a record of what we knew and did not know about insurgency, and acted as the milestones of their respective periods of conceptual thinking. They showed that despite starting each campaign badly the British usually managed to learn enough about their adversary to reverse the process of subversion before reaching the tipping point of a campaign.

Rightly or wrongly, the Maoist prototype provided the central concept for Western thinking. However, due to the stagnation of our doctrine, long after the post-colonial Cold War phase of insurgency was over, counter-insurgent techniques continued to emphasise the importance of traditional people's war even though many of the conditions which had previously defined the environment, and underwritten our success, had been overtaken by global changes. As a result, despite its apparent continuity of experience and willingness to adapt, the West was conceptually surprised by global insurgency, and despite many warning incidents prior to the drama of the 11 September 2001 attacks on America, had been unable to devise a concept or even a name for the insurgent form which has since so beset our way of life. At the highest level, our problems were greatly exacerbated by an absence of strategic conviction. But at a practical level there was also a lack of international structure and experience that would allow any strategy, no matter how brilliant, to be put into effect. Part I explains the reason for this crucial gap in our understanding of the evolving nature of insurgency.

While Europe was in the thrall of the Cold War and former colonial powers grappled with the narrowly national problems of post-colonial withdrawal, another form of insurgency was being explored by populations that were uniquely dispersed. Campaigns by the Irish Republican Army (IRA) and Palestine Liberation Organisation (PLO) were important milestones, not because of their political, religious or ideological significance, but as an emergent technique which might have informed us of a future trend. Several aspects of the PLO and the IRA were harbingers of a future era: the dispersal of migrant communities; the management of the narratives of their own misfortunes; and the exploitation of the virtual images of news events. Their significance lay above all in the virtual dimension of the campaign, which was becoming more important than the military value of raids and attacks on terra firma. While the terrorist groups became increasingly familiar with the practicalities of exploiting the news imagery of their activities, the West failed to see its significance as a dimension of future violence. Our collective failure to learn this has now cost us several years of reactive and ineffectual campaigning in which attrition rather than manoeuvre has been the guiding concept.[4]

Part I therefore offers the reader a context, a preceding narrative, and some definitions from which to launch the main hypothesis of this book. It shows that Western institutional experience is flawed and has failed to incorporate the lessons of campaigns that took place beyond each state's international interest and horizon. A measuring system and a conceptual tool were needed to identify what was missing from our understanding. Part I sets out to identify this gap, arguing that although insurgency has mutated at increasing speed and out-grown its post-colonial definitions, the term 'insurgency' should not be discarded altogether. What we face in the prevailing security era cannot be explained by the limited concept of terrorism—it should rather be seen as an evolved version of insurgency. Locating the gaps in our understanding is easier and more logical than creating a new blueprint, a new language, a new stampede of born-again experts and aficionados. These chapters do not therefore seek to redefine what we already know, or to re-label a long standing long-standing and widely established terminology. Their purpose is to mark the point from which to begin the central proposition of the book.

# 1

# MAO THE PROTOTYPE

*For more than 2000 years, primitive forms of insurgency had been used to challenge organised society. Mao's theory of people's war was a genuinely modern approach, which created a methodology for mobilising a population on an industrial scale. His distinctive contribution was to introduce a political dimension into what had previously been a largely military affair. In a successful Maoist insurgency the political took primacy over the military. This development provided a point in the narrative of insurgency from which to trace the evolutionary path towards globalised insurgency.*

## The Significance of Mao

If insurgency has been practised for more than 2,000 years, one is entitled to ask—why Mao? Why choose Mao's formula for people's war as the point from which to begin the evolutionary narrative? In the early 1900s, when Mao was testing his options for survival as a revolutionary leader, there were several other revolutionary styles to choose from. The metropolitan uprisings in Russia had succeeded in overthrowing the Tsar; the British faced insurgents in their empire, and closer to home in Ireland; and in Oxford, TE Lawrence was drafting his memoir of the recent Arab revolt. This chapter sets out to demonstrate why Mao has a compelling relevance to the present, and to explain why the success of his concept marks the start of a new era of insurgency.

China in the early 1900s combined the surviving elements of an ancient hierarchy with the incursions of a modern society influenced by ideas and structures imported from rich, industrial Europe. In contrast to the bleak deserts of the Eastern Mediterranean, which for so long had been the environment for insurrections, the Chinese countryside was productive and populated. Much of China was catching up with the modern world; its industries and cities were animated by capital, technology and the innovating influence of foreign powers.

In these circumstances, Mao's political survival and his military mobilisation of the Chinese had to be more than a guerrilla war of pin-prick attacks on isolated soldiers and their baggage trains. Nor would the process of insurrection be successfully initiated and sustained by a sudden uprising in the metropolitan areas as it had been in the previous century, and more recently in Russia. By necessity, it was a gradual affair that endured long periods of hardship and was continuously recharged by Mao's political energy. What makes Mao's contribution to the evolution of insurgency unique has little to do with his prowess as a military commander. Rather, his survival and later success relied on an ability to exploit the surrounding population and harness their manpower as his major war resource. However, as the Chinese revolutionaries had discovered to their cost in 1911,[1] harnessing a people was a far more labour intensive process than could be achieved with a few violent demonstrations in a crowded city.

In 1927 Mao seemed destined to be an unsuccessful guerrilla. The Hunan-Jiangxi border area where his small band of "rural vagabonds"[2] struggled to avoid a terminal confrontation with the vastly superior Guomindang (GMD) forces was supposed to be a classic wilderness where guerrillas thrived. Certainly the Jinggang Mountains challenged the larger, slow-moving GMD forces with their ponderous logistic train and their heavy guns, but they also presented problems for Mao's force. There was no reason for anyone to live there unless they were fugitives, and the only villages were "dens of bandits and deserters"[3].

For Mao and his fighters, campaigning in this area was becoming fruitless and exhausting. Hundreds of men living in the open required constant access to food and war supplies, and in the bleak unpopulated Jinggangshan none were locally available. Periodically, an element of his force had to make themselves vulnerable by moving down to the towns and villages in the plains to seek provisions and men. Although he managed to hold his force together, attract reinforcements and keep up the continuous cycle of re-supply, this was a campaign of attrition which he was certain to lose. The huge effort of existing in the Jing-gangshan was not compensated by any strategic advancement in the greater Chinese revolution. Mao and his rural vagabonds were merely struggling to stay alive—the bleak ravines of the Jinggangshan had become a death trap for his force just as the bare tactics of guerrilla warfare on their own had borne him no fruit.

It was this realisation that forced Mao to move his force to a differ-ent place and alter his concept of operation. Although change was forced on him as a matter of survival, his response gradually developed into an inspirationally successful form of insurgency. The Jiangxi where Mao moved in 1929 was a populated agricultural area. To survive, and in campaign terms to succeed, Mao needed to infiltrate his troops into the local communities. He decided to exploit local enthusiasm for land redistribution, and gradually adapted his Red Army to that purpose. In contrast to the predatory militias which also moved through the area, Mao's units demonstrated an egalitarian ethos towards each other and the local people. When this approach paid off, elements of the fighting force were formed into small cadres of political workers whose specific task was to educate and subvert the local population to the communist cause. Mao also needed a territorial dimension in his cam-paign and continued to operate from secure enclaves which he hoped were beyond the reach of the GMD.

The novelty of his concept of operations was that he reinforced the security of his territorial bases not by conventional military or physical means, but by surrounding them with a population that supported him. It became impossible for his adversary to move and campaign freely in the area. The local people became Mao's force multiplier—they supplied intelligence, shelter, stretcher-bearers, logistic support and manpower. Mao had rejected the classic guerrilla wilderness and adapted himself to survive and campaign in a populated farmland. His strength and his major asset was no longer the possession of territory, but the possession of a population.

An operational concept which relied on popular support for an ide-ology rather than control over territory succeeded more easily when the population in question lived in such poverty and despair that they had very little to lose by turning to violence. From the people's perspective, supporting the Red Army meant much more than just choosing an armed force which could overthrow an unbearable regime, this was a choice that could lead into a new era where the workers would control their own destiny.[4]

Mao did not seek to instantly transform these disaffected populations into armies and march them towards the government troops in the manner of an impetuous St Joan.[5] Mao's campaign was slower but more absolute—his aim was to gradually turn the population to his side. The arrival of Mao's cadres in a community initiated a process of subversion and the setting up of alternative structures to control, organise and mobilise. For families living at the edge of survival, the gleaming images of a secure and comfortable future had a compelling attraction. In communities where Mao's radical ideology collided with peasant conservatism, hardcore party members were at hand to keep up the momentum, to send the message that resistance might encounter violence.

Once this concept had been turned into a procedure it became almost irresistible. Mao's army was more than a military force, it was also a proselytizer and a political organiser. Initially it was not essential for the communists to hold the territory on which their supporting population lived. Rather it was more important to hold their beliefs and their allegiance. Government forces could come and go, occupying and reoccupying the villages and hamlets, but once they had passed it was important that the communist structures remained intact and reasserted themselves. Mao's guerrillas survived in basic military terms (as they had on the Jinggangshan) because they could organise ambushes and surprise attacks, but they distinguished themselves by becoming directly involved in a struggle to capture the minds and beliefs of the population. In his lectures he told his cadres:

…aid the popular masses…. help them to gather the harvest or cultivate their land and send our army doctors to prevent their epidemics or treat the peoples' ailments… hold joint entertainment sessions for the soldiers and the people…. smooth over any feelings of alienation between the army and the people.[6]

Mao's operational campaign was therefore pervasive, it deployed at every level, physically in the form of military action, subversively in the introduction of revolutionary structures within the community, and psychologically by holding out the prospect of a brighter future. His troops were indoctrinated to be more than just fighters, and they were urged not to rely on a few political workers to put into effect the propagation of ideology: 'the whole personnel of the unit had to participate in the struggle for popular support'.[7]

This is Mao's significance to the present. Previous insurrections had also involved a population, but the massive numbers involved in China and the methodology of their gradual mobilisation distinguished Mao's version. He had taken the concept of using the population as a resource to industrial levels.

As a process it was laborious and hard to get started, but once an element of the community began to move from onlooker to activist, the momentum of the campaign could not easily be reversed, and certainly not by military action alone. Mao was fighting above all for the people's minds and beliefs. If he won these the rest would follow. The poverty of his thoughts on military tactics when compared to the richness and enthusiasm of his lectures on the methodology of subversion reflects this emphasis. This "special ingredient"[8] was to have an international relevance, both as a ready-made concept for insurgency in other regions, and as the basis from which to write counter-insurgency doctrine.

## The Characteristics of the Maoist Model

After Mao reached Beijing in 1949 and established the People's Republic of China, his exploits as a commander and political helmsman became part of the mythology of the new state. Over the following years, Mao's writings on both communist ideology and insurgency theory were translated and republished, becoming widely available outside China.[9]

This dissemination of the Maoist model occurred at a time when the European powers, shattered by the trauma and expense of the Second World War, were at various stages of withdrawal from their colonies. Nationalist insurgencies were being waged across their territorial possessions, which covered most of the African and South Asian regions. In many cases, the nationalist insurgencies which instinctively challenged the colonial regimes in the 1940s and 1950s understood nothing of modern insurgency against a developed state. Mao's model for insurgency appeared at a critical moment in the spread of insurgency. However, while the concept of people's war exerted a great deal of influence over African and South Asian insurgent leaders during the period of Western decolonisation, not all of them adopted Mao's theories to the letter.

Insurgency was—and is—an evolving phenomenon. Throughout history, as the narrative of insurgency has progressed, so the concept has altered in line with the peculiarities of each era, place and social situation. New forms did not necessarily exclude the old ones—it was possible to encounter an old fashioned insurgency alongside very modern versions. But the concept itself underwent a constant evolution through its absorption of lessons and examples from the past and their re-application within the framework of the present. The evolutionary process which is central to this account therefore had guerrilla antecedents before the 1920s, but by the outset of the Cold War it was above all the Maoist experience which had left the most recognisable imprint on both the insurgents and the European doctrines for counter-insurgency.[10]

In the Western interpretation, Maoist insurgency, or people's war, could be defined by its characteristics and limitations. Firstly, insurgency was the expedient of the weaker side. A leader did not choose to be an insurgent—like Mao, he was usually compelled to be one because there was no other way to reconcile his towering political ambition with his completely inadequate power base. Furthermore, no commander would choose to be an insurgent because it was such an unwieldy, labour intensive military option, demanding a superhuman energy and huge charisma that he might not possess. He might also be daunted by the evidence of its frequent failure.

Secondly, after the Second World War, insurgency and counter-insurgency could involve at least two distinct populations. There was the local population at the epicentre of the violence, among whom the conflict was fought; and, in the post-colonial scenario, there was the population of the intervening nation conducting the counter-insurgency. Although detached from the violence itself, the support of this latter population was crucial, in particular to underwrite the continuation of a long campaign. Maoists strove to subvert the local population to their side and turn it against the government, and in an insurgency which involved a third party, they also sought to demoralise the metropolitan population of the intervening power. Insurgency therefore involved several distinct populations. For the insurgent and the counter-insurgent force, the support of the concerned populations was integral to their respective strategic centres of gravity. In military terms, these populations could be described as the 'vital ground' for both sides, meaning that the successful side would be the one which succeeded in winning over the people and isolating its opponent.

The third characteristic was the importance of ideology. Mao's political message was exciting. In the dark periods of his campaign it inspired individuals and entire communities to go the extra mile because they held a passionate belief. It was powerful enough to drive children to denounce their parents and married couples to betray each other. It crossed the divisions of language and race and drew together nascent revolutionaries from completely foreign cultures. In a rural society it undermined the ancient structures of privilege and ownership that regulated the land. It aroused such an emotional stampede that to stand in its path was to risk death, and radicalised locals might punish and even execute less than enthusiastic members of their own communities.[11] To be labelled as a revisionist or a backslider in a community gripped by the communist ideology carried the same fatal stigmatisation as the accusation of witchcraft. The communist slogans provided both a battle cry and a way of life. Their deceptive simplicity was their strength, they were hard to disarm or counter by using the complicated explanations of democracy.

The fourth characteristic was the insurgents' close relationship to the environment. In pre-industrial societies, insurgents had exploited the availability of wilderness areas, where they could over-extend their opponents and defeat larger more powerful forces, man for man, on their own terms. However, industrialisation diminished the military significance of the wilderness with improved transport technology and with expanding cities which joined together to become conurbations and townships. Insurgents have always been the product of their environment, and to be successful they had to change in harmony with the society from which they arose. Therefore, in response to this changing environment, successful insurgent leaders came to rely less on the military exploitation of terrain and more on the exploitation of popular support which flourished in the ungovernable slums of a crowded city—what counter-insurgency practitioners have recently taken to calling the 'human terrain'. Conversely, the counter-insurgent's recurring mistake was to assume that the insurgent-environment relationship was static.

The fifth characteristic was that exploiting this human terrain required an overwhelming sense of grievance to manipulate. A population that would support a successful uprising was a suffering population. In the case of the Chinese rural areas of the 1920s it was the mass of peasants, gradually starving to death, trapped on their unproductive land by rapacious officials, an unforgiving economy and an outdated farming system. In the case of insurgencies in richer societies the rebellious element of the population may have had a burning sense of their exclusion, of injustice or discrimination. So whether the suffering was a physical or psychological, in both cases it had to seem that the situation had reached the limits of the people's endurance. To move the community across the threshold from discontent to activism, there had to appear to be no reasonable avenue or process to redress the situation, so that they came to the conclusion that their condition could not be peacefully endured. The act of subversion therefore depended on getting the people to believe that their situation was unbearable, and furthermore, that there was no opportunity for redress, and that they had very little to lose by becoming activists. Success was not just a matter of practising the mechanics of subversion on a randomly selected community, it was driven by an overwhelming sense of misery and outrage in the target population.

The final characteristic was the tactic by which the response of the adversary became the key factor in this subversion process. Developing the supportive relationship required to sustain an insurgency depended on the existence of a target population that was already vulnerable to subversion and disposed to participate (as Mao's failure in the Jinggangshan had demonstrated). But even if a deep sense of popular outrage was present, exploiting it could not be achieved by a military campaign of surprise attacks alone. Mobilising a population to forge a common cause with the insurgent meant incorporating a strategy that painted the opposing security forces as enemies of the people.

The insurgents' pin prick attacks were therefore aimed at goading security forces to over-react, to lose self-control and lash out, to take revenge and use their weapons indiscriminately. The insurgent then had to make sure that these blows fell on the uncommitted population, driving them towards the insurgent. Conceptually, it was similar to the technique of a judo wrestler who throws his opponent using not his own strength but the gross weight and power of his adversary.

By comparison, old-fashioned guerrilla warfare was a simple cat and mouse affair, a military technique by which a small irregular force constantly harassed the unprotected extremities of a much larger and more powerful army. Guerrilla warfare in this sense was strictly kinetic, it referred to the constant use of surprise to overwhelm the isolated position, to kill the stragglers around the baggage train and carry off their supplies, to murder the solitary courier riding alone across hostile territory. In a modern society, insurgency was more complicated, focused not only on military techniques but on an entire spectrum of politics, terrorism, subversion, and persuasion.

## Western Interpretations of Maoism

During the Cold War some European states, along with the US, were engaged in large scale counter-insurgency campaigns. The revolutionary forces they faced were influenced by Mao's concept of people's war and many insurgent leaders adapted his principles to suit the culture and environment of their own particular nation. Consequently, Western writers studied his translated works with close attention. By the 1960s, Western armies (from, for example France, the United Kingdom, the US and Portugal) produced their own counter-insurgency field guides. The manuals published during the period of the Malayan emergency reeked of cordite and the dripping jungles associated with the recent campaign, but their immediacy made them a reliable measure of the preoccupations of the military.[12] During the Cold War both the US and British counter-insurgency manuals emphasised the subliminal impact of the Maoist concept and several decades later its influence remained.

By the 1970s, the pace of global change was accelerating and insurgency and counter-insurgency had moved into new fields. Nevertheless, the principles of Maoism and the primacy of popular support still lay at the heart of a genuinely sustainable campaign. After British forces had been in Northern Ireland for almost a decade, the 1977 *Field Manual* defined insurgency as 'a form of rebellion in which a significant part of the population instigates or acquiesces in the commission of widespread violence, sabotage and terrorism, and wages guerrilla warfare in order to overthrow the established government.'[13] This definition was qualified by the conditions that 'revolutionary movements need the support of a sizeable proportion of the population, and the aim is to involve everyone irrespective of sex, age or class, acknowledging no neutrals, and using any means of coercion or terror in the process', and that they flourished in areas 'where the regular forces of government are at a disadvantage, generally because the areas may be in rough, inhospitable country, or in towns and cities where revolutionaries can merge inconspicuously with the population.'[14] The British manual was describing an essentially Maoist version of insurgency. By 1995 the new *UK Army Field Manual* series continued to define insurgency as "the actions of a minority group within a state intent on forcing political change by means of a mixture of subversion, propaganda and military pressure, aiming to persuade or intimidate the broad mass of people to accept such a change".[15] Again this definition emphasised the concepts associated with a Maoist prototype, the idea that it involved a population and followed an operational concept that was essentially political rather than the strictly military techniques of guerrilla warfare.

During the Cold War the Western concept of insurgency was constantly influenced by a Maoist prototype of People's War and the long campaigns which continuously revitalised their experience. This continuity of perception, with its refinements, remained unbroken right up to 2001.[16] The campaigns involved organised labour, politicians and government officials, and their subversion was the key to the insurgent's concept of operations. This implied the use of propaganda, disinformation and violent pressure as well as holding out a brighter future in the form of a political manifesto and an ideology. The population remained centrally important for both the insurgents and the government forces they opposed, but the practical manifestation of the insurgency could take a number of different forms.

The British described terrorism as just one of several options that was available to the insurgent.[17] Throughout this period the relationship between terrorism and insurgency was seen in hierarchical terms, with insurgency an overarching concept that embraced a long list of activities, one of which was terrorism. Terrorism itself was not regarded or defined as a means by which to overthrow a regime on its own. Nevertheless, in the 1970s a number of politically disembodied extremist organisations had attracted public attention by using dramatic acts of violence, which muddied this otherwise clear distinction and encouraged commentators to confuse the technique of terrorism with the broader concept of insurgency. Paul Wilkinson restored the original doctrinal proposition by stressing that once a terrorist organisation 'demonstrated a capacity to win wider popular support among a substantial segment of the population... [and attract] a repressive campaign by the government leading to an increase in popular support', it was an insurgency.[18] This conformed with the Maoist view of terrorism as well as British military thinking.

## Maoism as Evolutionary Milestone

Mao's concept for people's war was set out in a widely published and translated version in 1967 which described the three stages of "protracted war" in general terms.[19] His guerrilla principles were derived partly from Sun Tzu. At the tactical level the principle was to avoid confrontation unless the insurgent could be sure of winning. But this did not mean their more powerful adversary should be allowed to enjoy a feeling of safety at any time, the insurgents were always well informed and ready to strike when an opportunity was presented in the form of a stranded vehicle or a lost patrol.[20] This constant predation by the insurgent kept up a sense of anxiety and drove up the cost of the counter-insurgency campaign. It meant that every official from the postman to the governor had to be protected. Each journey, each staff visit became a military expedition with escorts and contingency plans. The campaign against the government was a slow process of erosion rather than a series of violent blows.[21]

Meanwhile, the insurgent moved among the population with the ease of a fish swimming through water, unidentifiable and secure. To achieve this, it was essential that the insurgent was favourably distinguished from the rapine forces of the government and Mao instructed his fighters to "pay fairly for what you buy...speak politely...return everything you borrow…[and] pay for anything you damage".[22] However, the subversion of the population was an oblique process that took many paths, and terrorism was an important option for insurgents. It was used to demoralise a selected element of the community, to extort support from the uncommitted and, within the revolutionary movement itself, to maintain discipline and enforce obedience.[23]

Globalised insurgency was not a disembodied phenomenon that needed to be discovered or explained by a newly invented concept—it lay on the same evolutionary path as the biblical guerrilla. Along this long path, Mao's recognition of the population as the primary asset of a modern landscape was probably the most relevant event, and his concept for mobilising a population through the simultaneous processes of subversion, politicisation and an irresistible ideology marked the point in the narrative where the antecedents of global insurgency become apparent.

Although Western armies had come to terms with Maoist insurgency, they had failed to see that the evolutionary process was rampaging onwards at greater and greater speed as it rushed into the post-industrial era and the new millennium. Twenty-first-century global terrorism was largely explained as a consequence of the information revolution but its purpose and its relationship to a supporting community could also be explained by an extrapolation of Maoism.

# 2

# EVOLUTION[1]

*Mao's concept for exploiting populations so that they were the campaign-winning resource had become a central characteristic of modern insurgency. But the world was changing very swiftly. If globalisation had disturbed so many things it was hardly surprising that it also changed the Maoist prototype. Under these pressures insurgency proliferated into different forms, one of which was the globalised version of insurgency.*

Although Mao represented an evolutionary milestone in the development of insurgency theory and practice, his importance was bound to diminish in line with the rapid changes to the environment in which insurgencies were waged. In the short term, the environment was shaped by the Cold War superpowers' decision to continue their rivalry in the form of proxy insurgencies and counter-insurgencies in failing states. As the Cold War progressed, globalisation began thrusting its tentacles across national frontiers so that distant events increasingly altered the lives of isolated communities.[2] Long-term economic and demographic changes which had been barely visible in the 1970s, had by the 1990s become highly significant.[3] Globalisation changed the nature of the conflict area, strengthening some actors, weakening others and altering the conditions of the conflict between government forces and insurgents to favour the latter. This chapter concerns the impact of these effects in countries where governments were already weak, or in states that were poor and in many aspects also failing, and demonstrates how the changing environment led to the emergence of a number of diverging variations of insurgency.

In the short term, superpower rivalry beyond the European frontlines of the Cold War disturbed the simple equation of a Maoist insurgency. Mao had emphasised the need to husband the population, and both the insurgent and the government recognised the importance of capturing their support in the operational space. However, the Cold War reduced the significance of having the support of the population. When a superpower poured funds and munitions of every kind into the outstretched arms of their respective clients, it conferred a local autonomy on them. Whether they were insurgents or the opposing government forces, they were released from the obligation of winning local popular support—they no longer needed the people as a war asset if they had a constant supply of food, weapons, transport and funds from a superpower sponsor. As a result, the techniques of subversion and the need to woo the population fell into abeyance. When a regime faced a military challenge from within the state, the population found itself abused by both sides—the relationship between the uncommitted civilian and the armed band became predatory.

The deteriorating relationship between the insurgent, the government and the population in failing states was accelerated by the end of the Cold War. In the space of a few years the inner German border had been removed, the massively powerful Group of Soviet Forces in Germany withdrew from their decaying barracks and dispersed homewards, and in 1991 the Warsaw Pact was formally dissolved. Far from the inner German border the impact of these events was visible and immediate. Shutting down superpower support to the proxy war zones caused an urgent reappraisal. Insurgent leaders who decided to continue fighting without the cash and logistics that once came from a superpower patron now had to understand, as Jean-Christophe Rufin put it, that "their war economies ha[d] to change completely. They moved from relying on political assistance from abroad to a new, more business oriented attitude."[4] As a consequence, warring militias in a collapsing state had to become successful traders—they kept the conflict going by plundering local resources, which usually meant trading in precious woods, gemstones, protected antiques, ivory, jade and the production of drugs.[5] In this way they were able to maintain their autonomy, their independence from the population, and avoid a return to the earlier, labour intensive versions of Maoist insurgency. In the process of adapting to this new environment, they quickly discovered and exploited the advantages presented by new technologies, the proliferation of international communications, and the networks of traders who could transfer cash and weapons with great facility. Meanwhile, post-Cold War military downsizing released massive stocks of vehicles and weapons from both sides of the inner-German border onto a global market, where they could be bought by the newly rich militias.

## A Changing Environment

Four strands of development in particular had been altering the operational space in favour of the insurgent: transport technology; the proliferation of information and communications technology; the deregulation of the international economy; and the consequences of exposure to foreign cultures.

### Transport

Transport inflicted the most visible change on the geography of the conflict area. For thousands of years the wilderness had played a pivotal role in the evolution of insurgency, but the concept of what constituted a wilderness had been altering. Until the 1990s the wilderness referred to an impenetrable, largely uninhabited wasteland where people moved on foot carrying their possessions along river lines and footpaths. The transportation of materials in bulk was greatly limited by the need for mules and porters to carry their own food in addition to a cargo. This imposed a slow rhythm on the tempo of conflict. Only actors who could afford to use large helicopters and heavy transport systems that reached into the heart of the wilderness were able to override these limitations of time and space. In the under-developed tracts of sub-Saharan Africa, and in parts of Southeast Asia, this monopoly usually lay in the hands of international corporations and the more powerful armed forces.

But by the end of the Cold War several developments were eroding this monopoly. International aid was improving communications in developing countries. Engineering companies came to build roads, leaving behind construction plant and cross-country vehicles. Better roads attracted better vehicles, increasing the speed of movement and interaction. Powerful cross-country cargo lorries were penetrating the world's most isolated areas. Commercial vehicles were also being imported on the retail market. Nissan, Isuzu, Tata, Mercedes and Fiat became icons of a new era of greater movement and a shrinking wilderness.[6]

The disbanding Warsaw Pact forces were also a source of cheap and durable transport. The helicopters and chartered aircraft from the former Soviet military fleets now connected the remote airfields in an African conflict zone directly to the international systems beyond, introducing a two-way traffic that had either never existed before, or had been the monopoly of governments and international corporations. There was also an increase of small, privately-owned aircraft operating in these areas.[7]

At sea, containerisation dramatically lowered costs and speeded up the movement of cargo. This also enabled the small entrepreneur to move large, illegal items around the world with much greater facility than before. In some cases the transport costs of moving bulk materials against the stream of international export traffic were considerably lower than the real expense of the journey.[8] Containerisation was also anonymous, allowing illegal merchandise to pass more freely than before. An illegal cargo loaded simultaneously with six thousand other containers was unlikely to be found and in most cases impossible to open, until its turn came to be unloaded. Furthermore, a container was also large and versatile enough to carry stolen cars, armoured vehicles, helicopters and even human beings. Detection and interception became more difficult, anticipatory intelligence became paramount, and in many cases weak governments whose authority barely extended beyond their own capital city did not have the information or power to regulate this movement.

This penetration of the wilderness areas of the global periphery thus upset a monopoly hitherto exercised by a few armed forces and large international corporations. A small entrepreneur could now reach the innermost sanctuaries of a developing state, and carry away large quantities of that state's resources. Small entrepreneurs were trading where before it would have been impossible for them to operate, and the world could now reach into the wilderness areas.[9]

Communications

The second strand of technical development which altered the equation between insurgents and government forces was the proliferation of cheap and powerful communications.[10] In the 1990s, the number of main telephone lines had doubled to 1,100 million and an even greater proliferation of mobile phone users and Internet subscribers had begun.[11] In the remote areas of weakening states, distance no longer decided the cost of communicating electronically. Communications had become smaller, more portable, more mobile, easier to conceal and therefore less easy to control. Users enjoyed vastly improved access to networks, any of which could be increasingly interactive and carry other audio and visual services.

This proliferating flow of information acted against governments that were already weakening for other reasons. New communications monopolies were emerging, their reach and influence permeated across the world and their wealth and power considerably exceeded that of many developing states. The Internet opened up a new highway of evasion for seditious and criminal transactions which could

carry illegal material across international borders, covering its electronic tracks, and deliver it straight to the desktops of millions of individuals…Services could migrate to countries where laws were lenient or weakly enforced, creating offshore havens for pornography, gambling and tax evasion, and breaching international rules on intellectual property.[12]

The freedom of access, the surge of ideas and information could not be controlled and laws preventing the circulation of subversive material were impossible to enforce. Regardless of geography and political constraints, new ideas now took much less time to reach an optimum audience. In this way subversive ideas, radical ideologies and new technologies moved easily from rich to poor, from liberal democracies to down-trodden dictatorships, from exiled insurgents to supporting populations. In failing states, government malpractice became more and more exposed. The control of movement and communication, which sometimes went with the exercise of authority, was disintegrating.

The advantages derived from the communications revolution were not enjoyed solely by the insurgent. The compilation of voice features,

technical fingerprinting and credit card records all threatened the
clandestine operator. However, while such technologies might enable
a government to be excessively controlling, they were expensive—far
more expensive than the technologies being exploited by the criminal
or insurgent. As such, in critically unstable developing states where
government control was minimal due to cost, the communications
revolution favoured the small entrepreneur, the criminal and the
insurgent.

Economic Deregulation

The third destabilising influence was the weakening of the international commercial systems and markets. By 1980, many of the newly
emerged nations that were most susceptible to insurgency had fallen
into debt, their fragile economies disrupted by civil conflict or weakened by the collapse of the price of their exports. The old resource-
based economies in sub-Saharan Africa were now under severe
pressure from more efficient raw material competitors such as Malaysia and Indonesia. Synthetic substitutes from industrial countries also
increased competition. These developments widened the gap between
the rich and the poor.[13]

Meanwhile rich, money-lending nations were finding that IT and
digitisation now allowed a viable profit to be made from the mere
circulation of money rather than its transfer into goods and services.[14]
The consequence of this new mobility of wealth for poor and developing states was that capital became disconnected from trusting relationships—the obligation established between borrower and lender,
which had been an essential element of dealing, was removed. It was
becoming less and less common for capital to be transferred 'from
where it is concentrated and politically and strategically safer, to where
it is scarce and subject to political and strategic risks.'[15] The third world
had become 'unbankable', and the global economy was increasingly
focused towards the rich nations.[16]

The indebtedness of poor states gave international lenders—and the
non-governmental organisations (NGO) that acted on their behalf—
enormous leverage on weak state governments. Trans-national corporations, the international opinion-forming media, the global currency

market and international development agencies began to inflict their individual prescriptions, and the most intimate responsibilities of government ministries were subjected to international scrutiny.[17]

Furthermore, the communications revolution ensured that populations in poor states could now see how deprived they were in the global scale of social endowment, and in particular the inequality of the situation—the enormous wealth of the rich nations compared to the wretchedness of the poor. The speed and volume of capital flows from one country to another had no antecedent. Electronic money at the rate of more than a trillion dollars each day now passed from one side of the world to another at the click of mouse, destabilising the solid economies of one state in favour of a market trend in another. Some felt that a global community which condoned such inequality and exposed the weakest to the mercies of volatile economies must also expect that the most deprived elements of that society would in due course find a way of striking back.[18]

## Cultural Change

Social factors were also wreaking change in the rural areas that had once constituted the world's wilderness. In the 1960s populations increased rapidly after success in lowering child mortality rates and reducing the impact of malaria. The North African population, for example, increased from 280 to 640 million in 30 years. In Kenya it soared from six to 25 million in the same period.[19] Although the population was still largely rural based, a greater and greater proportion was becoming urbanised, and it is estimated that by 2025, 61 per cent of the world population will be living in cities.[20] Despite this migration, population increases meant that numbers remained relatively constant in the rural areas.

Much of the urban population already lived in dangerous and diseased suburban ghettos and shantytowns. Nevertheless, the pressures of rural unemployment, environmental damage to their homelands and climate change spurred migration to the cities, where perceptions of greater opportunity for survival were seldom fulfilled.[21] Urban areas were changing, with physical barriers reinforcing the vastly different lifestyles of rich and poor communities, protecting the wealthy in their gated communities and consigning the poor to their ghettos and squatter areas.[22] Civil society ceased to function when the more stable element of a community moved out towards the suburbs, leaving rampaging inflation, disease, starvation and banditry behind them. Survival depended on self-sufficiency, and families on the edge of the city cultivated small crops and kept livestock on every available patch of ground.[23]

Into this environment of physical and cultural upheaval and dislocation, radio, film, television and the Internet imported new values and cultures, with nothing to stop the flow of ideas.[24] In Barber's shorthand, the 'McWorld' ethos was assaulting pre-modern society, dictating how to dress, what to eat, how to do business, and even who to chose as a sexual partner.[25] Young people from traditional societies were uniformly confronted by the same global culture. This youth-driven, materialistic lifestyle reached them with varying intensity, and while in some cases it was resisted, universally it represented a confrontation to their traditional values.

In a community on the edge of subsistence, life was brutal but could be endured with the help of a traditional family structure in which the individual had an identity and a degree of support. But the images and lyrics of the McWorld ethos disturbed traditional societies—their conservative values were confronted by the brighter visions of a consumer culture in which young people of both sexes were heroes, leaders, and role models, and not fastened down by community and family convention. The same media also told them how very poor they were, and that they were destined to be excluded from the glamorous lifestyles depicted onscreen.

Satellite communications also meant that insurgents could be interviewed from their rural bases and their faces beamed onto TV screens throughout the world. New technology removed the need for the foreign correspondent to be in the same wilderness location as the interviewee. The BBC World Service and Voice of America were hugely respected and when the media deities reached out from distant cities and interviewed locals who opposed the government, they conferred a statesman-like aura on insurrection leaders, local warlords and even road bandits. The weak governments being attacked in these interviews had no idea how to deal with this media assault from another continent.

The strands of development associated with globalisation had made weak governments weaker and insurgent forces stronger. Outgoing colonial administrations had handed over a monopoly of power, which helped to control the movement of people, cargoes, electronic communications and the revenue from the state's resources. For the successor regime, this monopoly made up for their lack of competence and legitimacy. Technical advances, new means of communication and the impact of a less regulated global economy gradually eroded these controls. Losing control of the state's natural resources meant that revenue was now haemorrhaging from the national income and at the same time debts were starting to accumulate. This resulted in a shift of power away from the state, down into the hands of local commanders. Anti-government forces no longer relied on the local population for logistical supplies and funds. Instead they plundered the state's resources and commandeered the facilities to move them onto international markets. Military objectives became focused on the mineral mining areas, plantations, game reserves and the arteries which connected them to air and sea ports. The profits from stripping the state's resources and trading them on the international market were so enormous that they became the reason for war. Clausewitz was being stood on his head: conflict was becoming the continuation of economics by other means.[26] Successful plundering relied on maintaining a chaotic environment where the host government's writ had shrunk back to the perimeter of the capital city. In this environment, popular support was no longer essential and some insurgent forces now used communities manipulatively, either as human shields or to attract relief aid as part of their logistical resources.

### A Proliferation of Insurgency

For more than a thousand years insurgency had been a monolithic concept, and successive insurrections had followed more or less the same conceptual approach in their struggle to defeat their stronger adversary. Mao's strategy for mobilising a population that was spread across a large space was a response to a different environment. In China the "wilderness" where the government failed to exercise its writ also comprised rural areas with huge populations. The Maoist formula for people's war had moved the techniques of insurgency across a threshold into a new chapter but at the same time maintaining it as a monolithic concept for success. After 1948, in the early period of post war decolonisation, the majority of insurgencies in Southeast Asia and sub-Saharan Africa were essentially Maoist in concept and approach. The Cuban revolution had failed to establish a rival trend. Che Guevara's assertion that it was "not necessary to wait until all the conditions for making a revolution exist (because the act of insurrection would create them)"[27] was torpedoed by his own spectacular failure.

From the outset, the Maoist formula has been variously interpreted according to the differing tactical approaches of those insurgencies that have applied Mao's teachings. However, the control of the population has remained central to each successful variation. This concept came under serious pressure during the 1990s with the end of the Cold War and the ensuing rash of civil wars that tore through areas of the former Soviet Union, the former Yugoslavia, Southeast Asia, sub-Saharan Africa, Central America and, to a lesser extent, Western Europe. A number of quite different and successful insurgent strategies emerged during this period that challenged the centrality of winning over a population. With pre-modern and post-modern states co-existing in the same era, different branches of insurgency materialised that intuitively reflected the conditions in which they operated. The accelerating tempo of global change had altered the nature of the insurgent's operational space, his 'wilderness', his techniques, his logistics and funds and above all his relationship to the local population. Furthermore, the interference of superpowers as external patrons upset the simplicity of the old national model which at the local level had involved a host government, an insurgent force a population and possibly the former colonial regime.

As governments in developing states grew weaker it became easier for rebel forces to challenge them. The end of the Cold War witnessed a proliferation not only of the overall number of insurgencies, but also a proliferation of types of insurgency. During the Cold War, academics had defined insurgents and terrorists by their aspiration, but it became apparent to those drawing up the practicalities of a counter-insurgent campaign in the 1990s that distinguishing between insurgent forces was much better achieved by studying their capability, organisation and *modus operandi*. These factors were far more revealing than the vaguely worded manifestos of a group of self-aggrandising rebels. Clapham had categorised the African insurgents as liberators, separatists, reformers and warlords.[28] Eight years previously, O'Neill had identified insurgents as anarchists, egalitarians, traditionalists, pluralists, separatists, reformists and preservationists.[29] But such distinctions proved increasingly misleading in the post-Cold War world. Research showed that a rebel force's declared aims were rarely their real motivation for violence—that the rhetoric of insurgency was indeed just rhetoric.[30] The increasing number of insurgent methods could be more reliably understood and categorised by practical deeds rather than by political smoke screens. Crucially, there was no way that Clapham and O'Neill's lists of aspirations could include the concept of the insurgent as predator. And yet, in some cases, politics had become almost irrelevant to insurgent groups—they had no relationship with the population around them except as predators, and it was less and less valid to think of them as irredentists, preservationists and so forth, according to their supposed intent. For the purposes of organising a counterinsurgent strategy there had to be a better way of distinguishing one typology from another.

Assessing the environment in which the insurgent operated provided a far more useful way of distinguishing between insurgent typologies. First of all, if they survived for any length of time, the insurgents' military campaign bore a direct relationship to the strength of the opposing government and its security forces. At one end of the scale were rich governments with popular support, legitimacy and militarily competence. The insurgent attempting to challenge this government had to be extremely competent itself to survive. Its active cells had to be hidden with secure communications and untraceable sources of logistics and funds. It needed activists that were highly skilled and well organised. At the other end of the scale of competence, against a government that was so weak that it could no longer exercise control over its territory, the insurgent moved more boldly and more carelessly. If the government and its security forces were almost flat on their back with the debilitating effects of corruption and poverty, there was very little need for secure communications and clandestine logistical arrangements.

Secondly, geography imposed distinctions between insurgencies. Rich natural resources that could not be secured by the government regime fuelled a military campaign in which the population could be abused and disregarded. Conversely, campaigning in a bare wilderness devoid of portable resources imposed a more labour intensive, people-oriented approach. Rural areas required different skills and organisations to urban areas. Recent history also influenced the conduct of a campaign, particularly in states which had been the proxy war zones of the Cold War. Long after the active support of the superpowers had been withdrawn, their supplies, weapons and ammunition continued to circulate among the population. In an area where a saturation of weapons already existed (for example, Somalia), the supply of further weapons—or, conversely, the sanctions of an international coalition that attempted to shut off further supplies—seldom altered the degree of security or insecurity. But in an area which had escaped the peripheral violence of the Cold War and therefore had an unarmed population (for example, Nepal), the arrival of a case of AK-47s had a seismic effect.

The environment in which the insurgent operated was reflected in his motivation, form of leadership, organisational structure, methods of recruitment, military tactics and international reach. Emphasising the insurgent's environment allows us to form three broad categories—for ease of reference—which have been labelled here as Feral Militias, Popular Insurgents and Global Insurgents.

Feral Militias

At the lowest end of the scale of competence were the feral insurgencies, referring to the nature of the fighters, their cultural sources of motivation and their lack of sophistication. A feral insurgent was generally found in the element of the population that provided the backbone of the mob, the underemployed and unemployable, the sub-class devoid of social structure.[31] When life seemed unbearable they readily catapulted to violence and revolution—"nothing to lose, only the world to gain, so why not?"[32] Although their slogans were spiced up with Marx, Fanon, Castro and Guevarra,[33] they usually had no convincing political manifesto in terms of their actual relationship with the surrounding population. Many became insurgents as a reaction to a corrupt and despotic state that was too poor to pay its security forces, its writ diminished by mutiny, its legitimacy undermined by the armed bands holding territory on their own account.[34] Feral insurgents were characterised by their informal organisation—their fragile, *ad hoc* power structures that frequently fell victim to internal rivalries between battalions and between personalities within the battalions. They fought mostly for resources and supplies and in some regions fighting was ritualised in such a way that footsoldiers were unlikely to engage in fatal confrontations.[35] Where there was a vacuum of power and the state's security was ineffective, a feral force was dangerous and unhindered by humanitarian codes of conduct, but faced with experienced troops from a more professional army, the feral fighter had a poor record. Their ritualistic fighting techniques had evolved to drive off rather than confront an adversary. The feral unit had little popular backing and lacked a developed logistical and financial support structure, further limiting its chances of survival.

A sub-section of the Feral Militia category was organised by clans. In some regions an uprising might be based on clan structures and although the violence appeared to have the same disorganised and wild character as the strictly feral fighter, there were important differences. From the perspective of a counter-insurgency campaign organiser, the clan force needed to be distinguished from a less ethnically structured military force. A genuine clan was a biological corporation with long standing loyalties of blood, kinship and tradition; this was a powerful motivator for the individual. The loyalties of the clan fighter to his immediate group were dictated by his genealogy, which was visible to others and could not be changed.[36] Clans and tribes altered slowly and while a clan might be militarily defeated, the structures which were the source of its insurgent energy could be resuscitated. By the 1990s clan systems were under pressure from global changes and, in particular, urbanisation. Although these systems had survived for several hundred years, they were not socially isolated, they had to engage their environment. In urban areas clans were altering and becoming more ethnically promiscuous in character. But while urban migration may have diminished the clan force as a survival structure, this did not guarantee that the militant culture that replaced it was any less formidable, or easier to deal with.

## Popular Insurgents

In genealogical terms the popular insurgent evolved directly from the Maoist prototype and 'popular' therefore referred to the support of a population. Although global change had made it possible for insurgents in resource-rich states to challenge weaker governments without mobilising the people, popular insurgents still flourished in Asia, Africa and South America. The Maoist concept had also evolved under the pressures of global change. Towards the end of the Cold War popular insurgency had developed an international dimension. Individual recruits were better motivated and organised than feral militias. The empowering nature of ideology remained central to the movement. Without an irresistible cause, a popular insurgency could not survive in a strong state with an educated population and competent security forces. Popular insurgents living in urban areas dominated by the opposing regime needed to hold legitimate employment and carried on their insurgent responsibilities in a clandestine manner. Only insurgents living in areas beyond government control could afford to move and live as military bands. Young activists had freedom of choice, were more self-motivated than their feral peers. Popular insurgencies that were vigorously opposed had to organise themselves carefully, with complicated structures to achieve security. Their campaigns might last for decades, wearing down the population, eroding democratic institutions and brutalising the participants and, as such, they could only survive if they were supported by a sufficient element of the population to sustain them. The energy of their overt political organisations reflected the importance of this relationship. Although feral militias also displayed the organisational paraphernalia of political wings and associated NGOs, they were seldom genuine or effective. For the popular insurgent, however, the canvassing, subversion, coercion and organisation of the population were crucial, and had to succeed. Militarily, the popular insurgent was not seeking to drive away his opponents—he intended to kill them. To succeed, his attacks could not be impulsive, they needed weeks of careful planning and reconnaissance.

## Global Insurgents

By the mid 1990s the notoriety and, among some populations, the popular success of Osama bin Laden was challenging the definition of insurgency. Bin Laden's methodology had to be regarded as a crucially important consequence of global change and possibly even the leading edge of a new chapter of insurgent techniques. Certain elements bore organisational similarities to popular insurgents, with cellular structures and the constant need to cultivate popular support. But they were nevertheless distinct, separated by their global, as opposed to national, ambitions; their international following; and their horizontal, organically grown communicating structures.[37] To be defined as such, a globalised insurgent had to demonstrate an international reach by mobilising, subverting and engaging a globally dispersed constellation of different populations. This required a universally relevant message or a narrative of their circumstances that had transnational resonance. A successful global movement could strike the interests and assets of an adversary wherever it chose. It possessed no territory, building its constituency from a global community of followers; its strength and energy arising from a collective sense of outrage and the localised activism of its protagonists. This energy was continuously recharged and reactivated through a propaganda of the deed campaign (see chapters 3 and 6). The globalised insurgent faced military opposition in the form of internationally organised coalitions of developed states, which were the antithesis of the depleted national forces that customarily stood in the path of the feral and popular forces in developing states. The counter-terrorist efforts to eradicate them were complicated and had to include extradition agreements and the sharing of police, immigration and customs intelligence. Legal procedures had to be stretched to facilitate the unlawful traffic of prisoners, the re-monopolisation of satellite imagery by US agencies,[38] the monitoring of Internet traffic and the close supervision of global shipping, private aircraft and financial transactions. Just as the feral and popular forces were a response to particular failures of governance and security in their respective countries, the global insurgent could be seen as a consequence of failing global structures.

The above categories are no more than convenient labels, they do not claim to be definitive. Their purpose is to demonstrate how the concept of insurgency, which had been monolithic for so long had gradually branched out into several recognisably different manifestations. By the 1990s a spectrum of capabilities could be identified, ranging from the limited practical capacity of the feral militiaman to the highly-organised global activist. Deciding which theoretical label best fitted a real life adversary was a matter of identifying their working characteristics—their relationship to the population, organisational structures, motives for military violence, recruitment techniques—rather than their stated, and often disingenuous, political aspirations. At the lowest end in the scale of competence, the feral militia tended to focus on temporal concerns, on day-to-day survival and looting, while the global insurgent held loftier, more ideologically-structured motivations.

The purpose of chapter 2 has been to show that, after the Second World War, decades of global and strategic change had altered Maoism. Insurgency was no longer a monolithic concept—it had branched into several different categories whose disparity challenged the tenets of Western doctrine. Rather than addressing these emerging distinctions, the British and American doctrine writers of the 1990s seemed to be gazing backwards towards a previous era of insurgency in which the Maoist prototype was still dominant. Western analysts continued to define insurgents by their intent, failing to recognise that studying an insurgent group's environment and capabilities provided a far more useful structure through which to frame counter-insurgent responses. The West had failed to observe, react and rethink its counter-strategy at the same speed as the global insurgent was evolving. Regaining this lost ground might yet have been possible. The methods had altered, but the underlying principles were recognisable within Western military experience. Whether feral or global, these were still the actions of a minority group. The insurgents' operational concept still included a mixture of subversion, propaganda and military pressure, and influencing the disposition of the broad mass of people continued to be of central importance. This was not a historically disembodied adversary, an unprecedented anomaly which needed to be explained by new terminology and newly concocted definitions. Even the apparently novel global insurgency had emerged from the same evolutionary path as Mao, and Western experience and existing doctrine was still the richest resource by which to understand it.

# 3

# GAPS IN OUR KNOWLEDGE

*Governments and their security forces countered insurgency reactively and their doctrines trailed behind the leading edge of new insurgent ideas. Although the British Army had the most continuous experience of countering insurgencies, they had failed to recognise that their own doctrine had relied on a post-colonial environment which no longer existed. In common with the US they also failed to understand that the proliferation of communications was increasing the significance of populations which lay beyond the territorial space of the military campaign so that they now exercised a crucial influence in the virtual dimension.*

During the chaotic '90s there was a constant tension between the natural, effortless mutation of insurgency and the awkward struggle to develop a suitable counter strategy. Mao had established the importance of the population in a modern society. Insurgents from countries that were at different stages in their trajectory from pre-modern to post-modern each took what they needed from his ideology. The rash of failing states during the chaotic '90s has forced us to see that insurgency had been changing from the Maoist prototype into several different forms, which spread themselves along a spectrum that no longer corresponded to our narrow expectations of a people's war. This chapter explains why it has been so difficult for governments and their military staff to keep abreast of these developments.

## The Disadvantages of Being a Counter-Insurgent

There were good reasons why the concept of insurgency continually moved ahead of counter strategy. Insurgency was intuitive but counter-insurgency was counter–intuitive. The ideals and concepts of insurgency were internationally shared but counter-insurgency often took place privately behind the closed doors of a stricken state. Insurgency was intuitive because its options were so physically limited. Confronting a regime that was vastly more powerful actually made tactical decisions simpler—insurgents exploited whatever resources lay to hand, their actions and reactions following a consistent logic by which they focused their insurgent energy into whatever gaps and opportunities were afforded by the environment. The progress of the insurgency was naturally sequential. Their objectives, and the path they chose to realise those objectives, were dictated by the circumstances and surroundings in which they found themselves at any given moment. When insurgents failed to understand the characteristics of their environment they seldom succeeded, and this imposed an intuitive approach.

But from the perspective of those opposing the insurgency—the power holders, the government, the security forces—their campaign was far from intuitive. Once an insurgency succeeded and a subversive ideology took a firm hold and began to spread, the response had to be counter-intuitive if it was to stem the contagion. The power holder's natural reaction was to use the state's physical strength, intrusive policing and firepower. But that was precisely what the insurgent wanted and heads of state had to be careful not to fall into the trap of over-reaction. The politician's caution was counter-intuitive to the military, especially those commanders whose experience lay in large war fighting machines which accustomed them to deploy swiftly and destroy with powerful effect. Faced with insurgency they complained of fighting with hands tied, unable to prosecute what they regarded as the "real war" against the insurgent's military forces.

The political tactics were also counter-intuitive and demanded much more of state leaders than simply responding to their traditional constituencies. If the subversive campaign against them was exploiting a popular grievance, then the government had to seize the insurgent's political banners for itself. This was not an obvious move, but history showed that this is what had to be done. If they wanted to take the initiative they had to remove the steam from the insurgent cause by making good the perceived grievances in a more persuasive manner themselves. Counter-insurgent orthodoxy dictated that if the insurgents stood for minority recognition, then minorities might have to be recognised; if they urged for secession, then a treaty might have to be negotiated.[1] However, such an obvious *volte-face* raised objections. Besides demonstrating a wild inconsistency with previously held political positions, it forced the government to persuade its own supporters to alter their innermost convictions about fundamental issues of security and identity. In a colonial situation where the population did what it was told it was sometimes possible to do this, but closer to home few democratically accountable leaders could realistically remove the insurgent's political centre of gravity in this way. Whereas the insurgent was largely driven by a singular cause and motivation, the state had to accommodate an often impossible array of contradicting concerns among its constituency.

The development of counter-insurgency had also been an intermittent affair, with a ragged evolutionary history. Successful insurgents were intellectually experimental and at ease with a dynamic approach, but in most cases the opposing security forces were reacting to events rather than shaping them, and often found themselves conceptually surprised and struggling to adapt their mindset to the rapidly evolving circumstances dictated by the campaign. Counter-insurgent forces were not maintained in anticipation of possible future uprisings, whereas the state's need to resist a more traditional military threat ensured its war machinery was in a constant state of development. There were good reasons for this. In the post-Cold War security frameworks a state needed to participate with its allies in coalitions and international forces. To be capable of participating, a military force needed to be ready and have a necessary degree of interoperability, and to understand the techniques of cooperating in a war fighting engagement. Like the rules of football, the procedures for conventional war fighting were universally understood, either because there was a constant danger of an unexpected away-match or the possibility of having to play in someone else's team. By contrast, counter-insurgency, like incest, was a sordid private affair that spoke of a dysfunctional community. Individual governments were uniformly unwilling to discuss it in much detail, each state had its own values and these dictated a national *modus operandi*.[2] It followed that there was no NATO or international concept for counter-insurgency.

For 2,000 years the nature of rebellion had remained essentially unchanged: a rebel's purpose had been to overthrow the rulers of a particular society or nation. The fact that the colonial regime might come from Rome or Britain did not alter the territorially defined nature of the actual rebellion—it was an internal affair focused on the overthrow of a government with a particular population that was fastened to a particular place, insurgency did not refer to a mass movement or a mobile war of conquest. Right up to the 1990s counter-insurgency was a matter for the individual government being challenged. Each nation state was unique and followed its own idiosyncratic response when threatened by insurgency. Although in the 1970s national counter-insurgency doctrines appeared to have a degree of uniformity, in reality there remained distinctions resulting from differing national and cultural interpretations. Reduced to their basic components, counter-insurgencies involved a ruling political regime, whose assets included the security forces and their political narrative or manifesto. Despite the uniformity of these basic components, each nation applied different social values to the relationship between the state, the population and the security apparatus, such that the *modus operandi* of each nation's counter-insurgency campaign took on the character of its host culture.

The condition which above all distinguished counter-insurgency responses from one country to another was the varying degree of their democratic accountability. A government which had a popular mandate to govern and was therefore highly accountable to its electorate became constrained in its counter-insurgent campaign. Public scrutiny and an aggressive media ensured transparency. The constitution protected individual freedom of speech, association, movement and communication and therefore prevented the government from indiscriminately spying on its own people and denying them the right to oppose the military campaign. Laws prevented the unlimited use of force against civilians who might or might not be part of the insurgency. Both national and international laws dictated how a government treated its prisoners, particularly on questions of detention without trial, the use of torture to extract information and the use of images of prisoners as part of the propaganda campaign. In some cases history has shown that an insurgent population could be subjugated by the use of overwhelming and ruthless force,[3] but this was not an option for a government striving to present itself internationally as a liberal democracy. Only the regimes and individual dictators that did not have the constraints of seeking re-election were free to use force indiscriminately and disregard the individual freedoms of the population.

For several centuries rich secure states of the northern hemisphere had participated in military alliances, which increasingly compelled them to share their military procedures and doctrine. In the case of NATO it had taken four decades to move towards commonly accepted standards of equipment and operating procedures for war fighting.[4] However, the deployment of NATO-led coalitions to Bosnia, Kosovo and Afghanistan (where, broadly speaking, their task was to restore a monopoly of violence to a legitimate government) demonstrated that although a degree of uniformity existed on questions of war fighting, internal military operations and counter-insurgency were still an intensely national issue and lay well beyond the authority of the rulers of the NATO alliance.

## The Limitations of British Doctrine[5]

Chapter 2 reached the conclusion that Mao's version of peoples' war had been altered by global change and by rapid advances in technology. These mutations emerged in an intuitive fashion from the crowded suburbs of Latin America's slum towns, and later in the Eastern Mediterranean region, in places and situations which did not directly involve the rich and secure NATO nations. Chapter 2 also suggested that globalised insurgency was not a disembodied form of terrorism and lay on an evolutionary path that was directly connected to Mao. Globalised insurgency could therefore be understood and explained from the perspective of our existing experience. But counter-insurgency was an intermittent affair and the problem was to find a continuous thread in our own experience which connected Mao to Osama bin Laden. It was perhaps for this reason that the post-colonial expeditions of the British were so enthusiastically rediscovered in the first decade of the twenty-first century.[6] If a solution to contemporary problems lay somewhere in the evolution from Mao to bin Laden then the British, with their continuity of counter-insurgency engagement throughout this period, had a unique perspective from which to understand globalised insurgency.[7]

While the British army had certainly become a repository for an extended experience, significant gaps remained. By the time NATO forces were engaged in Iraq and Afghanistan in the early 2000s and attempting to comprehend and explain global jihad, it was clear that something was missing from their conceptualisation of insurgency. The gap had opened at the end of the 1980s when the characteristics of insurgency had continued to alter vigorously, but in conflict areas that lay beyond the direct interest of Western states. In the following decade, NATO armies had failed to think about these changes or develop a counter-insurgent thinking by which to address them. The concerned departments in Whitehall were engaged in peace support operations or counter-terrorism, and insurgency had acquired a fixed insignificance in the British government's priorities. Their *modus operandi* had not moved on except superficially since the Maoist principles derived from their post-colonial experience. Moving from this era of doctrinal stagnation to the early 2000s, young British and American officers now returned from the front lines of the insurgency in Iraq and Afghanistan declaring with some asperity that the coalition could never find the answers to global insurgency from a "stretched version of the Malaya campaign".[8] Perhaps they were right. Britain's was the longest continuity in counter-insurgency operations, but there had been scant effort to understand what specific value this extended experience offered to the contemporary situation, and, crucially, why it should not be overestimated.

In the role of imperial policeman, faced by centuries of low-level operations,[9] the British had evolved a tendency to think in terms of battalions rather than brigades or divisions.[10] The experiences of the regiment through its long and substantial history were recorded in battalion orders, standing procedures, and in the living memory of the individual officers and non commissioned officers who served alongside each other in the same units for many years. To some extent these institutional characteristics continue to provide a British battalion with its operational continuity and intuition.

The British experience began after 1945 against a global background of imperial collapse. While the imperial powers were gradually recovering from the social cost and physical damage of war, the populations of each colony urged for their self-determination. From the perspective of an aspiring rebel leader the Maoist concept for people's war seemed to provide an off-the-shelf formula for insurrection. Among the colonised populations, the sense of outrage that Mao spoke of in his 'strategic defensive' phase was already establishing itself, and the Maoist formula provided an eminently adaptable road map that could be adapted to national circumstances.[11] The British defeat of what was essentially a Maoist model of insurgency in Malaya was doctrinally significant. The Malaya campaign demonstrated that despite the stark predictions of domino theorists, the Maoist formula was not, after all, irresistible. Malaya did not change the course of history but at a national level it gave the British a central concept for their counter strategy in later campaigns (in particular, North Borneo, Oman and, to a lesser extent, Northern Ireland), reinforcing their position in the small group of nations that held counter-insurgency expertise.

For the purpose of this account, the Malaya campaign provided several important lessons. The counter-insurgency started badly and the British initially succumbed to a wartime obsession with deploying large military formations into the vast tracts of rubber plantation and primary rainforest, which proved counter-productive. An experienced caucus of colonial civil servants and military officers saved them from a bad situation that was rapidly approaching its tipping point. They devised a manoeuvrist strategy that focused on the political dimension of the campaign—the Chinese population and their support for the insurgency—rather than the strictly military problem of killing terrorists. The government plan was to address the swamp rather than the mosquitoes that continuously emerged from it.[12]

This experience established a list of institutionally accepted principles and prerequisites such as:

– politics had to take priority, the imperative was the political plan and the military purpose was to support it;
– an operational structure had to be created to execute that plan that was multi-agency and multi-functional, under civil control and capable of putting into effect a delicate strategy;
– an uprising following a people's war strategy could not be countered by military attrition alone;

- when the population was successfully engaged and subverted by insurgency, there was a point in the campaign after which no lawful counter-strategy was likely to prevail;[13]
- at the tactical level the conduct and quality of junior military leaders involved in counter-insurgency was crucial;
- low-level tactics and procedures of counter-insurgency were in principle much the same for each operation;
- intelligence-led operations required a risk-benefit approach to low level operations which were the antithesis to a "send the bullet and not the man"[14] dictum for dominating territory by fire;
- the Maoists aim was to subvert the population to their side and the British counter-strategy sought to persuade it back to the government side.[15]

The concept which lay at the heart of the British experience could be explained as I + POP > SF + GOV. In this equation I represented insurgents, POP—population in the operational space, SF—the security forces and GOV—the government of the opposing regime. The Maoists aim was to subvert the population to their side of the equation and the British counter strategy sought to persuade it back to the government side. Depicted in this way the equation stressed the centrality of the population and the fact that the outcome of the campaign was generally decided by their disposition and support for the winning side.

In the decade that followed the dissolution of the Warsaw Pact, the utility of British counter-insurgency doctrine was challenged by the swiftly evolving nature of insurgency. Although the central importance of the population was still reflected, there were assumptions in British doctrine and in the unchanged British way of thinking at battalion level, which were now dangerously misleading. In the field manuals that appeared in 1977 and 1995 there was a serious failure to recognise the importance of having operated in a colonial or a post colonial environment and the consequent dangers of imagining that the *modus operandi* that evolved in this relatively familiar situation could be transferred to a place where none of these conditions existed.

During the postwar dismantling of empire and the political stampede to erase every aspect of Britain's colonial past, the imperial conditions that had been the essential planks of their counter-insurgency doctrine were neither understood nor recognised as factors of success. The desire to throw away the whole experience obscured the significance of the colonial presence and its legacy in British counter-insurgency doctrine. Doctrine writers understood that winning the consent of the population was, and still is, the primary objective in countering a Maoist style insurgency but failed to see that even in a colony, consent was a key condition for success. In many cases, once established, British colonies functioned peacefully only with the tacit consent of a sizeable and influential element of the population. The ratio of coloniser to colonised—of the tiny British contingent to the vast numbers of the native population—suggested that a degree of consent to their presence was already inherent. The officials in each colony were competitively selected from an educated and ambitious British upper class, in many cases they were talented and intrepid men, used to living and campaigning in the field, with an intelligent grasp of their territory, its people, languages and culture. They survived and succeeded on their wits, natural authority and knowledge. When the colonised population rose up in insurrection and a military force was rushed to the scene, it was subordinated to these same British administrators who became responsible for the direction of the campaign.[16] All the problems of devising a political strategy, ensuring the legitimacy of the military actions and restoring the structures of governance were taken care of by a familiar hub of individuals. It was a continuously reconvening club in which personal relationships tended to override the ambiguities of their civil-military partnership. It was therefore the colonial administration, and versions that replaced it after de-colonisation,[17] that played a most important part of the counter-insurgent strategy. The engagement between the government and the military tended to follow a comfortingly similar pattern whether the incoming British battalion found itself in sub-Saharan Africa, Southeast Asia or the Middle East. The battalions which rushed to the epicentre of the insurrection found themselves locked into a familiar system of English-speaking officials with an unsurpassed knowledge of the land and its people. It was the resident colonial staff who designed the counter-insurgent strategy and provided the political insight to design the campaign objectives and resuscitate the state's authority.

When it came to transferring this experience to a field manual, the authors focused on the military *modus operandi* and failed to appreciate that the crucial lessons of their experience lay in the nature of a civil-military understanding that had existed long before the military campaign. But this was never formally identified as an essential factor. Although British doctrine emphasised political primacy and civil-military cooperation it was designed as a military handbook, and its style and focus reflected its intended military readership.

By the 1990s the colonial officials who had been the key element in every operation since Cardwell were now missing. Coalition forces were intervening in countries that were the antithesis of the former colonies, where the incoming military were regarded as occupiers and where there was no familiar structure of colonial officials and district officers to be seen. Moreover, the diplomats who belatedly attempted to fill this role, although no doubt intellectually brilliant, crucially lacked the derring-do, local credibility and natural authority[18] of their colonial era predecessors.[19] A few extra hands from the Foreign Office or the State Department could not compensate for this loss, a problem which was only exacerbated when Britain and the United States found themselves embroiled in even more complicated terrain of the twenty-first century campaigns. As Rory Stewart explained in 2003 from the impeccable position of a newly appointed Coalition Provisional Authority's deputy governor of Maysan Province in Iraq, "Our position reminded people of colonialism. But we were not colonial officers."[20] In Baghdad's Green Zone, during the American administration there was also a sense of moral vacuum—scenes of drinking, dancing and despair in that surreal citadel[21]—which recalled a previous genre of doomed expeditionary forces.[22]

The post-Cold War strategic environment opened a new era of low-level violence for the NATO nations in the Balkan and African emergencies, where the restoration of order required what was essentially a counter-insurgent approach. Although at local level the British counter-insurgent techniques proved to be successful, broader problems presented themselves as a result of an absence of strategy and a failure of campaign design, particularly in the civil-military structures. It was simply not a realistic option to fill the void left by the departure of a national government—with all its natural expertise and authority—with a band-aid package of contracted officials and flat-pack embassies. By the 1990s NATO armies were intervening in hostile

foreign countries that lacked the comforting framework of recognisable political leadership and local authority, and this urgently required
a new operational approach. Ad hoc efforts to replace the missing
superstructure of national government with a spaghetti tangle of international organisations and high officials rushed in from the UN had
serially failed. From a military perspective, the rich, secure states which
habitually contributed their military forces to these missions frequently found that the demands of peace support operations required
them to cross thresholds that their national parliaments were not will-
ing to countenance.[23] As General Mike Jackson put it, they simply
"held up their red cards."[24] What was distinctly lacking at the highest
levels was a compact between the multitude of international actors;
they needed a common political agreement that could uphold a campaign directing authority, provide a unity of purpose, and authorise a
structure for co-operation and a methodology for addressing the
vacuum of governance on the ground. Unless the highly independent
actors which made up the international response habitually subordinated themselves to a single authority, each campaign had to start
from a blank sheet of paper. Interdepartmental rivalries and failures
of cooperation also raged in Washington and Whitehall and these
tensions transferred down to the ground and created self-defeating
situations for the young men and women who represented them in
the field.

The civil administration, which had been an essential part of the
campaign, was lost, and it was dangerous to imagine that a few extra
pages in any field manual could restore it. No commonly agreed *modus
operandi* was ever established between the Western nations as they
grappled with the complex emergencies of the 1990s—they were never
effectively organised to function as a single operational force or in
harmony with the array of civil agencies who played an equally important part in the drama. Although it seemed as if there was a doctrinal
continuity from the Maoist era of insurgency and counter-insurgency,
in reality there was not. The international dimension of a new era of
coalition forces was an obstacle to operational effectiveness that was
never addressed with conviction. Expectations were too high; it had
taken NATO states several decades to agree how to direct and fight
a conventional engagement in the relatively small operational space

along the inner German border—why should anyone imagine that the 75 nations and several hundred civil agencies who poured into these new, byzantine scenarios could achieve the same degree of operational co-operation in just a few years? A concept to overcome the problems of the international dimension was completely missing from our doctrine.

### The Growing Significance of the Propaganda of the Deed

The other missing dimension in our doctrinal thinking concerned the central importance of the media and the exploitation of imagery. Although the British understood the use of propaganda and psychological operations, in common with the other NATO armies they did not understand how it was distinguished from the propaganda of the deed or the fact that for some insurgencies the latter had become the primary instrument of the campaign. Towards the end of the Cold War, before NATO armies began to grapple with the problems of peace support operations, a dimension of insurgency began to emerge and grow that was to have a huge significance after 9/11.

The propaganda of the deed began as a nineteenth century anarchist concept which prescribed a process to arouse a population from a state of sullen endurance to uncontrollable passion by committing visible acts of violence. In the crowded industrial cities of that period there was good reason to believe that a defiant deed could trigger off rioting and lead to wider insurrection. Faced by overwhelming state security forces, these urban revolutionaries had to proclaim their message by deeds not words "for this is the most popular, the most potent form of propaganda."[25] Several decades later this crude idea was developed into a more formidable insurgent technique by Patrick Pearse and the Irish Republican Brotherhood. In their view "agitation propaganda was needed to awaken the masses from their unpatriotic slumber and lead them into violent action."[26] Pearse's target audience was the element of the Catholic Irish who already hated the British as a sacred duty and were ready to believe his glittering generalities about the future because they appealed to an existing animosity and a common narrative of injustice and deprivation.[27] This deeply prejudiced audience was Pearce's entry point into a wider Irish population through which he could spread his message and his activism.

Half a century later in the 1960s two quite separate insurgent campaigns began to demonstrate the significance of this technique in a post industrial society and how it was a logical development of the Maoist approach to insurgency. From their Ulster enclaves Northern Irish nationalists were using it to mobilise distant elements of the Catholic Irish diaspora, and in southern Lebanon Palestinian militants were using it to mobilise their refugee communities in the Eastern Mediterranean. Although separated by territory, culture and aspirations, the Irish Republican Army (IRA) and the Palestinian Liberation Organisation (PLO)—and their respective derivations—had several things in common. Israel and Ulster were small, populated and highly developed territories. In these crowded areas there was no space or sanctuary for the popularly misconceived "guerrilla fighter" to survive and carry on a traditional military campaign of harassing attacks. Both cases involved populations of dislocated or outraged activists who were in effect "prepared audiences", who already had a cultivated hatred for the adversary state (the United Kingdom and Israel) and impossibly high expectations for the outcome of the insurgent campaign.[28] Armed with the huge optimism and resourcefulness that is essential for any successful insurgent, the respective leadership of each insurgency endeavoured to bypass the obviously disastrous military-attrition option and opened a more political dimension of the campaign. In principle their aim was to move gradually towards their objectives by mobilising popular opinion around the world as well as within the national boundaries of the insurgency. The PLO and the Provisional IRA (PIRA) both succeeded in placing the concept of the propaganda of the deed at the centre of a new chapter of insurgency. And in both cases the military staff that opposed them and whose job it was to monitor doctrine failed to understand the significance of what was happening.

The Palestinian exodus from what is now Israel began in 1948, initially as a trickle of displaced farmers moving to existing communities in the surrounding Arab states; but after the 1967 war and the Israeli seizure of the West Bank and the Gaza Strip, the trickle became a torrent, instinctively heading for closer sanctuaries in Jordan, Syria and Lebanon. During the period in which the Palestinian population fled and then re-congregated, a leadership emerged among the refugee camps in southern Lebanon. Its purpose was to improve the lives of refugees and represent their case to the rest of the world. The PLO vowed to restore the Palestinians to their former lands in Israel. Within its structure was a miscellany of terrorist groups whose purpose was to strike Israel's population, territory and interests. They seemed to be driven by an instinctive urge for retribution rather than a carefully thought out, stage by stage campaign strategy. Their attacks against fortified Kibbutz systems, the Israeli military and the public—and more randomly against civil aircraft, cruise ships, embassies and even sports teams—appeared to be a list of disconnected acts. However, against a rapidly altering social environment in which individuals and disparate communities were increasingly banded together by the radio news and TV imagery of the media, there was an important connecting factor. Each act, usually in its final stages, became highly visible to the world and often encouraged the interest of reporters, press photographers, and television film teams. The attacks were becoming irresistible as news stories, visually sensational and carried out with a desperate conviction. Much later, the involvement of suicide bombers emphasised the despair of the terrorists; the young men dressed like kamikaze pilots, became a story within the story and the plight of the Israeli victims was eclipsed by the shocking imagery of the act.

The purpose of this drama and visibility was ostensibly for the attackers to articulate some (usually impossible) demand or condition relating to their ongoing campaign. But crazy demands often turned out to be less interesting than the aura of celebrity surrounding the act itself, initially generated by the nature of the incident but ramped up to a much higher pitch by a frenzied international media whose headlines propagated it throughout the world. Individual hijackers began to take on the same public notoriety as footballers and pop stars, and with celebrity came the subliminal narrative of what was happening and what had happened to the Palestinians. The media stampede was now sensationalising, multiplying, translating and dispersing this message to important audiences—the Palestinian diaspora, Arab states, the international Muslim community—and across the northern hemisphere the protest generation of students and young liberals were now thinking and agitating about Palestine. The misery and degradation which was unintentionally communicated by the hijack story tapped into Arab and Muslim concerns. Among audiences were groups and individuals who, in Pearse's logic, had already been subjected to the constant pre-propaganda of their circumstances and who therefore shared a common narrative of the Israeli occupation and a hatred that was practically a religious duty. These people became the entry point through which to reach a wider audience. A growing awareness of the conflict brought benefits for the Palestinians—sympathetic states offered cash, weapons, training, logistical support, international places of refuge and diplomatic protection. Above all came recognition; the Palestinians began to develop an international personality and were now conspicuous at the UN General Assembly among the non-aligned members.

The gurus of counter-insurgency missed the significance of this technique. In reality it was the only viable plank of a campaign in what was otherwise a hopeless situation for an uprising. While reluctantly acknowledging that the PLO factions were successfully promoting a cause, the insurgency experts of the period[29] felt that, except to the most biased observers, the Palestinian protracted popular war strategy was a failure.[30] The Israelis had, after all, prevented the PLO from implementing a shadow government in the occupied areas and the movement itself was beset by disunity and was therefore unable to function as a government. In the 1980s, the success of an insurgency was still measured in orthodox terms by territory controlled, government forces physically defeated and shadow regimes installed. By this measure, the PIRA campaign in Northern Ireland also failed.

These processes were not understood or conceptualised by Western military staff as they moved through the chaotic '90s into the twenty-first century. Although several writers explained the armed propaganda effect,[31] the experience of insurgency and counter-insurgency as a Maoist phenomenon was too strong to allow fundamental changes to doctrine or to even consider the relevance of Palestinian events.[32] British doctrine cautiously referred to "media" and "propaganda" but made no attempt to fasten these ideas together and explain how the propaganda of the deed had taken on a new significance in line with the growing power of communications and the dispersal of populations.

From the West's perspective, the Palestinian movement of the 1960s had taken on a fixed insignificance as a rabble of counteracting factions, which had little hope of achieving its stated objective of eradicating the Israeli state or even more realistically to challenge its presence on Palestinian land. In terms of body counts and territory, the Palestinian campaign had failed. But this characterisation refused to see the evolutionary importance of what was happening. It was not so much their nationalism or their ideology which was important—their long-term significance lay in the methodology they employed, the intuitive use of a dispersed audience that could only be reached through the media, which itself was rapidly proliferating at the time, its technological advancements matched by an increasing taste for the sensational and immediate. Focusing on the statistics related to military attrition and territorial gain had blinded Western doctrine writers to the developments occurring in the propaganda of the deed. The Palestinian insurgency opened a new chapter, which is essential to our understanding of how the propaganda of the deed was later adapted to the needs of the global jihad.

Several decades on, the significance of the PLO and PIRA campaigns and the value of the propaganda of the deed ought to be clearer. However, by 2001 there were still several lessons that were crucially missing from British doctrine. The apparently senseless bomb blasts in Ulster and the PLO campaign of hijacks and bombings had successfully exploited the growing energy of the media and thereby aroused a wider awareness of what was happening. In the case of the PLO it was becoming a people's war by proxy and the millions of sympathetic Muslim viewers and readers were not necessarily activists but, like football supporters watching their teams on TV, the insurgent's goal-scoring moments also became their own. The appalling nature of the attacks and the catastrophic brawling within the PLO hierarchy were airbrushed away; fanaticism and notoriety were seen as conviction and celebrity. In the 1920s Irish nationalist concept of "pre-propaganda" they were audiences that were already persuaded, they saw what they wanted to see. The images, print stories and the international nature of the drama became a source of mobilising energy that boosted the morale of migrant communities and acted as a call to arms for young men seeking to escape the grinding misery of the refugee camps. The media-marketing age made it both possible and credible to mobilise a dispersed and disaffected population. The news value of an act of violence now outweighed its tactical value and this was altering the definition of insurgency.[33] Recognition, notoriety, activism—these were the factors by which an insurgent campaign measured its success, not the amount of territory it held or the number of governments it had overthrown. By 2001, British military doctrine briefly recognised the "dangers of Islamism"[34] and insurgents' exploitation of the media, with particular reference to radio, TV and the press.[35] But there was nothing in it which went on to ask: "so what?" No one was keen to find out how images of bombs and troops and screaming civilians were reaching and moving vast audiences and were therefore probably the most influential instrument in achieving the strategic purpose of the insurgency. No one was looking at how these images, which regularly reached the Palestinian viewers and their supporters, were so damaging as to override the benefits of day-to-day success stories from their counter-insurgent opponents, whose weapons searches, cordons and one-day-brigade raids could only deliver short-term results. It should have been possible to see that, boosted by the rampaging power of the media, the propaganda of the deed had moved from Cinderella obscurity to centre stage. And yet according to the British military doctrine of July 2001, the end-state by which insurgency should be measured was still the ability to achieve "a straightforward seizure of power" or to establish an autonomous state.[36]

Recognising this virtual dimension as the overriding objective of a post-Maoist insurgency and counter-insurgency had awkward consequences. It disturbed the comfortable categorisation of insurgency as something done by guerrillas in distant wildernesses that seldom intruded upon rich and secure societies. In reality, the power of the propaganda of the deed was forcing an inversion of tactical priorities. Military commanders would have to think about the visual effect of what they did under the floodlights of the world media. Recognising the importance of the virtual would also alter the equation (I + POP > GOV + SF) which lay at the heart of counter-insurgency philosophy. A new version of the equation would have to show that the vital ground—the target population (POP)—did not refer simply to a territorially defined population but to several populations spread across the region, as well as a globally dispersed migrant constituency. The PLO campaign had been both laboratory and forerunner for a

powerful new strain of insurgency and added additional complications
to what was already a complicated problem. In the case of the Palestinians, the Israeli military and the retributive nature of their counter-
action had taught us nothing about how to deal with what was in
effect a progression in the evolution of insurgency. The only people who
seemed to have learned from the experiment were the insurgents.

4

# THE CHRONOLOGY OF NEGLECT

*By the 1990s the consequences of strategic change had forced the West to rethink their approach to low-level military interventions. But, instead of studying and revising their existing knowledge of insurgency and counter-insurgency, they were persuaded by the 'peace-activities' lobby to develop a* modus operandi *for peace support operations. Consequently all thinking and doctrinal development of counter-insurgency was discontinued during that crucial decade in which the insurgents raced ahead of us in their understanding of global insurgency.*

Because the rich, safe countries of the NATO alliance had failed to monitor how insurgency was changing in other parts of the world, they were destined to be surprised. During the 1980s and 1990s they had ignored insurgency and failed to spot the embryonic versions of what was to follow in the next millennium. Although being surprised is inherent to counter-insurgency, by the end of the Cold War the pace of change was speeding up, insurgents altered faster than the ponderous military alliances which sought to contain them, so being surprised was becoming a condition from which it was doctrinally less and less easy to recover. Insurgency was mutating aggressively like a flu virus searching for potential weak spots in its environment. It was outstripping its opponents' ability to observe, conceptualise and respond. Nevertheless, there were individual academics and military officers who certainly understood what was happening. From the unchallengeable perspective of the media staff in Headquarters Northern Ireland, Brigadier Maurice Tugwell had conceptualised the significance of the propaganda of the deed in his 1979 PhD thesis and later publications.[1]

Similarly there were observers who understood how Palestinian insurgents were subverting a sympathetic regional audience through the media. However, the degree to which these prescient figures actually managed to sway government and military thinking is less obvious. Institutional wisdom is buried in the fabric of government departments and military units and only emerges according to needs and fashion that are dictated by public interest and the political climate. This chapter describes how the military staff and research academics in NATO armies responsible for counter-insurgency doctrine were constrained to focus on the peace-building and state-building aspects of peace support operations and failed to monitor the swiftly changing nature of counter-insurgency.

Staff colleges are the barometers of fashion and the selections and omissions that comprise their course manuals therefore provide a measurement of contemporary military attitudes. There were two particular periods when it was important to see where fashionable thinking had reached. The first was at the end of the 1980s when military institutions were intellectually rousing themselves after forty years of stagnation and the fruitless hypotheses of nuclear strategy. The second stage was at the end of the 1990s. By this time, coalitions of post Cold War alliances[2] had deployed their newly reorganised forces to complex emergencies in Africa, Asia and closer to home in the former Yugoslavia.[3] As part of a new genre of peace-supervising forces, they had experienced casualties, frustrations and failures, despite the primitive nature of the local militias which opposed them. Global change had been gradually altering the environment of the insurgent, but in the West, fashionable thinking was focused on peace operations in which there was apparently no adversary—only "spoilers". Western forces were therefore badly surprised when insurgency re-emerged centre stage in its global manifestation.

## Moving Beyond the Colonial Version of Countering Insurgency

The Cold War and its procedures were intensely demanding and little intellectual engagement beyond its needs seemed to take place. The study of counter insurgency was at a standstill, so that by the end of the Cold War the colonial *modus operandi* for counter-insurgency training was still reverentially followed. Young British officers spent little time on this discipline, but when they did, a frequently used scenario for practicing the restoration of law and order in an overseas setting began with an incident in which a howling mob was advancing towards the district courthouse (a building which seemed to feature in most training events).[4] In the routinely used storyline shops were burning, bands of looters were out in the streets, the police had disappeared and the only force that could prevent the total destruction of the town and its local government was the recently arrived 1st Battalion of the Blankshire Regiment (of which the student was the commander). The problem which had to be solved invariably began with the following narrative: "…from the smouldering doors of the courthouse steps the dishevelled figure of the district magistrate who hands you a letter containing the urgent and lawful request for your troops to restore order with immediate effect. What is your next move?"

In the 1960s and 1970s the significance of this scenario, and the derivations played out in British training centres during the Cold War, lay in the magistrate's letter. It was a subconscious hangover from an era when the government regime to be restored was most likely to be either a British colonial administration or an independent state based on the same familiar structures. Long after the end of the post-colonial run down, the 'magistrate's letter' narrative continued to represent a syndrome, an institutional state of mind, that refused to be shaken by reality. The handbook for the counter-insurgency element of the 1989 British Army Staff Course still bore traces of this scenario and its associations.[5] Although the magistrates letter is not used as an exercise device, the concept of requesting military assistance because the incumbent government and local forces "are no longer able to deal with an existing or developing threat" is central to the counter-insurgent response in these notes. And the continued presence of the government implied the existence of a residual team of officials who would take care of the political aspect of strategic planning.

The significance of the 1989 handbook is that it shows how far the British had reached in their understanding of the evolution of insurgency—the Staff College instructors who put it together were the cleverest officers of their year and their teaching represented the cutting edge of military thinking,[6] and what they were still advocating was an essentially Maoist scenario. The population continued to be "the key to the entire struggle."[7] The insurgent's end state was reassuringly territorial and their operations were designed to meet orthodox political objectives. The campaign was presented as a protracted affair in which the insurgent would gradually replace the writ of a failing government with their own "local administrative network". Mao's phases of revolutionary warfare were still regarded as the classic formula.

From the perspective of the intervening force's response, the Staff College emphasised the integrated nature of counter-revolutionary warfare and made the point that the military was but one element of the campaign. The host government was in charge, they would provide the political aim, the public information strategy, intelligence and security tasking and the necessary emergency legislation; they would also resuscitate the local police and military forces and establish a "framework for joint civil and military control of security operations"[8]. In a nod to prevailing fashions, the Staff College also recognised Tugwell's ideas and the course handbook explained a psychological dimension of operations[9]. However, whereas Tugwell had implied that media operations were becoming increasingly central to the *modus operandi* of a counter-revolutionary force, the Staff College writing team was more cautious. Their handbook categorised these functions as the management of propaganda and psychological operations, which put them at the edge rather than the centre of a commander's plan.[10]

In the 1980s it was, however, not possible for the Staff Colleges to ignore the extra-territorial phenomenon of the Palestinian insurgency against Israel. The 1989 handbook explained this entire genre of operations as "international terrorism" and defined the insurgent movements in southern Lebanon and the Palestinian Territories (as well as parts of the IRA) as "international terrorist groups".[11] Terrorism, according to the handbook, was a crime and did not lead towards a legitimate revolutionary end state. It recognised that terrorists exploited the vulnerability "of modern technological states ... to draw attention to a neglected cause," but it did not specify the example of the PLO and the particular significance that terrorism held for a group of its nature. In the twilight period of the Cold War, international terrorism was still seen as an extension of East-West rivalry, an instrument whereby certain states supported terrorists in order to pressurise or cajole their opponents.[12] But in 1989, the British Army Staff College along with most of its NATO partners was unwilling to see that their list of international terrorist organisations had confused large and operationally effective insurgent movements, such as the PLO and Hizbollah, who enjoyed the sympathetic support of many thousands of people around the Eastern Mediterranean, with tiny isolated groups, such as the June 2nd Movement in Germany and the Japanese Red Army. If they had addressed this contradiction with greater rigour they might have concluded that the large insurgent movements associated with the Shia and Palestinian populations were not acting for the same reasons or organised in the same way as the minute groups of wild young men and women with whom they were being categorised. This might have led on to the proposition that Amal and the PLO were far more than terrorists—they were insurgents for whom terrorism represented only one path to their ultimate goal. But this line of reasoning was ignored by Western defence institutions who could only recognise insurgency when it had the familiar appearance of protracted Maoist guerrilla warfare. They were intellectually careless that beyond their established concepts, the nature of insurgency was altering and the part played by terrorism and the propaganda of the deed in the overall campaign was evolving among the stressed and expectant communities of Palestinians and Irish nationalists. Postmodern insurgents were reaching their goals by gaining international recognition and global sympathy. With these, they had successfully outflanked the counter-terrorism forces lined up against them, whose inventory of purely kinetic, muscular responses lacked any kind of political imagination.

What were the consequences of this continued blindness? The 1989 Staff College handbook was a competent document. It reflected a marriage of the Maoist concept with recent operational experience, which for the British was in Northern Ireland. It acknowledged the as yet unchallenged idea that the population was the vital ground for both the insurgent and the counter-insurgent forces. It emphasised political primacy in the formulation of counter strategy. It conceded a subordinate role for the military and explained the multi-faceted nature of the response and the need for the government to take responsibility for political tactics and the resuscitation of government structures. It also acknowledged the significance of propaganda and psychological operations. But the problem with any staff college handbook or military doctrine was that it had to look backwards in order to be acceptable as a teaching text; for this reason it was no more than an accepted version of past experience. As General Alastair Irwin, who in 1989 was a Lieutenant Colonel and leader of the Counter Revolutionary Warfare writing team, recollected:

"each new version (of the counter revolutionary warfare manual) appeared shortly after the conclusion of the last campaign. So the version in our hands when we went to Northern Ireland was the version that was substantially based on the Aden experience. So sub-consciously the collective mind was set in the immediate past rather than the immediate present. Past experience is surely bound to affect the way people approached a new problem, even if at times this could be misguided."[13]

Irwin, and his co-authors (outstanding officers who were meteorically successful in their army careers) could not have known that they stood on the threshold of a chaotic decade in which there would be a dramatic reconfiguration of the security environment.

## Fusion and Confusion in the Chaotic Nineties

In the 1990s seismic international events and long-term trends converged into what turned out to be a decade of continuous surprises. The Warsaw Pact and NATO armies were still physically and mentally configured for mass warfare on an intercontinental scale. Amid the shambles of downsizing and restructuring, the war fighting formations of the Cold War moved across a threshold into a new chapter of global security in which peace support operations, and the restoration of order in collapsing states became the only show in town for most European defence forces. The social impact of these events is described in greater detail in Chapter 2. This assessment focuses narrowly on the intertwined narratives of counter-insurgency thinking, peace support operations and international terrorism. Across Europe a discontinued generation of nuclear strategists flung aside their textbooks on mutual destruction and became born-again peacekeeping experts. There were plenty of problems for them to solve. Military coalitions made up from the former war fighting units of NATO and the Warsaw Pact now found themselves together in the same expeditionary forces, facing situations that in some respects were reminiscent of the 'magistrate's letter'—the riot control exercises used to train young British officers since the 1960s. However, things had changed, for there was no longer the friendly, dishevelled magistrate—nor the entire regime of familiar officials and local forces which he represented—to provide the political dimension of the campaign plan that was vital in order to win over the population. This aspect of the operational framework had disappeared by the time NATO armies found themselves in the collapsing states of Cambodia, Kosovo and the other disintegrating parts of the globe. Their political leaders enthusiastically deployed them to these hostile places, but they made no effective provisions to replace the crucially missing element of the campaign planning structure or to achieve a sufficiently binding alliance that would compel the various forces and agencies involved to work together.

By 1993 the doctrinal pioneers of peace support operations, were also instructors at the British Army Staff College.[14] The central problem they had to address was that, in a collapsing state, the intervening military had to restore a monopoly of violence into the hands of some form of legitimate government. Although in terms of the breakdown of law and order this was a familiar narrative, the obvious nature of the solution became obscured by a hugely convoluted and unmanageable international dimension. In the "new world order" the strictly national approach had to be cast aside. The Foreign Office, egged on by Clare Short's[15] department for international development, was obsessively fastened on the UN peacekeeping scenario as the framework for military action. As a result the Staff College writing team were compelled to put aside forty years of campaign experience which was entirely relevant to the problems of restoring a monopoly of violence to a weak state.

However, the UN's consent-based approach was designed for situations in which peacekeeping troops policed inert buffer zones to keep old-war combatants apart[16] and the contingencies of the 1990s did not fit this model. Despite serial ceasefire agreements and truces of every kind, the international forces in collapsing states often found themselves thwarted by local militias who refused to allow the peace process to succeed. On the ground there was a political vacuum at both the strategic and operational level and no caucus of friendly officials to represent the host state and provide a political strategy. As a result, young NATO officers found themselves standing in the wreckage of European, African and Asian towns, having to act as mayor, police chief, fireman, ambulance provider, housing officer, prison warden and market economist.

Despite serial failures to address problems of operational coherence, by the mid-1990s, peace support operations had moved up in our scale of priorities to become irresistibly fashionable, while counter-insurgency moved down into total obscurity. In 1996 the publication of a redrafted version of the *British Army Field Manual* on counter-insurgency was limited to only a few copies in favour of the production of a peace support operations manual.[17] Counter-insurgency was by now irretrievably consigned to the jungle trails and mountain passes of history and its unsavoury connections to colonialism set off alarm bells among the politically correct officials who now dominated the new era of humanitarian operations. However, while fashionable thinkers fixated on peace support operations, the British forces that found themselves plunged into the wreckage of failed states intuitively applied the counter-insurgency experience that survived from Northern Ireland.[18] Towards the end of the decade this approach was finally gaining recognition. British generals commanding the international forces in Bosnia and Sierra Leone now had sufficient confidence to say publicly that their first priority was to re-establish security and that what they were doing was essentially counter-insurgency by another name.[19] Gradually, military fashions were changing as it became increasingly difficult to deny that the international community was facing local forces who had no interest in a peace process being imposed upon them. Although humanitarians continued to call these adversaries "spoilers" so as to preserve their neutrality, development agencies who were committed to a successful peace process now took a more robust view of those who sought to kill them or loot their assets. It was clear, even to the high priests of UN orthodoxy, that intervening troops could no longer rely on the significance of their blue berets and white vehicles to protect them when they sought to restore order in the face of a determined and unprincipled adversary.

Throughout this period, the insurgent had been altering at the same pace and intensity as the environment, spurred on by the pressures of global change, migration and the proliferation of cheap communication technology. But the military staff trailed behind these developments, failing to understand the consequences of a more globalised operational space and distracted by the UN enthusiasts in Whitehall. In 2001, British military staff were still failing to interpret what was happening in the operational space as a significant evolutionary progression. In the orthodox environment of the Staff College and Westminster, peace support operations and counter-insurgency were regarded as separate antithetical disciplines, whereas on the ground a fusion had been taking place for some time. The physical truth of this fusion was demonstrated in their own downsizing arrangements. The Northern Ireland Training and Advisory Team (NITAT) which prepared units for Northern Ireland, and the United Nations Training Assistant Groups (UNTAG) which did the same for units destined for complex emergencies, had originally been doctrinally and physically separated. But in 1998 it was finally conceded that the two had to merge, probably for administrative reasons but as a corollary, it now became impossible to deny the similarity of techniques being used for both operations. Furthermore, that year saw the publication of a new Army handbook for "Operations Other than War", which explicitly brought together the two hitherto separated concepts of peacekeeping and counter-insurgency under the same cover.[20] This demonstrated as nothing else could, a reflection of what troops were finding on the ground—that the two disciplines were merging, and that the understanding of insurgency and counter-insurgency was highly relevant to the complex emergencies of the 1990s.

What the 1998 handbook and its revised counter-insurgency doctrine failed to anticipate were the wider implications of insurgencies on a global scale. By a supreme irony, it was published in June 2001 just months before the Al-Qaeda attacks on New York and Washington. After the towers fell on 11 September, the actions of the internationally organised jihadi activists were universally regarded as a form of sensational terrorism whose perpetrators were so desperate that they could not be politically engaged. This attitude discouraged any thinking that might recognise this movement as an evolutionary progression of insurgency.

The discourse now focused so obsessively on international terrorism that it excluded the evolutionary perspective. While some academics and military doctrine writers continued to recognise the connection between insurgency and terrorism, the aficionados of terrorism had turned up the spotlights to illuminate a strictly kinetic dimension of the campaign. In spite of all the institutional experience to the contrary, by the 1990s, terrorism and counter-terrorism were being regarded as stand-alone activities. Government agencies associated with counter-terrorism had developed their own short-term responses which were not led by a political strategy. These consisted of practical procedures involving special police departments, surveillance, heightened security, extra protection for public events and transport, intelligence targeting and so forth—all of which aimed to catch or kill terrorists. It was an immediate and narrowly kinetic response and in the longer term failed to recognise that terrorism was invariably part of a larger insurgent campaign of political violence and propaganda. There was now a tendency to see terrorism as a disembodied event and not as one part of a larger campaign of subversion, which in this thinking could therefore be dealt with exclusively by physical counter measures. Government officials did not want to see it as a form of insurgency, it was politically more acceptable to categorise it as something which had no support or realistic objective. Counter-terrorism was therefore apolitical, there was a complete absence of strategy in its conduct and the "Global War on Terror" represented the ultimate stage in the elevation of counter-terrorism.

## Updating the Insurgency–Terrorism Relationship

Although the distinction between terrorism and insurgency was becoming blurred by a surge of popular theories which arose from an over-promoted view of terrorism during the 1970s and 1980s, in practical terms the relationship had not changed. Their relative positions were set out with greater authority and some care in military doctrine during the Cold War.[21] The distinction was also reinforced by individuals[22] who argued that groups which used bombing, assassination, hostage-taking and similar acts, but failed to combine these acts with a broader subversive campaign, quickly found themselves fastened in a cycle of violence that seldom succeeded in gaining the sympathy of a wider population; they could therefore be correctly regarded as terrorists. But a movement which in addition to committing acts of terrorism also had a political strategy to subvert the population to such an extent that it attracted a reciprocating political response from the government, amounted to something more than terrorism.[23] By successfully involving a substantial element of the population they raised the game from terrorism to insurgency. This was not just a matter of academic labelling, the significance of the distinction lay in the need for a political as opposed to a narrowly kinetic response by the government. A strictly counter-terror response did not address the possibility that the terrorists had attracted popular support. It assumed that if they were locked up or shot there was no longer a movement which could threaten the state; the surviving rump would be nothing more than a diminishing band of hard core extremists, posing a short-term threat. The government's counter-terrorist operation was therefore physical, the responsibility of the counter-terrorism units, the police, special intelligence agencies, customs, immigration, treasury and so forth. When this effort succeeded in accounting for the nucleus of activists, the emergency was over. Without a political dimension, the group had no popular sympathy to speak of and therefore lacked the capacity for regeneration,[24]

However, if a group had a political strategy, attracted public support and demonstrated that it had a serious regenerative dimension, then they were more than terrorists. Their violent acts might be described as terrorism, but by investing a great deal of energy into their subversive capability, their overall campaign was insurgent. In this case, the government had to do a lot more than lock them up or shoot them—it had to reverse the effect of the adversary's political engagement with the people. This required the campaign to have a political dimension in addition to the physical procedures of counter-terrorism; most of all the government would have to create a strategy, a political narrative that could win back the disaffected element of the population. To succeed they would have to combine the techniques for restoring security with an overall political strategy that stripped away the political banners from the insurgent[25]. In British experience this involved a diversity of civil departments and agencies in addition to the instruments of counter-terrorism. These very different actors needed to become part of the same operation and their combined task was to alter the conditions which the insurgents had been exploiting.

Governments therefore tended to insist that within their own territory this form of low level violence should be labelled terrorism, because insurgency was associated with despotic regimes and downtrodden populations. In addition a counter-terrorist campaign was less complicated to execute and did not require a political strategy and an array of additional departments and agencies to put it into effect. The government could treat terrorism like measles or chicken pox—it might leave a scar but it would eventually pass. On the other hand countering an insurgency was like treating a cancer, its removal would involve life-changing surgery.

## Recognising the Evolution of Insurgency

In real terms the relationship between insurgency and terrorism had nevertheless been complicated, not by the aficionados of sensational terrorism, but by the effects of globalisation and mass communications. Insurgencies based on a people's war and its derivations, which were potent and successful throughout the Cold War, no longer represented the entire span of activity. The mainstream people's war concept which influenced our doctrine of response for so long had mutated into an the array of different insurgent campaigns that looked and acted very differently. Although the process of mutation went unnoticed for several decades, the different typologies were visible during the 1990s and, by 2001, insurgency could be better explained as having spread into several categories. These are shown below as a spectrum.

In doctrinal terms (referring to chart on page 73) the true successor of the Maoist model was "popular insurgency".[26] The "feral militias"[27] which, as previously explained, lay further down the scale of military competence, were also insurgents because they involved populations, but in a different way. Ending them was not a matter of simply destroying the fighters—feral militias were a consequence of a wider condition threatening the state, specifically a vacuum of governance, a collapse of civil society that encouraged the emergence of lawless

The Proliferation of Insurgent Categories

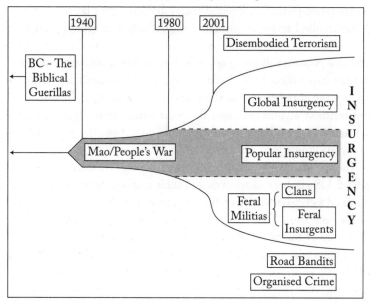

militias. Destroying the militias without attending to the wider mis-fortunes of the state would simply leave the door open for the same affliction to reassert itself. For this reason the required multi-agency, multi-disciplinary response was very similar to a form of counter-insurgency. It entailed political initiatives, state-building programmes and confidence-building measures, as well as a military intervention. So, following Wilkinson's distinction between terrorism and insur-gency, it was the nature of the required response rather than the armed rebel group that determined how a movement should be defined. In the spectrum band beyond the feral militias lay a category comprising road bandits and organised criminals who had no popular following and whose eradication was largely a physical affair.[28]

At the opposing end of the scale of military competence, global insurgency involved a more elaborate version of "population"—not just one or two populations as in the traditional Maoist sense, but a whole array of communities spread across the world. In this case the counter strategy would have to involve an international campaign that addressed the extent to which elements of this supporting diaspora continued to be subverted and thereby provided the movement with regenerative potential. Beyond the global insurgent lay a category of "disembodied terrorist", isolated individuals and groups that committed acts of self-promoting violence which failed to engage or attract a popular following and which therefore lacked any real regenerative capability. They could be eradicated without any effort to engage the population or develop a political campaign. The disembodied terrorist at one end, and the road bandit and organised crime syndicate at the other, can rightly be placed outside the general category of insurgency.

The speed at which insurgency was evolving remained unacknowledged. US strategic directives and their counter-terrorist campaigns adopted a one-screw-driver-fits-all approach which anticipated a hostile organisation that in evolutionary terms had remained static. Furthermore at the outset it had confused several categories of genuine insurgents with politically disembodied extremists which lay at edges of the chart above. This lack of rigour became more evident in the rhetoric which accompanied the "Global War on Terror". British and US experts continually fixated on the supposed end state of the global jihadist movements, rather than understanding the environment and the very modern societies from which they arose. Doctrine staff failed to acknowledge the centrality of the propaganda of the deed, and as a result, no official effort was made to design or investigate the sort of government campaign that would be required to counter a movement driven by a propaganda of the deed-strategy. Furthermore, British doctrine continued to make completely wrong assumptions about the framework within which the military campaign would take place, assumptions which were now decades out of date. In the twenty-first century it had become more difficult than ever before to conduct counter-insurgency in a foreign state. Furthermore an expeditionary counter-insurgent campaign was a political, military activity that should flow from a broad national framework, but in the US political leaders had completely failed to provide one. Excellent though it was, the new US doctrine of 2006 was in danger of becoming a moon without a planet around which to orbit.[29]

Had the West been continuously engaged with the changing nature of insurgency and absorbed its implications, it would not have been such a problem to explain the evolutionary trajectory from Mao to Osama bin Laden. But institutionally, there was now a failure to see bin Laden's strategy as a development from a previously understood concept of insurgency. Instead the media and public interest became engrossed by terrorism, the inconsistencies of Islamism and physical solutions. Despite the historical gaps and the absence of an overarching national security structure, Europe's experience of counter-insurgency rather than terrorism was still the obvious perspective from which to understand the developments which seemed to follow in close succession after 11 September 2001.

These were the reasons why the rich, safe countries and most of the remaining world were destined to be surprised by global jihad. It would take several lost years for us to understand that counter-insurgency was the stronger discipline from which to interpret the violence of the new millennium and not counter-terrorism. But by the time fashionable thinkers began to see this, counter-insurgency doctrine had been standing still for more than thirty years. When it was rediscovered, it was too late; counter-insurgency doctrine, the horse on which we now bet all our money had become a pathetic and neglected creature, blinking in the floodlights of public expectation after decades of obscurity and neglect.

The West had not only been caught out by the timing and ferocity of the attacks on 11 September 2001, they had been caught out intellectually. When the most visible icons of US power and prosperity were smashed, the instinct was to brand the attackers as a disembodied phenomenon with almost no following that did not require a highly visible campaign of political refutation. The idea that they might be part of a global movement, and that millions of Muslims might rejoice in their success, was unimaginable to a nation recovering from psychological shock. The cost of the damage was measured in physical and emotional terms but not political. The discourse focused on what could be more easily absorbed—the casualties, the damage and the dollar cost of restoration—none of which significantly disrupted the functioning of the US. There was very little response to the concept of this act as a successful propaganda of the deed-strategy. Indeed, several years later, the West still had no definition or nomenclature by which to describe the adversary or the concept of operations which distinguished globalised insurgency. The absolutist nature of the "Global War on Terror" discussion got in the way of identifying an intelligent as opposed an intuitive response.

In September 2001, the US doctrine for counter-insurgency had not been amended for more than twenty years. The Germans had no counter-insurgency doctrine whatsoever, and the French doctrine was no more than a list of tactical procedures that were relevant to its specific post-colonial scenarios.[30] The British had recently rewritten and republished their counter-insurgency doctrine, in June 2001, but this version failed to move beyond the Maoist or national interpretation that had resulted from their experience in the former colonies and Northern Ireland. The evolutionary consequences of global change on the nature of insurgency were not addressed, had not even been properly considered by the US, the British and NATO. The movement which now attacked them had grown and developed from beyond their horizon. It was a more complicated phenomenon than any previous form of insurgency, bringing together political activists and fighters from many different countries and cultures. On 11 September 2001, if doctrine writers were thinking about insurgency at all, they were gazing comfortably backwards to the continuing possibility of a "magistrate's letter" scenario and to the wild figures swathed in belts of machine gun ammunition in the dripping jungles of a bygone colonial era.

# PART II

# POST-MAOISM

## INTRODUCTION

For NATO and the Warsaw Pact armies, the dismantling of the Berlin Wall in November 1989 marked the threshold of a new security era. European nations began to reduce their constant state of readiness and demobilise their huge continental forces leaving a smear of empty tank sheds and derelict barracks along the alignment of their former deployment. The East-West mindset of the Cold War had to change. Staff colleges had to rewrite their exercises so that imaginary battle groups no longer faced provocatively towards former enemies who now sat together in the same classes. Intelligence collection plans had to reflect the fact that former adversaries were now free to tour and photograph the highways, rail yards and bridge complexes that had recently been nuclear targets in a primary strike plan. However, although the progression from Cold War to post-Cold War had suddenly imposed a starkly different regime on organised military forces across the world, in the evolution of insurgency the process was more gradual and continuous.

Crossing the threshold into a new security era was an institutional shock for the US and Europe, but their societies and political values had been constantly altering for some time through the effects of new technology, rising prosperity and globalising forces. Insurgents too, had been moving with these changes and had become part of the twenty-first century, its technology and its networked society. The institutionalised counter-insurgent, on the other hand, had remained stationary since the 1960s. Although military forces had changed as a result of the end of the Cold War, their view of insurgency and their expectations of the insurgent were still rooted in a previous age. Society had moved on and insurgency had gone with it. By the first decade of the twenty-first century, modern forms of insurgency were unrecognisable from the 1960s versions that continued to fixate counter-insurgent thinking. The 2006 US doctrine was not a new concept, it was a repackaging of the Maoist campaign. While Western society had been moving at the speed of an express train, the study of insurgency had been standing still.

Part II describes how a globally-dispersed movement, which could be described as a globalised insurgency, has successfully pushed the whole concept of insurgency into a new chapter in its development. It aims to explain the characteristics that distinguish an increasingly globalised era from its Maoist antecedents. Part II is less about the particularities of radical Islam and the technicalities of terrorism and more about how an entire span of globalising activities has advanced the concept of insurgency into a new form that we scarcely comprehend and have failed to meet in a manoeuvrist fashion.

Globalised insurgency is not a uniquely Islamist phenomenon. In its current form it exploits Muslim migrant communities and the communicating structures which fasten them together, but there is no reason these same characteristics of migration and mass communications which distinguish any post-modern society cannot be exploited by another global movement. Global insurgency is the convergence of a vigorously altering post-modern environment with a brilliantly exploitative insurgent genius, which, at the time of writing, happened to be Islamist. The insurgents are jihadist activists but the origins of their operational concept are distinctly Maoist. Although Mao and his peasant army were the pioneers of people's war that did not mean that it would remain forever a Chinese or a communist technique. Post-Maoism has to be regarded as a concept that could be used by any similarly inspired global community.

It had always been possible for the smaller, weaker and militarily less powerful to challenge a regime by mobilising the concerned populations. But in post-modern societies, where security forces were so much stronger and where the wilderness no longer existed, a traditional insurgent could not expect to succeed. Principles that had long been the back-bone of an insurgency were being altered by new technologies and global changes. Insurgents no longer had to accept that the overwhelming strength of the opposition and the absence of a wilderness precluded a successful offensive; their altered social environment provided the means for a different way of uprising. If they could no longer survive as Mao had in his Jiangxi Soviet by subverting the local population, then they had to transfer their campaign onto a different plane by subverting the beliefs of a very much wider audience. Whether this was a deliberately planned strategy or an instinctive diversion from a blocked path, the end result was the same. The surge of mass communications had for the first time given the insurgent the opportunity to mobilise an international array of migrant minorities and nations, there was no longer just one or two populations involved but many and they were spread across the face of the globe. It was not necessary for insurgents to achieve tangible results—soldiers killed, ships sunk and territory seized; it was now possible to attack the government through propaganda of the deed which communicated an insurgent energy to populations which lay far beyond the supposed "operational territory".

Part II sets out to describe how mass communications allowed the insurgents to exploit an archipelago of migrant populations, to unify them, and mould them into a vital resource. The campaign ceased to be a matter of territory and of having a tangible contact with a population but instead had become a struggle for the mind, in this particular case the Muslim mind. Locally in areas where modern and pre-modern societies continued to flourish, the tactics of insurgency appeared to be unchanged, but above the street level there was another form of insurgent energy that campaigned with huge success because it could exploit the dysfunctions of our global system.

Post-Maoism could not be explained without understanding the perspective of the socially displaced migrant communities from which it largely arose. The vital ground for Europeans was not the hopelessly poor masses associated with a Maoist uprising but among the more adequately housed, fed and educated citizens of their own countries.

A new battlefield was being defined by mass communications. Guerrilla tactics had been replaced by the logic of the propaganda of the deed. Televisual atrocities animated audiences whose relevance to the campaign was far from obvious until one started to see events in their global context. It was not the dollar value of the targets they destroyed which was important but the image of the deed and its subliminal message. Academic obsession with the technical minutiae of terrorism and the particularities of radical Islam turned out to be false trails that obscured the grand evolutionary stages that brought us from Mao to Osama bin Laden. Coalition leaders proclaimed the front lines of their counter strategy to be Iraq and Afghanistan and engaged in old-fashioned wars of attrition while the adversary fought in a completely different dimension where his objectives lay in the archipelago of disaffection.

# 5

# MULTIPLE POPULATIONS
# AND MASS COMMUNICATIONS

## THE INTERNATIONALISATION OF INSURGENCIES

*Towards the end of the Cold War, the scale of insurgency and counter-insurgency campaigns grew. As the number of populations which exercised a leverage on the outcome of the campaign began to increase, so did the number of actors involved in the counter-insurgent response. The interconnectedness of the participants on both sides meant that the campaign could no longer be managed by a traditionally structured authority. The centre of gravity had moved from the national to the international.*

When the British reduced the Maoist doctrine to something that could be thrust into the pocket of a soldier's 1944 pattern jungle trousers, the concept which lay at the heart of their simplified version could have been explained by the symbols I + POP > SF + GOV. In Maoist thinking, if POP was persuaded to move to the side of the insurgents they would win and therefore the government and security forces had to campaign to draw it back to their side. Mao's importance had been to recognise the population as the campaign-winning resource. This chapter concerns the profound effect that mass communications had in re-defining POP, and the significance of the population as the fulcrum around which the equation is poised.

In the twenty-first century campaigns in Iraq and Afghanistan, doctrine experts and commanders in the field recognised that the population was the vital ground for both sides. However, when military

commanders said, "the population is our vital ground"[1]—which population did they have in mind? In 1927 when Mao had begun to practise what later became the principles of modern insurgency in Jiangxi
province, 'the population' was an uncomplicated factor. It referred to
the people living in his campaign area and—prior to the arrival of the
Japanese invaders—it was therefore the population of one nation, and
in the case of Jiangxi the local population was contained within a
manageable territory. As insurgency progressed into the post-colonial
or Cold War era, the population continued to be the centre of gravity,
but its monolithic nature was challenged by the possibility that there
were now other states and their populations involved in addition to
the one in the conflict area. Although some of these might live several
thousand miles away in Britain or the United States, in a democratic
system their disaffection and their voting power could exert a termi-
nating influence on a counter-insurgency campaign.

This chapter explains that as we moved through the post-colonial
era into the chaotic '90s the number of population areas involved in
the basic equation was rising. Some were contiguous to the conflict
area, as Syria is to southern Lebanon, as Cambodia and Laos are to
Vietnam and the southern Indian states are to Sri Lanka. There were
also intervening colonial powers from distant regions such as the British, the French and later the US in Vietnam. The significance of the
increasing number of populations which now comprised POP was
that their dispersal altered the centre of gravity of the campaign. If the
population was still "the vital ground", its geographical spread no longer corresponded to the physical territory of the conflict area. Democratic processes within the intervening powers, and the wider
awareness of global populations, meant that a campaign could be
overwhelmed by agitation and political violence from much farther
afield. The political dimension beyond the conflict area was growing
larger and more complicated than the campaign on the ground; both
the insurgent and the counter-insurgent needed to think and act globally as well as locally. This process was accelerated and further complicated by a parallel strand of developments in communications. The
proliferation of linkages between insurgents and populations meant
that more and more people living beyond the conflict area were
becoming actively involved in the outcome of an insurgency. This

included the diaspora or the overseas element separated from the population within the conflict area. In the mid-1970s the Irish and Palestinian communities beyond the conflict area demonstrated a leverage on the insurgencies in Northern Ireland and Palestine/Israel. Into the new millennium, the implication of this trend was that the outcome of either the insurgent or the counter-insurgent campaigns lay to a much greater extent in political events taking place thousands of miles away, that success could no longer be determined simply by the campaign on the ground in the territory of the beleaguered state. This chapter sets out to show that the population was still the vital ground but that its composition had changed enormously and therefore insurgency and counter-insurgency had become much more complicated than a set of practical techniques related to a defined territory. The dispersal of communities and nations and the growing mesh of communications that potentially tied them together had mobilised people who were previously not even concerned spectators, but who now related to each other and distant events with a new sense of immediacy. These relationships compelled us to rethink the continuing relevance of the Maoist equation (I + POP > GOV + SF). If POP had now become such an untidy constellation of states and communities scattered across the world, to what extent could it be the "vital ground"? The traditional Maoist formula seemed to be eroding. The campaign's centre of gravity had evolved from the nationally defined epicentre in the operational space into a mosaic of concerned states and communities spread across the world. There were still traditional Maoist insurgencies that were defined by a particular nation or territory, but these existed alongside globalised insurgencies which were no longer contained in a particular space. Post-modern societies were crossing an evolutionary threshold from Maoism to post-Maoism and it was now crucially important to know which version was involved.

## Multiple Populations

In the 1950s and early 1960s, when insurgents rose up against a colonial regime, the population which was central to winning or losing the campaign was territorially defined. Usually it lay in a space which corresponded to the conflict area of the insurgency. Although in every case there was a diaspora element, this migrated part of the population was physically too far removed from the epicentre of the insurgency to exert an influence. Communications were tenuous and expensive, news travelled slowly and migrants tended to be fixated by their immediate circumstances rather than the agonies of their abandoned homeland. At the epicentre of the insurgency, the rewards of having the population on your side were immediate and tangible. If the population supported the government they would be empowered and the conflict area would become more dangerous for the insurgent. The population was a potential force multiplier for both sides. In the case of the insurgent, having their support provided an essential component alongside the military backbone of the uprising. The population boosted their fighting strength, but probably more importantly, they were a source of manpower which could be activated on an on-call basis to carry equipment or messages, pre-position demolitions, supply intelligence, provide storage space and conduct local reconnaissance. Being an activist was the natural consequence of being part of a particular population. If you were an insurgent the local people involved on your side intuitively concealed you, fed you, warned you about approaching enemies, looked after your wounded, spirited away your precious weapons after an attack, lied for you in courtrooms, misinformed the police, sweet-talked the press and generally created a hospitable and morale-restoring environment, while making it a very dangerous one for your enemies.

In the insurgencies of the early Cold War, the involved populations were not always contained neatly in a defined territory and there were often strands of foreign influence and cross-border activity. Nevertheless, in the scenario of a national insurgency, the centre of gravity (in the Clausewitzian sense of that idea) lay in the state where the uprising took place. The outcome was decided on the ground where the insurgents struggled to overthrow a regime or government. The pressures and assistance of the diaspora or of outside states were seldom a deciding factor. In the 1950s, when a European army was deployed to restore order in its former colony, their behaviour and the conduct of their campaign very rarely became issues that could bring down their government back home, or spark riotous protests thousands of miles away from fighting. During the early Cold War period, isolation ensured that the outcome was decided much more by events on the ground. The nature of popular support was local, physical and immediate—and only very exceptionally found itself assisted by political advocacy groups in the lobbies of nascent international organisations in the far away cities of Europe and America.

However, this characterisation of the 'population' (as in the equation's POP) as locally determined was already under pressure in the early 1960s, with the number of populations connected to a distant conflict zone multiplying with increasing speed. Fast-forward to 2001, when insurgency moved emphatically into a post-Maoist era, and the activated diaspora and the involved states now represented a much more globally dispersed web of connected and interested populations. There was no longer just one or two concerned populations on the vital ground but an array of differently disposed communities, who were spread across the world from Stockholm to Jakarta. Insurgencies were becoming a concern of so many external parties because indigenous populations were spreading out and away from the actual conflict zones. The response to these insurgencies now demanded a far broader cast of actors.

Often, those indigenous populations had migrated to escape earlier, bloody conflicts. Enterprising individuals caught up in the incipient violence of Africa, Asia and the Middle East during the 1980s and 1990s had seen the writing on the wall early enough to get out. They would have had many reasons to leave: personal security, cultural oppression, depleted environment, famine and epidemic and the absence of economic opportunity. At the same time, migration to safer, richer places was now far more possible than ever before. Improved transport technology had dramatically increased mobility. Moving from one continent to another was cheaper, easier and swifter and offered a chance of escape from the warlords and robbers that predated their lives back home. Small boats were lost at sea but if they could gain the mainland their passengers could pick up the well-worn paths of previous migrants towards more comfortable lives, leaving behind countries that were collapsing into insurgency. Enterprising families from the North African coast, the Horn of Africa, the war torn states of the Middle East and Southeast Asia were escaping from the poverty and violence of their home states and spreading out across the world. Counter-insurgency Doctrine Moves Backwards  during the Chaotic '90s.

At the same time as these migrations were taking place, the greater awareness and interconnectedness of populations was altering the established concept of insurgency and counter-insurgency. During the Cold War the isolation of the British colonies had ensured that an uprising was an internal matter. Any counter-insurgent campaign was planned either by the colonial administration, or in the case of recently independent states, by the new national government. By the 1990s, more and more nations were getting involved and it was increasingly rare to find an exclusively national campaign. For some time the former colonies were becoming connected to the wider world. Global change and interconnectedness were making weak states more vulnerable than before. Their populations were growing fast and becoming concentrated in urban areas.[2] The leaders that had taken over after the exodus of the colonial regimes found themselves unable to provide even the basic needs of their constituent populations, making further conflicts inevitable (for example, in West Africa, Sierra Leone and Liberia). Rising debt, increasing competition in the world markets, weak economies, collapsing internal security and dysfunctional governments ensured that eroding security became the catalyst for humanitarian disaster.[3] And whereas in the past their isolation would have put them beyond the media horizon of most of the world, now Western voters were emotionally involved and demanded their governments "do something".

The interventions which took place on this basis during the late 1980s and early 1990s were not regarded as countering insurgency and the actors who deployed to these distant places did not feel that what they were doing was part of a military campaign to restore security.[4] UN officials reinforced this delusion, euphemistically and incorrectly referred to it as "peacekeeping". In military terms the international interventions of the 1990s were incompetently planned and launched with a credulity that was at times surreal, characterised by terrible tragedies on the ground and ineffectual directions from distant officials.[5] International aid agencies promoted themselves as being part of a separate moral order so that they could be distinguished from the intervening military force. Many claimed that their activities had the consent of all the parties to the conflict and that somehow the large quantities of logistic assets they brought into the heart of the barren conflict zone had no bearing on the continuation of violence. The real nature of these long-term disasters was obfuscated by an epidemic of sanctimony and by the self-interest of the irreconcilable elements of the international response and, above all, by the sheer complexity of the events themselves.

What is important for the understanding of the evolutionary narrative of insurgency is that there were two conditions which now altered the previously established concept of Maoism. The first was that the international civil servants of the UN, along with government officials from participating states and the executives of civilian agencies, in very many cases failed to see that these conflicts were not a new phenomenon in military terms—that they had antecedents and could be explained to some extent by what was already known about insurgency and counter-insurgency. Sadly, Western politicians and agencies were not particularly interested in taking a pragmatic approach to security. Their concern for humanitarian doctrines—and their adherence to the rhetoric that accompanied such concerns—left them unprepared for the fact that in many cases their presence was certain to be opposed by local forces who stood to gain from the continuation of lawlessness. Many of the senior international civil servants who planned and supervised UN interventions came from liberal societies with no instinct for insurgency. They understood nothing of how to restore a monopoly of violence, or of the tactics which had been developed and understood by generations of the now-excommunicated circle of counter-insurgency experts and doctrine writers. British and US doctrine teams were frozen into silence by their respective foreign ministries. "Complex emergencies", as they would later be named,[6] became the fashionable explanation of what was happening and the intellectual property of the humanitarian and development communities.[7] The civilian actors on the ground rejected the principle of operational coherence that had been the hallmark of counter-insurgency for so many years. Instead, with the assistance of co-opted military staff, they invented new doctrines and practices, and demanded autonomy in the "humanitarian space", arguing that they should be free from any idea of a 'campaign' and above all from the tainted associations with a UN force or any intervening military presence.[8]

As a result, counter-insurgency thinking moved backwards during the 1990s. The US counter-insurgency doctrine was not rewritten until 2006. In the case of the British, their revisions, which might have grappled with these swiftly evolving ideas, were postponed until 2001. Instead, the British created "Wider Peacekeeping"[9] which described with excruciating correctness a reactive, multi-agency, multinational response to a complex emergency without providing any concept of how it might succeed in restoring the secure environment which was the essential first step in the process of "peacebuilding". Western planners should, first and foremost, have anticipated the attitudes and dispositions of the local forces they would encounter after the intervention, rather than assuming that all parties would welcome a restoration of order with open arms.[10] They failed to appreciate that before any restoration strategy could begin some form of internal security had to be established, and this required a level of military engagement that they were not prepared to countenance. To find out what such a campaign should have looked like, they needed to look at the forty years counter-insurgent expertise and institutional experience that had so recently been brushed under the carpet. These assets would have provided the framework by which to understand the hierarchy of tasks which had to take place to recreate the monopoly of violence within a conflict-ridden state. However, for the crucial period of the '90s, the counter-insurgent experts had remained silent, and policymakers instead turned to peacekeepers, nation builders and peace studies aficionados for inspiration. It took them almost a decade to acknowledge the importance of restoring security and tackling those who oppose the peace process,[11] and to abandon the excruciating euphemisms of the 1990s.[12]

## Multiple Actors

Complex emergencies required a large number of actors, each with their own specialities and disciplines. The Inter Agency Standing Committee's (IASC) 1994 definition emphatically recognised complex emergencies as something so complicated and on such a scale that the response had to be "beyond the mandate or capacity of any single agency and/or the ongoing United Nations country program".[13] Whereas in the conflicts of the 1950s the humanitarian needs of the population, the failures of governance and the absence of security were dealt with by a single colonial administration, forty years later these tasks had been taken over by a panoply of different actors. However, the basic task—of scraping back together the torn-apart elements of a collapsed state—was essentially the same. Putting Humpty back together again, so to speak, was no more a purely military task in the 1950s than it was in the 1990s, and the fashionable thinkers of post-Cold War Whitehall and Washington who felt they were breaking new ground with their civilian-led operations were in fact fatally missing the evolutionary connections.[14] The invasion of Afghanistan and Iraq, in brutal fashion, made this connection for them. It could no longer be denied that confronting complex emergencies was simply counter-insurgency by another name. Faced now by what was so evidently and unavoidably an insurgency, political correctness finally yielded to the imperative of resuscitating Britain's neglected counter-insurgency experience and taking proper account of how the operational space had changed.[15] For, despite the links to the past, there had been changes—in particular, responding to a collapsing state in the twenty-first century meant addressing a completely different constituency than it had half a century earlier.

In the early 1990s the IASC had rightly recognised that putting Humpty together was a many-faceted problem. Their definition of complex emergencies implied that in the case of an insurgency or civil war, each sector of the political-humanitarian-security problem attracted different sets of donors and actors. This meant that the international response not only comprised many elements but that they had to represent a span of completely different functional disciplines. Each of these disciplines had opposing views of how to organise an international response.

In addition to the diversification of the response, a national insurrection had become an increasingly international affair. By the 1990s there were many conflict areas in which the disaffected population had internationalised themselves. Migration and the concept of a global labour pool had transferred the earning element of the population to foreign countries. Both the I + POP and GOV + SF factors in the original equation—the insurgents and the counter-insurgents—were internationalised to a much greater extent. They both extorted funds from the overseas element of the population by putting pressure on relatives who remained within their respective areas of control. In some cases the actors in a collapsing state also owned sizeable businesses and funds and investments overseas.[16] In some cases the dissident factions and the opposing government forces systematically stripped and exported national resources directly on to the international markets to fuel the war and maintain their lifestyles.[17] Their ability to recruit, raise enormous sums of money and organise their logistic supplies from far beyond the margins of the state added a dimension to the problem which lay completely outside the reach of the intervening forces and agencies on the ground.

The deployment of coalition forces to these conflicts meant a dramatic increase in the number of foreign actors involved in conflicts. Broadly speaking the foreign element of the international response fell into four different functional sectors. In the military category there could be up to twenty different national contingents making up the multinational force, and in particular messy cases, there might be a multinational observer force operating there as well.[18] As for civilian agencies, there might be up to two hundred non-governmental organisations and international groups deployed into the operational space to provide the humanitarian and development aspects of post-conflict recovery. In a third category were the major bilateral donors who financially underwrote the campaign. Each bilateral donor might be responsible for a particular aspect of the recovery plan.[19] Above the operational level were various political levers being pulled by concerned states, which exerted external pressure and advice on the parties in the conflict. The concerned states might keep up the momentum of the negotiations, organise peace talks and design the peace process itself.

From this, we start to see how an increasingly international response and the multiple strands that connected it to the operational space had altered the once simple notion of 'population' as expressed in the original equation. By consecutive stages the concept of POP was becoming less and less manageable as a campaign asset: first in the

Maoist prototype as several local communities; then in the colonial/ post-colonial world as two or possibly three national populations; and finally in the Cold War version as seven or eight different national populations.[20] The Commonwealth response to the Rhodesian insurgency involved contingents from Britain, Australia, New Zealand, Kenya and Fijii. The popular response in each of these countries had to be taken into account, as did the reaction of peoples in each of Rhodesia's neighbours, not to mention the disparate groups in Rhodesia itself.

In the late 1980s popular support was a still a manageable factor in the campaign, but the huge operations of the 1990s, which now involved twenty or thirty nations and an additional host of agencies, finally torpedoed the idea that you could base a counter-insurgency campaign around the single-nation premise of the Maoist era. Global coalitions brought a vastly larger scale to insurgency and counter-insurgency at precisely the time when Western policymakers were abandoning years of accumulated military knowledge and experience that might have helped the West draw a path through this new chaos. Doctrine, as we have seen, was poorly maintained and not officially recognised. It had failed to acknowledge the internationalised element of the campaign, or the importance of propaganda of the deed (see part I, chapter 3), while UN guidance offered little help for troops who found themselves having to engage adversaries in combat.[21] Each new deployment was planned on a blank sheet of paper and the individual agencies and military forces taking part were left to find an operational concept which could bring them together on the ground. Proliferation led to an overwhelming loss of coherence both for the elements of the international response and for the forces arrayed against them. By discarding the evolutionary process taking Western engagement up to this point, policymakers had conceptually disembodied these interventions leaving them without a name or a doctrinal identity. Without a structure or a clear idea of what they were facing, the response was disorganised. We had arrived in the post-Maoist era without any language or definitions by which to understand what was happening and there were no milestones to mark the beginning or end of the violence which characterised each contingency. In the previous era, the coherence of a campaign had been imposed by limitations of scale and territory; in the post-Maoist era coherence was destroyed by the disorganised swarm of states and agencies.

## Communications and Connectedness

This chapter has so far presented the difference between Maoist and post-Maoist insurgency as a loss of coherence caused by the increasing number of populations which now exercised an influence on the outcome of the campaign. The distinction was also reinforced by another phenomenon, the simultaneous proliferation of communications. In the past, a Maoist insurgency had been distinguished by its isolation. Cold War government officials had regarded it as a form of violence that took place in far away dripping jungles and remote mountain passes. Similarly, from the perspective of the beleaguered nation beneath the jungle canopy, the insurgents, the population and the government did not instinctively reach out to the international community for assistance. Distance and isolation prevented them, just as they had discouraged foreign populations from intervening. Orwell describes this isolation when, having been wounded in the Spanish civil war, he returned in a semi-traumatised condition to England and found a population that refused to believe "anything really happened anywhere else", a population that would never wake from its slumber until they were "jerked out of it by the roar of bombs".[22]

During the 1950s and early 1960s news and images of distant events reached people through radio, newspapers, newsreels, the cinema and, later, television. This information was controlled at the highest level by authoritarian governments and then by news editors whose primary concern was to feed their audiences with stories that also had enough commercial appeal to shift units. Production time was extremely slow, particularly for images. The public watched wars on newsreel film that had to be physically carried from the jungle into studios in the US and Europe before they could be transmitted. The majority of a population—un-travelled and under-educated—were unmoved by news of distant insurgencies and war. Even when their closest family were involved in these events, distance and time imposed a huge sense of separation. Communications between individuals, usually by letter or a specially booked long distance telephone call were sporadic and limited by cost, and in many cases they reinforced rather than reduced the sense of dislocation.

If poor communications between continents characterised the strategic environment of a Maoist insurgency, the opposite condition—a veritable deluge of communications—defined its post-Maoist successor. The slow technology, controlling structures and limited availability which had helped to impose the isolation of the 1950s and 1960s were disappearing during, and finally swept away after, the Cold War. Telephones became smaller, cheaper and mobile and allowed individuals to speak direct from the jungle floor to offices in New York and London. Print, images and moving pictures were suddenly being transmitted digitally by related systems. The flat metal cans of newsreel carried by special couriers from the war zone to the studio had disappeared from airport terminals. The Internet found its way into every household and allowed the once isolated individual to access foreign markets, enter institutions, watch events unfold, participate in social networks and interrogate a growing, spreading, invading mountain of information. Digital communications had already altered—if not revolutionised—so many aspects of our lives, it was hardly surprising that they would have the same effect on the concept of insurgency and counter-insurgency.

The proliferation of involved populations went hand in hand with the explosion of digital communications. The problem was to understand their relationship and its consequences. The individual had now become a part of the news-gathering process, each mobile phone and digital camera user became in Nik Gowing's terminology an "information doer",[23] the passing citizen whose record of a split-second event, the bungled arrest of a terrorist, or the individual soldier's video diary of his daily routine in Afghanistan, when connected to a website could command public attention on a huge scale. Besides empowering the individual, this development had a revolutionising significance for the vertically structured news industry. The huge numbers of "citizen journalists" whose stories and images conveyed a direct but sometimes wildly inaccurate account of an event created the possibility of an "information asymmetry".[24] On the government side the information machinery was ponderous and vertically structured, its strategies, briefing policies and the efforts to over-simplify and obscure could be unravelled in an instant, not so much by small groups of malevolent adversaries as by the crowds on the streets with mobile phones or a fifty dollar digital camera whose images of an event could be uploaded at the press of a button. In an old-fashioned Maoist campaign, poor technology, censorship and the news editor could assist the government and security forces by moderating the debate. The arrival of mass communications blew these controls out of the water.

By the 1990s the relationship between populations and communications had altered the centre of gravity for both the insurgent and the counter-insurgent campaign. The insurgent could reach out to a long-migrated diaspora and show them how their culture and homeland were being violated. These populations, once unmoved by such distant events, were suddenly alert, accessible and animated—and they became a resource for the insurgent, perhaps not in the physical manner of a local population but by giving the insurgent international leverage. Prior to the digital communications era the Palestinians and the Irish had already demonstrated how an insurgent campaign that was faced by military impasse on the ground could exploit populations far beyond the territory of the beleaguered state. Insurgency had gradually acquired a new dimension in which migrant communities, concerned nations and the overseas labour force were all part of the equation.

Mass communications brought some big disadvantages to the counter-insurgent forces. They eroded cohesion: the establishment of open-source networks[25] removed the government information managers and the news editors which previously stood between the voting public and events on the ground. "Information doers" and their "user-generated content" had unleashed a torrent of blogs and imagery. Everyone—farmers, shopkeepers, front line soldiers, leaking officials, abused prisoners—all added to the flood of information, pouring into the new consumer-generated pool. The protest and debate which in the 1970s would have taken place in a labour intensive fashion on the streets of American and European cities now erupted minute by minute on the Internet. Bloggers, leakers, clandestine photographers and the general public all added to the wild, assertive discussion which challenged governments and tore apart the cohesion of the response. In this environment how could there be a single strategic narrative for the multitude of nations and agencies which made up the response?[26]

Information anarchy favoured the insurgents. Their visibility was augmented by the unlimited and uncontrollable traffic. Its bottom-up direction had for them a self-proclaiming, self-activating and self-recruiting effect. Without information controls, activism flourished; the proselytising initiatives had no collective structure, no command chains and no decision-making cycle. It stemmed from local enthusiasm which could not be easily controlled and interdicted by counter-insurgent forces. Using mass communications, an insurgent's support could be globally dispersed, it could take on the organic quality of a social movement rather than the "hard wiring" of a clandestine guerrilla force.[27] However, for the coalition which opposed a global insurgency, information anarchy had an opposite effect. Their vertical structures were undermined by user-generated content; information asymmetry became an uncontrollable nightmare and over-reactions—such as shutting down the blogs of frontlines soldiers or punishing unregulated statements by officials—only served to stimulate the debate beyond the coalition's control.

## Consequences

The increased number of populations involved in a counter-insurgency campaign, and the surge of communications that connected them to each other and to events on the ground, had altered a formula which had been central to Western doctrine. Insurgency had moved across a threshold from Maoism to Post-Maoism. Increasing the number of actors as well as the mesh of communications between them had changed the nature of the counter-insurgent campaign, not so much at the tactical level where soldiers and civilians continued to think and act locally, but beyond the operational space where insurgents were exploiting globalisation and the disarray of the international response. The evolution of counter-insurgency had been a series of sporadic reactions by different nations to the same evolutionary process. The successive stages of the Maoism to post-Maoism process were not mutually exclusive and it was possible for different types of insurgency to coexist in the same region, so that one found post-Maoism manifesting itself in Afghanistan while next door the traditional version flourished in Nepal.

The four main consequences of multiple populations and mass communications were therefore that:

- vastly improved communications allowed the insurgents to develop into a global movement and mobilise more and more communities and individuals to their side (to a lesser extent, the same principle could work for the counter-insurgent forces and coalitions),
- the growing numbers of civil and military actors involved in the counter-insurgent campaign eroded coherence and reduced the possibility of a genuinely international counter strategy against globally organised insurgents,
- the growing torrent of information was uncontrollable and promoted the visibility of the insurgents' actions in the eyes of their supporters,
- and that the campaign centre of gravity had shifted from the national to the international level. It was now hard to identify and there could be a number of critical points in the international spread of the campaign.

The deluge of communications now connected the scattered elements of a population and the struggles of their kinsmen in their home state. It made it possible to motivate them as a resource in the campaign. This combination of increasing migration and the proliferation of communications was probably a major factor in moving insurgency across the threshold from the Maoist to the post-Maoist era. For the insurgents the benefit of achieving global involvement, besides the obvious funding and logistic support, was that it moved the epicentre of the struggle from the local, where they could be technically defeated by military attrition to the global, where muscularity on its own was absolutely not a feasible counter-insurgent approach. Al-Zawahiri reinforced this principle when he proclaimed that military coalitions led by the US would never allow a Muslim movement to reach power in an Islamic country and therefore "....to adjust to this new reality we must prepare ourselves for a battle that is not confined to a single region..."[28]

By internationalising their campaign the insurgents exploited a coalition's weakest points—its inability to achieve cohesion and legitimacy. In principle an overseas intervention had to be more unified than the insurgents it opposed. The huge cost of sustaining a sophisticated military force in a hostile foreign environment was a burden that might become unbearable, especially when the bombers could reach the home constituency. When the insurgents attacked a particularly weak partner or a selected coalition population it could upset the cohesion of the coalition, whereas it was almost impossible for the coalition to attack the emotional bonds between the supporting nations and the insurgent.[29]

The growing torrent of news and imagery inflicted a loss of information control on both sides. The insurgents seemed to thrive on a tsunami of Islamist materials, the passionate response it generated and the animosity of the Western press. The deterritorialisation of Islam had put global jihad beyond "the politics of local causes and intentions"; the energy of the networked society had created an international community that had become the engine rooms for violent insurrection. But for the opposing coalition the same loss of control was a negative factor that led to a loss of coherence between actors at the operational level.

The idea of the centre of gravity as a manageable factor that could be attacked or protected was no longer valid. It didn't seem to matter for the insurgent, for whom it was enough to survive and proclaim a cause, but the counter-insurgent had to do more than survive and proclaim, they needed to have a structured campaign with objectives and an exit strategy. Instead, they came up against a vital ground that had been impossibly complicated by the twin forces of migration and mass communications, and this had subtly but crucially shifted the centre of gravity. Whereas in the Maoist insurgencies of the Cold War it was in the territory of the threatened state, in the post-Maoist era after the Cold War, it lay to a much greater extent in the global domain.

The Maoist equation $(I + POP > GOV + SF)$ had altered. Each symbol now had a local, national and global dimension. The government and insurgent factors had also proliferated. The wild energy of the virtual dimension now favoured organic movements, which seemed to grow and survive in the torrent of information, while the ponderous movements of the vertically structured state organisations failed to engage them. The deciding factor was still 'the population' but it was not at all the same population as before. A small part of it was still the national or local population in the host state, but there were now larger and more influential overseas populations. A whole new range of factors had to be taken into account. In a US-led campaign, for instance, the voters and their representatives on Capitol Hill had a huge influence over when the operation should be terminated. POP was the vital ground but not any longer in the sense of a traditional Maoist insurgency. The focal point of the decision-making process, if there was one, lay somewhere in the internationally dispersed constellation of communities and populations. The entire campaign acquired an additional dimension that hugely multiplied its complexity just as a third dimension would on a chess board. The international civil servant, the staff officer, the government planner—they could no longer dismiss insurgency as an arcane form of violence. Insurgency and subversion had become a post-modern phenomena. The insurgent was part of the new millennium: he or she power-dressed, worked in high-rise air-conditioned offices—they were culturally deterritorialised and digitally interconnected. The image of them as wild young men in dripping rainforests and distant deserts continued to exist only in the minds of those academics and officials who had failed to recognise the leap into a new, post-Maoist era.

6

# THE MIGRATION FACTOR

*The scale of recent migration and its social consequences were becoming a condition of disaffection. To some extent, revivalist Islam had generated activism, however there was also another factor that many twenty-first century activists had in common—the cultural isolation associated with migration. This condition cut across a span of cultures, languages and territories. The problem for the counter-insurgent was to understand the universal grievances which could animate an archipelago of different communities.*

After the attacks on New York and Washington, the English-speaking media became fixated by Islamism and the convulsions of the Muslim World. The invasion of Iraq followed the invasion of Afghanistan and the appetite for the Global War On Terror animated every sector of politics and the media so that 9/11 and the events that followed became the only show in town. A media stampede had silenced thoughtful opposition and peripheral conflicts were neglected. Public interest for complex emergencies diminished, popular enthusiasm for the UN multinational forces that had been deployed in the 1990s now evaporated. Analysts and their patrons were irresistibly drawn to the sensationalism and visibility of 9/11, the next project was "global terrorism", "super terrorism" or "new terrorism" and in the rush to claim and re-label this apparently unexplored intellectual territory the adversary became detached from any evolutionary process that might connect it to our previous experience and doctrine. Military experts proclaimed its asymmetric qualities, terrorism experts revealed its kinetic secrets, but no public figure seemed anxious to point out the less sensational truth that 9/11 and the concept of insurrection that it represented could be explained by previous experience, that it was a logical development of what we already knew, and as such already had a position in the widening landscape of contemporary violence.

Fortunately, by 2006 the stampede to promote and re-label 'Global Terror" abated and the idea that we were involved in a longer campaign that might be informed by our experience of insurgency and counter-insurgency acquired greater resonance in Whitehall and Washington. The US published their COIN doctrine, which had not been revised since Vietnam.[1] The British followed with a major overhaul of their own doctrine, which since the 1960s had been a continuously revised version of the same, traditional Maoist paradigm.[2] It seemed as though the prescient element of the US and British military staff was at last about to grasp a nettle that involved defining and responding to a post-Maoist era of insurgency. This shift away from the terrorism-fixated reaction to radical Islamism and 9/11 allowed military staff and academics on both sides of the Atlantic to explain the al Qaeda phenomenon in a more intelligent and holistic manner.

But this surge of enthusiasm for insurgency among Western thinkers did not address the evolutionary significance of what was happening. The larger issue was whether this convulsion was a uniquely Muslim phenomenon or, more significantly, whether post-industrial societies had crossed the threshold into a new era of insurgency. Was there something about the Muslim culture—the dispersal of its communities, its grievances, the energy of its outrage and its global personality—which was not so much unique, but uniquely exploitable from the perspective of a global insurgency? Doctrine writers had to answer these questions, because if global insurgency was a strictly Islamist phenomenon it was less likely to be replicated by any other movement. If it was in a single category of its own then it could be regarded as ephemeral and therefore not a trailblazer for successor campaigns by other cultures and other ideologies. And if that was the case, the global insurgent phenomenon was not so doctrinally significant. On the other hand, if that was not the case and global insurgency was not uniquely Islamist and was more accurately described as a set of levers that could be pulled and pushed by any global movement, then it would have to be recognised as a hugely important development, something that would have to be understood not only by the US but by every participant in the successive counter-insurgent coalitions.

Chapter 5 explained that post-Maoism is defined by a transformation of the operational space, in which the centre of gravity for insurgency and counter-insurgency moves from the national to the international, superseding traditional forms of conflict in which the outcome is decided 'on the ground', and creating a myriad of influential factors spread around an archipelago of concerned states and communities across the globe. To achieve this global transformation the array of involved communities had to be linked together at every level by mass communications.

This chapter suggests that global insurgency is not a uniquely Islamist or Muslim phenomenon. It accepts that initially the long-term migrations of the Muslim populations seem to have made them a uniquely dispersed culture and that the global spread of radical activism has recently been confined to Islamism. It also agrees with the prevailing institutional wisdom that through the exploitation of mass communications a tiny element of radical Islamists has succeeded in developing into an insurgency according to the authorised US and British definitions of that technique, but in this case they appear to be attached to no particular territory. However, it does not follow that global insurgency is a uniquely Islamist phenomenon. Global jihad and radicalisation are more convincingly explained as part of a larger generic reaction to global changes. At a superficial level it is the autoimmune response to the McDonald's restaurant in Riyadh.[3] More profoundly, in Muslim states, it is the refusal of a resurgent society to accept their despotic rulers, and in the archipelago of Muslim communities dotted around world, it is a reaction to the immense consequences of migration. The tendency, post-9/11, was to blame an opposing ideology for the spread of this insurgency. But the narrow peculiarities of revivalist Islam—its rhetoric about Western attacks on Islam and the victimisation of the Muslim world—are not enough to explain this phenomenon. They may well have been a useful rallying point, but deeper forces had to be at work. For the insurrectionist impulse to spread through so many languages and cultures, for it to succeed in animating such widespread spectator sympathy and individual activism, requires something more substantial, some huge and widely experienced trauma. The answer lay in a range of mass global experiences, mass migration, the inequalities of the global economy and the extraordinary social revolution that has manifested itself in the nature of post-industrial society. It was more logically these universally experienced conditions which encouraged so many populations around the world to head for richer, safer regions, animated dislocated communities and created vast numbers of vulnerable people.

## Muslim Migration

Muslims generally accept that regardless of ethnicity anyone who has publicly announced that "there is no God except Allah" is a Muslim and to this effect there may be between 1.3 and 1.5 billion Muslims, making it the second largest religion in the world today.[4] Of the 57 member states which comprise the Organisation of the Islamic Conference (OIC), 46 have a Muslim majority and most have an Islamic constitution and government.

Beyond these frequently cited figures, an important characteristic of Islam is the unique dispersal of its followers. Although Christians, Hindus and Buddhists are also spread around the world, Muslims have reached and penetrated into so many non-Muslim states and in such vast numbers as to be incomparable. Eight European states each have a Muslim population of several million and, including Russia, Islamic population experts estimate that there are now more than 50 million Muslims living in Europe.[5]

But the pressures which compelled so many Muslims to come to Europe also applied to non-Muslims, and after the Cold War the Muslim communities who migrated were merely part of a universal trend. By 1991 one million people were migrating permanently each year from poor to richer countries alongside a further traffic of 27 million migrant workers and 30 million irregular migrants moving constantly between states.[6] The reasons for these mass movements on such a global scale arose from a span of interconnected factors. Improved technology was transforming production techniques and competition was forcing companies to move their factories in search of cheap labour, low transport and infrastructure costs, and abundant raw materials. The logistic problems of relocating a huge production process were greatly reduced by better communications, and in addition international mergers and acquisitions were being transacted more swiftly and simply due to the increasing facilities for transferring capital. The new production centres that emerged became part of a network of globally connected industries which in turn created a need for a global labour pool; across the world manufacturing processes were concentrating into economic zones where goods could be produced cheaply on a global scale. However, focusing production into specific areas removed capital, opportunity and labour from others. Economically weak countries which had failed to become part of the global factory system lost out, and contributed to a widening gap between rich and poor, a gap that was exacerbated by the demand for an educated workforce who could operate in the ever-evolving world of modern industry. For the individual, becoming part of the global labour pool meant being in or moving to a country with a modern education system. It also meant having the financial security to stay at school long enough to reach qualification. The demand for constant re-qualification entrenched a divide between and within countries, between the prosperous areas which were part of the global manufacturing system and the social wastelands where it was almost impossible to survive. These developments, in addition to the migration arising from environmental change and continued violence and insecurity, compelled families in disadvantaged societies to seek a better chance for survival.[7]

Migrating communities naturally chose to move to host states which already had particular cultural and historical connections: Turks went to Germany, South Asians went to Britain and North Africans to France and Spain. They tended to migrate in family chains, following each other to the same destinations where in some cases they created a social replica of the community that they had left behind.[8] The states they abandoned were often in the grip of undemocratic regimes. The Islamist revival of the 1980s and 1990s sought to reform, resist, and in the most ambitious cases, to overthrow these regimes. Many Islamist supporters found themselves fleeing for their lives and when they left, they took their insurgent energy with them into their adopted host state; migration flows were transferring nationalist insurgencies from the Muslim world into Europe. North African states such as Egypt, Libya, Tunisia, Syria and Algeria, which were beset by insurgency and Islamic revitalisation were growing closer in travel time to Europe's major cities. Many migrant families in France and Spain were only a ferry passage and a day's car ride from their previous homeland. The mass of individuals and families arriving in Europe were becoming an uncharted population, the host states where they settled serially failed to investigate or record their diversity, their culture, their politics.[9] By failing to authorise a methodology for making this assessment and failing to understand their patterns of resettlement, European governments were destined to be surprised by the consequences of migration.[10]

Mass migration was not an exclusively Muslim phenomenon, and it is clear that displacement is set to continue and accelerate, and that the demographic make-up of those involved will cut across all social, political and religious divides. The Intergovernmental Panel on Climate Change (IPCC), together with Christian Aid and the UN's Populations and Climate figures showed a global total of 155 million people displaced by conflict, natural disaster and urbanisation in 2007, and forecast that this was set to rise to one billion. These predictions were echoed at the 6th IISS Asian Security Summit in June 2007 when Singapore's prime minister, Lee Hsein Loong, pointed to the consequences of climate change as the initiator of mass migration, falling food production and humanitarian crises on a huge scale in the Asian regions.

While Muslim populations have not yet been matched by any other major culture or religion in the scale of their global movement, they are merely the vanguard of far greater displacements to come. The problems associated with migration—social dislocation, lack of security, poverty—are common to all. If it could be shown that global insurgency was in fact a response to these problems, then the potential exists for it to spread far beyond religion.

*Distinguishing Global Insurgents from National Insurgents*

During the Cold War when uprisings were distinguished by their apparent political intent, their different categories ultimately referred to how their leaders wished to change a society that was defined by territory. According to this measure they were labelled as secessionists, reformists, anarchists and so forth. In the post-Maoist era the reasons why men rebel and the long-term goals they espouse have become opaque and less easy to explain. Insurgency has spread into several different categories (described at the end of Chapter 4) and this means that there can be different groups with different causes operating in the same place. In recent years in Afghanistan and Iraq there have been insurgents who fight for traditional reasons: to overthrow despotic rulers, to resist foreign occupation and to uphold themselves as stateless minorities, and to achieve this, they have sought to change the tactical situation on the ground in a particular place. But there have also been fighters in these same places who are not territorially limited in this way, whose nationality is irrelevant and whose cause has a more universal character. In the case of Afghanistan and Iraq these fighters could be described as globalised insurgents, animated by pan-Islamic issues and shared strategic narratives rather than the need to protect a particular tribal interest or overthrow a particular regime in a particular territory. Generally speaking, it was the active presence of this global element that compelled the rich, safe countries to participate in the counter-insurgent coalition.[11] As long as an insurgency remained a Maoist affair that was nationally determined and contained within the boundaries of a single state, Western countries could afford to be unconcerned; but when the global tentacles of the post-Maoist version threatened to reach out into the heart of their own cities, they had to take action.

Unfortunately, the US and its coalition partners in their initial interventions in Afghanistan and Iraq took a one-screw-driver-fits-all approach towards both traditional Maoists and global insurgents, especially where they operated in the same space.[12] According to his 8 February 2007 statement to the Foreign Affairs Committee at the House of Commons, Robert Springborg maintained that US and British leaders had blurred the distinctions between the different forms of Islamism which happened to operate together in the same country. In both Iraq and Afghanistan there were several versions of insurgency, distinguished from each other by their relationship to the state, but only one of these variants was exclusively transnational. More important, the US had until recently failed to acknowledge that the agenda of the transnational category was antithetical to the territorial versions of Islamist resistance operating alongside.

According to Springborg's definition each category had different interests and therefore exercised a different impact on coalition strategy. In the first category, al Qaeda, Hizb ut-Tahrir and the remnants of the Zarqawiyyin (which were then still active in Iraq) were global insurgents or transnational jihadists who believed that the resuscitation of the state was inherently in opposition to their concept of Islam. In their deterritorialised view of the world, Islam should consist only of a single Ummah, and therefore Western states and apostate heads of Muslim states are legitimate targets for attack. The second category of Islamists were the national liberationists that included Hamas and the Palestinian Islamic Jihad in, Hizbollah in Lebanon, many of the Sunni insurrectionists as well as followers of Muqtada al Sadr in Iraq and some Shi'a activists in the Gulf, especially those in Bahrain. In the main, these groups believed in the legitimacy of states and their purpose was not to destroy them but to liberate them from despots and occupying forces. In a third category were the national Islamists who more specifically sought to Islamicise existing Muslim states. They included the Muslim Brotherhood in Egypt and its offshoots in Jordan (the Islamic Action Front), Syria, Morocco and elsewhere. There were also the Salafis in Kuwait, the AKP in Turkey and possibly the neo-Khomeinists grouped around President Mahmoud Ahmadinejad in Iran. They tended to be less direct in their use of violence to achieve their aims and, although they had extensive links to similar organisations in other states, their focus was national, not transnational. The fourth category was a hybrid of the national Islamists who were distinct because they did use direct violence in their campaign to reform or liberate their respective states. Examples in this category were the Gama'a al Islamiyya and Islamic Jihad in Egypt and the Islamic Salvation Front in Algeria.

In Springborg's view the vast majority of Islamist groups, as defined above, had a national or local focus and their engagement alongside global insurgents meant that although they shared the same operational space and probably therefore the same adversaries, they did not necessarily have the same ambitions for the population and its locally influenced version of Islam. The intent of the three non-global categories of national Islamists was to gradually democratise states which were the focus of their respective campaigns and reach out to other political actors with similar interests. In the long-term many of them would, according to Springborg, exercise a moderating influence which would restore and reinforce the state, its institutions and its civil society. If this succeeded, it tended to oppose and fragment the efforts of the global jihadist.

So how does the first of Robert Springborg's categories—the global insurgent or inter-state jihadist—successfully engage and exploit the social vulnerability of a predominately migrant population in Europe and beyond? According to Marc Sageman "global salafi jihad" grew in three phases.[13] The first wave consisted of the original fighters who went to Afghanistan to become part of the resistance against the Soviet occupation in the 1980s. They were the smallest group and in many cases met and even knew Osama bin Laden. The second wave—"the best and brightest from the Middle East"—were young professionals who became radicalised in Western countries and had probably never met or seen bin Laden or any of his associates. The third wave were the less educated children of migrant families who in some cases moved at the edge of the criminal classes in Europe and became self-radicalised before being caught up by more formally organised subversive Islamist organisations searching for recruits. Because they had shared the Afghanistan experience the first of Sageman's waves were a relatively small and identifiable group, but as time passed and the migrant communities became larger and more established, each wave of insurgent activists grew correspondingly, becoming less identifiable, less manageable and less cohesive with almost no shared experiences or common organising structures. From its military origins in Afghanistan the hard-wired vertical organisation chart of an old-fashioned insurgency had melted down to a tiny nucleus of hardcore followers. Beyond that, the widening array of sympathisers and activists had become organic, it had no definition or shape and could only be recognised as a bottom-up social movement rather than the rigid structures of an insurgent organisation. It was the second and third of Sageman's waves which now defined globalised insurgency; not the top-down nucleus of Afghan veterans. Like other global movements, individual activists had no common ethnicity or social background but in many cases they shared the long-term consequences of dislocation which arose from their experiences as children in a migrant community.

## The Migration Factor

Although it must seem that year zero for all research on Muslim exclusion and Islamic activism was initiated by the spectacular events in New York and Washington in September of 2001, in reality alarm bells had been ringing in Britain long before.[14] Tensions had already boiled over in May 2001 with rioting between Muslim and "white youths" in the Greater Manchester area. After an escalating series of incidents, a large crowd of Muslims set fire to the tragically misnamed Live and Let Live pub in Oldham and then blocked the surrounding streets with burning cars to prevent the arrival of the fire services and the police. Outbursts of rioting continued through the summer and spread to other regions of the United Kingdom where there were large Muslim communities and by July the sum of incidents in the Manchester and Bradford districts amounted to the worst inter-communal violence in Britain for twenty years, costing £25 million in damage and injuring more than 200 police officers.[15] The 2001 riots greatly increased the pressure on the Home Office to understand the causes of Muslim exclusion and three months later 9/11 hugely intensified public interest and speculation on the whole question of Muslim migration and its relationship to radicalisation. A string of reports explaining these events appeared in 2001. The first in July 2001 was Lord Owsley's *Community Pride not Prejudice*,[16] presciently commissioned by Bradford City Council before the 2001 violence. Owsley, the former chief of the Commission for Racial Equality had been tasked to report on the exclusion and interracial violence in the Bradford district of West Yorkshire prior to the first outburst in Oldham. Next came David Richie's report, published in December for the Oldham Metropolitan Borough Council, on the underlying causes of the violence. In the same month Professsor Ted Cantle, chairman of the government's Community Cohesion Review Team, published his report, addressing the need for a more coherent national response to what had happened. Since then there has been a more or less continuous debate involving research from university departments, the Home Office and local government in addition to an energetic interpretation of events by the leaders of the concerned Muslim communities.

In sum, the reports presented a bleak long-term picture of a Muslim migrant population living in the poorest urban areas throughout Britain, excluded by location, circumstances and to some extent by their own insularity from the opportunities and values of British mainstream society. The thorough isolation of the Muslim was captured in the opening pages of Cantle's report by a Pakistani migrant who, after giving evidence to the Commission, told them "when I leave this meeting with you I will go home and not see another white face until I come back here next week." He spoke as if he was about to travel across a border into a foreign country. Cantle's findings were endorsed by the Home Office. Although his report was essentially an action plan, it also described the circumstances and grievances which fed into communal violence in Britain. The committee's views in this respect are summarized below:

- The communities lived separate but parallel lives reinforced by educational arrangements, community and voluntary bodies, and employment. They were also separated by having their own places of worship, language, and social and cultural networks, so that many communities did not seem to interact at any point.
- There was ignorance about each others' communities that could easily grow into fear especially when exploited by extremist groups determined to undermine community harmony and foster divisions.
- Although some communities had responded to this challenge with determination, this commitment was not shared by the principal agencies and community leaders. Some agencies were not used to working together, or had not even met together previously. In most institutions, including the political parties and voluntary organisations, there was little evidence of an inter-communal debate and a reluctance to confront the issues and to find solutions.
- There was little attempt to develop clear values which focus on what it means to be a citizen of a modern multi-racial Britain.
- The committee members were inspired by many young people they spoke to who seemed to be participating in regeneration and other

programmes against the odds and with very limited and fragile resources.

- Some communities felt particularly disadvantaged, and thought that the lack of hope and the frustration born out of the poverty and deprivation all around them meant that disaffection would grow. Yet they were not always well targeted, nor even identified.
- Opportunities were also far from equal, with many differences in real terms, in respect of housing, employment and education.
- There was an inconsistency in the approach to policing and in the extent to which communities felt supported and part of a positive vision for the local area.

These general statements were reinforced in a much more explicit manner by Muhammad Anwar in 2005.[17] He saw Muslims, particularly the Pakistani and Bangladeshi communities as the most deprived groups in Britain and with the benefit of the EU Commission's research in this area explained that British Muslims were generally failing or discriminated against in the five key social areas of education, employment, housing, politics and day-to-day discrimination on the street.[18] In education, Muslim GCSE results were consistently lower compared to white, Chinese and Indian groups. Muslims felt the British education system was hostile to their needs and that there were not enough Muslim teachers and education managers in local government. In their efforts to seek employment, first generation Muslims had gravitated towards industries which had been all but wiped out in Britain by the globalisation of manufacturing processes. The 2001 United Kingdom Census and Labour Force Survey showed unemployment was three times higher for Muslims than for whites. When searching for employment Muslims felt disadvantaged by their separate culture and discriminated against when competing for promotion. They didn't fit into the secular lifestyle of the British, found it hard to develop contacts with their work colleagues and found wearing the hijab and declining to drink alcohol was seen as a rejection of the norms of the work place. In housing, the Muslim preference for living together and maintaining their traditional family structures acted against them in a nuclear family housing system. Exercising these preferences meant that Muslims were crowded together in city centres and became the lowest owner-occupier communities in Britain

as well as living in poor, congested areas.[19] Obviously Muslims had
the right to vote and stand for elections, but because they were concentrated into a few specific areas they produced only a tiny handful
of Muslim politicians. As a result, they felt nationally and locally
under-represented and saw Muslim issues consistently ignored by the
major political parties. Anwar's survey showed that at school and university, at work, in the media and on the streets, Muslims felt discriminated against whenever they came into contact with the host society.

British Muslims' reaction to British foreign policy was summarised
by the Foreign Office in a policy letter to the Cabinet Office:

a particularly strong cause of disillusionment amongst Muslims including
young Muslims is a perceived 'double standard' in the foreign policy of western governments (and often those of Muslim governments), in particular
Britain and the US. This is particularly significant in terms of the concept of
the "Ummah", i.e. that Believers are one "nation". This seems to have gained a
significant prominence in how some Muslims view HMG's policies towards
Muslim countries.

Perceived Western bias in Israel's favour over the Israel/Palestinian conflict
is a key long-term grievance of the international Muslim community which
probably influences British Muslims.

This perception seems to have become more acute post-9/11. The perception
is that passive 'oppression', as demonstrated in British foreign policy, eg non-
action on Kashmir and Chechnya, has given way to 'active oppression'—the
war on terror, and in Iraq and Afghanistan are all seen by a section of British
Muslims as having been acts against Islam.

This disillusionment may contribute to a sense of helplessness with regard
to the situation of Muslims in the world, with a lack of any tangible 'pressure
valves', in order to vent frustrations, anger or dissent.

Hence this may lead to a desire for a simple 'Islamic' solution to the perceived oppression/problems faced by the 'Ummah'-Palestine, Iraq, Chechnya,
Kashmir and Afghanistan.[20]

The reports on the Muslim riots of 2001 represented a variety of
British and Asian views, from conservative government officials to the
strident advocacy of individual investigators. Notwithstanding the
disparity of their approach they all seemed to agree that British Muslim communities had legitimate grievances that could in part explain
the violence of the summer of 2001. According to the historian
Michael Howard the streets of British towns had become the front
lines of a head-on clash of values between secular post-modern British

and non-secular traditional Muslims.[21] Surrounded by a flamboyant
and aggressive Western society, Muslim communities were striving to
hold on to their cultural identity while at the same time trying to
establish themselves against the seemingly insurmountable hostility
of their alien hosts.

What the reports neglected to mention, and what would only
become apparent four years later when bombs ripped through a bus
and three trains during the London rush hour, was that this siege
mentality was also a breeding ground for a more concerted form of
rebellion. In the years between those riots and the attacks of 7 July
2005, amid the struggles and isolation of their daily lives, many British
Muslims would find themselves privately uplifted by the triumphs of
Islamist activism and the failures of the Americans in their War on
Terror.[22] Few of those investigating the 2001 riots were prepared to
make a connection between the generic despair of British Muslims in
their city ghettos and the possibility that some of them would go on
to detonate themselves on packed commuter trains. It is not surprising
that this connection was not made. The issues at hand had a familiar
ring to them—education, housing, jobs, discrimination. These brought
rioters to the street in every corner of the world, and even when ampli-
fied by a howling mob, they were not sufficiently compelling reasons
for a young man to carry out such an appalling act of mass killing.
There had to be another chapter in this narrative.

Research into the psychology of terrorism and suicide bombing has
suggested that each British domiciled terrorist on MI5's list of "more
than 1,600 suspects"[23] moved from disaffection to extremism along
an individually determined route.[24] This torpedoes the idea of a uniform industrial method of recruitment and forces us to look beyond
the psychological make-up of the individual for explanations of this
descent into violent extremism. What all these individuals did share,
however, was the experience of dislocation as first, second or third
generation migrants. That common experience ties people together,
often in entirely positive ways, but often in shared disaffection.
Informal groups in which the individual starts as a casual sympathiser
can quickly mutate into a unit in which they become a frontline soldier. Despite the ambition of a well intentioned Home Office to reach
out to the Muslim community and include them in a British way of

life, the social and material challenges of overcoming exclusion are simply too great.[25] The first generation had avoided cultural engagement with their host populations and it was their children who had to bear the consequences of being at the frontlines of two different cultures. For many, the rites of passage turned out to be a traumatic journey through isolation, rejection and then the possibility of subversion or radicalisation.

## Isolation

In the case of Asian migrants to Britain, their separation from the mainstream culture was partially self-enforced. In the 1980s they had come from Bangladesh, East Kashmir and Eastern Punjab in extended families and village groups to industrial towns in the United Kingdom and recreated the communities they had left behind. To some extent they lived together instinctively but it was also imposed on them by a lack of alternatives. They came from the total seclusion of a South Asian village to a life lived out of a suitcase, and they sought out relatives and former neighbours as the only familiar foothold in their strange new environment. For these reasons the tendency for migrants from particular Asian villages and districts to congregate into the structures that they had left behind became self-reinforcing. It encouraged them to carry on in their previous lifestyles and removed the need to learn the language and customs of the host. If you were constantly surrounded by your own kinsmen, you could dress, eat, converse, worship, marry, have babies, die and be buried in the customary way of the community that had been left behind at home. Furthermore, to the newly arrived migrants, Britain seemed like a wasteland of moral depravity and maintaining the rules and culture that had defined the family in Asia became doubly important. However, living under such strict moral codes in Britain required them to follow a lifestyle that became frozen, so cut off from its origins that it no longer evolved. Back home in Silhet and Mirpur, social values were moving with the pressures of global change but in London, Manchester and Bradfield self-enforced isolation was making these communities culturally more orthodox than the societies they had left behind.[26] Later, satellite dishes and international television stations allowed

migrants to shut down completely whatever tenuous links they had
to British culture. Many had felt their culture and home countries
were unfairly represented by the host's media, and now they could
switch off the BBC for good and transfer their loyalty to more acceptable Muslim-generated versions of the world and of themselves.

## Rejection

Withdrawing into a replica of the culture that they had left behind
was more feasible for the parents than for their children. The Muslim
environment in which they sheltered provided most things, but not a
school. So from an early age it was the children who learned the language and the social characteristics of their host. In Britain the ratio
of Asian pupils at primary and secondary schools varied greatly from
town to town, but even where there was an overwhelming majority of
Asian children, the teaching staff, syllabus, materials and exam system
followed the British national standard. The Britishness of their education continued when they left to attend A level college and university.
With very few exceptions the children of migrant families spoke and
wrote and probably dreamed in English. They were not only far more
savvy about the British than their parents, they were British. In their
mixed classes at school they had white friends and were animated by
the visible aspects of British cool—the clothes, the music, Manchester
United, David Beckham and the panoply of brand names which shone
down from every high street arcade. But each day after this relatively intensive encounter with the host culture, they returned home
to a 1980s version of an Asian family; in many cases they had to
change out of their day clothes to attend the mosque and after a traditional family meal they might sit together and watch an Asian film
in the front room.[27] There was not much opportunity to hang out in
the street and if they had white friends they left them at school. By
comparison to the bustle and energy of an average British classroom,
the children's madrassa could be a disappointment. The rooms set
aside for the purposes of religious education beside the mosque were
austere compared to the brightness and colour of an average state
school. The religious teacher, recently arrived from the same homeland
community as the parents, would teach by rote, speak no English and

have insufficient theological knowledge to present the Koran in an interesting way.[28]

All children go through periods of rejecting their parents, it is a normal phase of the growing up process, but the children of Muslim migrants were trapped between post-modern Britain and traditional Asia. There were many additional reasons and complications why they might reject their parental culture and their local, territorially defined versions of Islam. Life behind the front door of the Asian family home might have seemed decidedly un-cool compared to the social freedoms on the street, the un-chaperoned association of young people, the bright lights and the loud music.[29] In their parental culture adolescents, especially girls, were the property of their parents; they were not free to decide socially where they might go or whom they might meet. The consequences of rejecting traditional values at best meant an intense family drama and at worst physical retribution or even death.

But rejecting or being rejected by the parental culture did not mean that the other culture, that of white Britain, accepted them with open arms either. Very often Muslim children experienced dual rejection from both their parents and the host society. As they drew away from childhood they encountered prejudice and discrimination in the street and exclusion from opportunities that had seemed so attractive from the perspective of their homes.[30]

Life between two repellent cultures took several forms. In Shiv Malik's account of this problem in Beeston, the street gang could provide a sanctuary for a particular category of Muslim youth.[31] Malik's description focuses on a local gang—the Mullah boys—which had around twenty members. They had formed initially in response to the encroachment of drug suppliers and users in an otherwise traditional Muslim area of Beeston. The Mullah boys understood the situation better than their out-of-touch parents and had decided to take action by kidnapping local addicts, holding them in a vacant flat and forcibly cleansing them of the habit with their parents' consent. Like many of their Muslim peers, the Mullah boys "got religion" after 9/11. In their born-again manifestation they now found themselves between the suffocating orthodoxy of their parents and the completely unacceptable nature of their *kufr* hosts, so they forged a lifestyle of their own.

Racially tolerant, their membership included white and Afro-Caribbean converts. In a direct confrontation of their parent's ethnically and territorially determined religion, they lived in the discipline of a gang that existed between the British and the migrant culture. They associated freely, they conducted their own mixed race marriages in a local bookshop and justified their lifestyle by arguing that as long as it was between Muslims it was acceptable to their version of Islam. This was an intuitive street-level response to the problems of being a second-generation migrant on Beeston Hill. In his careful intrusion into the gang, Shiv Malik found no obvious linkages or controls leading to a hard-wired subversive organisation. The Mullah boys were a completely British phenomenon, a deterritorialised version of Islam available to all comers.

Ed Husain on the other hand had a completely different response to the problems of rejection.[32] His personal journey began in the rose tinted multiculturalism of his infant school with *Peter Pan* and *The Jungle Book*, a caring teacher and a peer group of white middle-class infants. The next stage of his education at Stepney Green (boys only) school was a much tougher experience, where the vulnerable Husain had to start making decisions about how to survive in a landscape of Asian gangs and schoolyard violence. Hanging out with the boys was not an option for the solitary, short-sighted "boffin" and he moved instead towards Islam. Husain enjoyed a privileged introduction to religion, learning the Koran at the feet of his saintly and much respected "grandfather" and so had every reason to grow up comfortably in the norms and traditions of a Sufi-oriented version of Islam. However, intellectual restlessness and an attraction to challenging ideas and personalities led him on and on into a tangle of subversive organisations; wherever he turned there always seemed to be an irresistibly compelling figure waiting to take him further towards the threshold of violence. As a young teenager he grew out of the folksy communal Islam espoused by his family and was attracted to increasingly politicised versions. He turned first to Jamat-e-Islami and then progressed to the more activist Young Muslim Organisation, whose members were deeply intolerant of British culture and aggressively proselytised in the schoolyard and the college campus. Moved by the plight of the Bosnian Muslims during the 1990s Ed became increasingly attracted to radical personalities, finally joining Hizb-ut-Tahrir and falling under the spell of its most visible communicator, Bakri Mohammed.

There are several aspects of Husain's personal journey, which have a wider significance. His disengagement from his grandfather's Sufism in favour of more radical forms of Islam completely traumatised his family. His father, alternating between rage and tears, regarded his son's conversion as an unforgivable betrayal; espousing radical Islam was much more shocking than espousing the faintly disgusting habits of the surrounding British. And yet, within the Husain household there was a stoic internalisation of their grief. As a family they were so removed from British society and its institutions that the idea of seeking help was unthinkable. Even in the darkest moments of the family drama when they must have suspected their son was involved in something highly dangerous, consulting with the police was out of the question. From the perspective of an ungovernable son in a deeply orthodox Asian family, becoming an activist in a radical Muslim organisation also sent an acutely rebellious message. The equivalent in a white British household might be the formerly demure, home-loving daughter arriving back late at night in a dishevelled mini skirt, sporting a fresh tattoo on her belly. In both cases, over and above the yearning for a better religion or a better appearance, the intent is to send a signal of defiance. Unlike the Mullah boys, Ed Husain lived a solitary life by day, moving between the institutions of East London, meeting in the secretive cells of Hizb-ut-Tahrir and at night sleeping with his agitated but resigned family. Mohammad Sidique Khan who blew himself up in the London rush hour on 7 July 2005 was also one of the Mullah boys and later a youth mentor in the Hillside Primary in Beston where he appeared to be a "tower of strength to the community". According to Shiv Malik the Khan family had known for several years before his attack that their son was a violent radical and their "traditionalist efforts to stop him just made things worse".

## Subversion

Although Khan is portrayed as a different type to the bookish Ed Husain, in the initial part of their journey they both shared a conceptually similar process of isolation, rejection and subversion. In a post-modern society, subversion was no longer a mass process which could be conducted uniformly on an industrial scale. The population had become too complicated and in the comparative security and prosper-ity of a European city there were too many survival options for young people who fell between the culture of the host state and the ortho-doxy of their parents. The Mullah boys roaming the streets of Beeston in their feral gang had developed one way of dealing with the prob-lem, but for the less self-assured individuals who hung around the mosque, the book store, the gymnasium and the college the politicised version of Islam promulgated by radical organisations was another answer to cultural dislocation. The parents' generation, clinging to the moral standards of their abandoned village community, at least knew who they were and where they came from, but their children, living at the interface between two cultures, often found themselves rejected by both, and this left them uniquely vulnerable. Hassan Butt, who claimed to have subverted thousands of young Muslims into the Brit-ish jihadist network, exploited their identity problem.[33] As a Hizb-ut-Tahrir recruiter, so did Ed Husain. When his team of canvassers entered the crowded halls of an orthodox mosque looking for a recep-tive audience they ignored the elders who came to listen in Urdu and instead targeted the young who sat listlessly on the floor waiting for the English translation. The humble, untrained Muslim officials who ran orthodox mosques were no match for the sharp debating skills of Husain's team.[34] The young Muslims they targeted were highly sus-ceptible to their approach. As Butt put it, their message was "....here come the Islamists and they give you an identity ... You don't need Pakistan or Britain. You can be anywhere in the world, this identity will stick with you and give you a sense of belonging." For the rudder-less immigrant children in Britain's urban classes this was the height of cool and wonderfully defiant. It seemed to give an identity to the generation of young people who stood in the no-man's land between two cultures. It was saying that Muslims "should not be divided by race or nationalism and that all Muslims are one."[35] It also offered an Islamic alternative to living in the suffocation of the family, to the chaperone system, to having to marry your cousin or some ugly illiter-ate from the village back home. It was the solution for those who wanted to follow Islam but throw off their parental culture. Of course, those that followed this path into the jihadist network—throwing off the protective ties of family and kin as they went—found themselves locked into a way of life from which there was no way out.[36]

The Mullah gang represented one end of a spectrum of different responses to the problems of having to find an identity. The British, French, Spanish, Belgian and Dutch versions of the Mullah gang were an organic response that emanated from the street. Another point on this spectrum were young Muslims with less aptitude for the street who drifted around the mosque, the campus buildings and the bookshop. The first generation immigrants who arrived in Europe looking for jobs and to attend university courses were another point on the same spectrum. Moreover the range of possible responses to isolation, from the Mullah gang to the fire-bombing doctors in Glasgow, was replicated in European cities. Radical Islam or political Islam offered irresistible answers to the widely experienced problem of identity, it was defiant and cool and many young Muslims seemed to be doing it.

But to what extent was this a social movement or a subversive campaign orchestrated by a vertically controlled insurgent organisation? Some like Hassan Butt and Ed Husain had been part of an effective recruiting organisation that was linked to extremist movements. However, there also seemed to be very many individual exponents of jihad who would recruit not because they were part of a sinister organisation but in a random, instinctive manner.[37] The attendant who handed out the towels at the health spa, the football coach for the local boys team, the outdoor activities leader—all of them dealt with a constant flow of receptive listeners to whom they could plug the jihad.[38] The same process was also going on in the bookshop, in the local Islamic association, at the gymnasium, in the student canteen and outside the mosque. In addition to the recruiters, a considerable element in this traffic of conversion was self-radicalised. Young people were exposed to jihadist ideas through the Internet and through pamphlets and notices in the public spaces of their school or university. The problem was to locate the interface where the individual's search for an identity met with the genuinely hard-wired tentacles of an insurgency.

In the vast majority of cases the process was harmless; the heat and noise of the second and third generation children of British Muslims beginning the confrontational process of establishing themselves in the wider population in the same aggressive way as the waves of Jewish and Afro-Caribbean migrants which had preceded them. It was they and not their parents who had been the first to engage and then challenge the local culture and to speak the language as the native British spoke it. They had not accepted their parents' assumption that they were guests, they were British and for most of them there was no question of one day returning "back home". But first and foremost they were Muslim, more keenly aware than their parents of their separate identity, more politically alert and responsive to any perceived injustices done to Muslims across the world. And therefore being moderate was decidedly un-cool. It meant being identified with the despised kufr,[39] government, police and local authority. Moderate Muslim figures were regarded with suspicion and it was hard for them to deliver their moderating message to the young second and third generation activists. Although radical Islamists challenged the host culture with shrill, provocative and at times violent demonstrations, their actions were mostly legal; it was not the crowded, angry, questioning and at times seditious meetings that were the problem, it was the more vulnerable groups and individuals who hovered on the edge of these gatherings and met and enacted their fantasies in private who were likely to move on to violent extremism.

The purpose of this chapter has been to describe some of the social consequences of migration and to make a greater connection between the vulnerability of the migrant and the processes of subversion. The populations that migrated to Europe were divided by ethnicity, language, politics and their territorially defined versions of religion. Only some of them shared radical Islam, but they all shared the trauma of displacement as first, second or third generation migrants. They had all encountered some degree of racial prejudice—on the streets, in the classroom or workplace, at the hands of police or welfare officers—and these small but recurring shocks built a profound influence on their day-to-day attitude towards the host culture. Moreover, every individual on MI5's list of 2,000 extremist suspects had these two attributes: radical Islamism and the consequences of migration in some form.

This account cannot show conclusively that it is the consequences of migration and not Islam that are the main reason why young people attack their host state with such hatred and ferocity. But it is probable that the migrant adolescent who has faced a crisis of identity at a personal level is vulnerable to radicalisation. The art of the post-Maoist insurgent has been to seek them out, exploit their loss of identity and snare them irretrievably into a violent organisation. However, the idea of a global network of vertically organised jihadist cells and action squads reaching down on to every European street is no longer credible. There is a powerful organic dimension at work which has not been fully recognised or understood. In reality, very many vulnerable young migrants find a new identity in radical Islamism, not because they were recruited by a sinister organisation but because they have been swept along in the powerful current that exists wherever there is a migrant community—in fact wherever young people move and gather. In the current iteration of globalised insurgency, the jihadist message has been a perfect cause for the young person with an identity crisis: it draws them into a global community, it gives them an ideology, restores their self-esteem and encourages them to reject cultures which have rejected them, all without the penalty of forsaking Islam. For the counter-insurgent and beleaguered government, the first question must be the source of the identity crisis, not the panacea they reach for once they have fallen. The overwhelming significance of the migration factor compels rich, safe nations to recognise that the globalised insurgent is more than a passing convulsion in the Muslim world. To understand post-Maoism, the current obsession with the peculiarities of revivalist Islam must yield to the greater ramifications of global change.

# 7

# THE VIRTUAL BATTLEFIELD

*On their own, the shared hardship of migration and a revivalist religion were not enough to activate an archipelago of different communities, there had to be a more compelling instrument. Global change and the information revolution ensured that propaganda of the deed (POTD) would become that instrument. This chapter sets out to show how POTD became a concept of operations and by the third millennium was central to a post-Maoist campaign. Meanwhile, the counter-insurgents had failed to dominate the virtual battlefield or understand the social structures in which a global movement existed.*

Abuthaabit: This media work, I am telling you, is very important.
Very, very, very, very.
Irhabi 007: I know, I know.
Abuthaabit: Because a lot of the funds brothers are getting is because they are seeing stuff like this coming out. Imagine how many people have gone [to Iraq] after seeing the situation because of the videos. Imagine how many of them could have been shadheed (martyrs) as well.[1]

During the Cold War the Palestinians and the IRA had promoted their cause more successfully through the international media than by the military impact of insurgency. Faced by powerful governments with effective security forces it made sense for them to exploit approaches that were not overwhelmingly blocked by their adversaries. Both movements advanced their political campaign by engaging and animating populations, which despite being dispersed across the globe managed to find ways of exerting pressure that furthered the insurgent campaign.

The significance of the insurgent campaign moving into a virtual battlefield was largely lost on the '90s generation of Western defence experts. When governments and security forces tried to follow them into the virtual realm, they did so reluctantly and without much success. The unfamiliar environment favoured the insurgent, whose intuitive approach and informal organisations were more suited to penetrating social networks and engaging the emotions of a huge audience, an audience to which they themselves belonged; whereas the opposing security forces could not overcome the barriers created by their separate ethnicity and authoritarian structures.

The population continued to be the prize, and in the context of the post-9/11 security era the Muslim migrant communities in the EU and across the world comprised the vital ground for both sides. But by the time the second and third generations of migrant children in Europe were going to school in the 1990s it was a population that lived increasingly in a virtual dimension and it was here that their beliefs and emotions were being fought over, rather than in the field. Because the adversary—the global jihadist—represented a strong cultural alternative to the host state, there were many reasons why the predominately white Christian coalitions of the West were unable to gain the initiative. This chapter explains how the "propaganda of the deed" had evolved since the Russian anarchists first used that expression to describe a revolutionary technique, how that technique became an operational concept with the evolution of insurgency and how after the Cold War the proliferation of mass communications meant it would become the chief instrument by which to subvert sympathetic populations that were spread across the world.

## Deeds

Propaganda of the deed refers to the incitement of an animated or potentially violent audience through dramatic actions, rather than words. Whereas any government or party might use propaganda, propaganda of the deed was the expedient of a weaker side that was compelled to use desperate measures to challenge a stronger opponent.

The records of the weak rising against the strong showed how a local act of defiance could trigger off a wider insurrection. In 17th century Britain, when Charles I decreed the Common Prayer Book would be used in both the English and Scottish churches, the implementation of this order at Edinburgh's St Giles' Cathedral fell to John Hannay, the Dean. And on the particular morning when he began to read for the first time from that reviled prayer book, Jenny Geddes, an Edinburgh street vendor seated in a prime position in the congregation, hurled her stool at his head shouting "… duar ye say Mass in ma lug!" (or "dare you say the Mass in my ear", referring to the reading of a supposedly Catholic order of service to a stridently Protestant audience). Her disrespect electrified the normally restrained congregation who rose up and flung their stools, chairs and prayer books towards the chancel until the Dean and his officials retreated. Rioting in Edinburgh led to civil wars, which gripped England, Ireland and Scotland. Although at the point of its initiation the nationwide insurrection involved nothing more than a disturbance at St Giles' Cathedral, this small act of defiance had set light to a very much wider population that was already outraged and expecting trouble. The incident of Jenny Geddes and her stool is one example of small deeds with huge consequences that have become key moments in history.

However, every small act of defiance did not necessarily set off a huge insurrection, and triggering off such a volcanic response required a population with a number of particular characteristics. First, it had to have a mutually perceived grievance which arose from a shared account or narrative of the circumstances. The narrative did not have to be factually correct but it did have to be widely accepted and imprinted on each individual in such a way that it became a constant refrain in their everyday affairs. Second, the population had to communicate within itself and to the world beyond and this was easier in a densely populated city than in the countryside. Third, there had to be an expectation of violence. The deeply conservative churchgoers at St Giles' Cathedral were not revolutionary material but in the circumstances they were already deeply upset and prepared for a confrontation. Finally, and most important of all, the deed that triggered off these expectations had to be visible, dramatic and ignite the emotions of the prepared audience.

## Propaganda of the Deed

Towards the end of the nineteenth century as European populations concentrated into urban areas, radical politicians felt their efforts were too easily thwarted by increasingly efficient state security organisations. In rising desperation they resorted to "spectacular acts of individual terror [that] could shake the existing order to its foundations."[2] Although there was plenty of combustible human misery around in the streets, the trigger mechanism was still a matter of chance and it was possible that a moment of unbearable discontent might pass before it could be exploited. The Anarchists decided it was no good randomly waiting for a suitable act of defiance to take place; matters had to be reduced to a more deliberate process.

As discontent in Russian cities grew, many populations began to assume the characteristics suggested above (discontented populations with a broadly communicated, common narrative and violent expectations) so that a random act of defiance was increasingly likely to trigger off greater and still greater violence. The relevance of the Anarchists was that they had understood the process which brought together the conditions needed to push a population across the threshold from stolid endurance to uncontrollable rage. Instinctively they realised the importance of identifying a narrative, a shared sense of misery, of having the facility for speedy multilateral communications and emphasising the personal tensions that created an expectation of violence. But instead of waiting for a Jenny Geddes figure to release this energy by chance, they repeatedly triggered it themselves. In 1905 when Georgi Gapon organised his workers to participate in the Russian General Strike, he proclaimed: "Now is the time for bombs and dynamite, terror by individuals, terror by the masses ... an immense sea of blood shall be shed."[3] Peter Kropotkin declared that a single deed was better propaganda than a thousand pamphlets; for him words became "lost in the air like the sound of church bells,"[4] It was acts, acts, acts which exploited existing hatreds and awakened the spirit of revolt. This evolutionary step in the development of propaganda of the deed was, according to Neville Bolt, an early form of "'shock and awe' ... to create state implosion, somehow, through terror."[5] The Anarchists had refused to accept the casual circumstances by which an unplanned deed might or might not trigger off the revolutionary energy of a suitably conditioned population. In their crude fashion they had devised a trigger mechanism that they could control and continuously operate themselves and it was this principle which was later exploited by insurgents.

Two decades later, propaganda of the deed was brought into a new chapter of development by the Irish Republican Brotherhood (IRB), in particular by the poet, politician and staunch nationalist, Patrick Pearce. Bolt maintains that the IRB conjured up an "imagined political community" of Irish nationalism by selecting the heroic and tragic moments from the history of the Irish people. The IRB took this historical view of themselves and extended it towards the future so that it became a symbol or metaphor that would communicate a story and an aspiration. Although this was conveyed in the language of state overthrow it was also fused with a Gaelic and religious identity that enabled them to engage an agrarian, Catholic population.[6]

During the period leading up to the Easter Rising, and the British counter-insurgency efforts which followed, Pearse was the IRB's spokesman, orator and information campaign manager in a very modern sense until his execution by a British firing squad on 3 May 1916. Pearce's significance as a propagandist was exceeded by his genuine brilliance and his passion for Irish nationalism. Awaiting execution in Dublin he brought his talents to their most potent form; in "A Mother Speaks" he imagined his own mother addressing the Virgin Mary, and their shared experience of pain and loss and martyrdom:

> Dear Mary, that didst see thy first-born Son
> Go forth to die amid the scorn of men
> For whom He died,
> Receive my first-born son into thy arms,
> Who also hath gone out to die for men,
> And keep him by thee till I come to him,
> Dear Mary, I have shared thy sorrow,
> And soon shall share thy joy.[7]

The IRB understood the power of martyrdom and the importance of the valedictory address long before it became the instrument of the jihadist bomber. After his Court Martial verdict on 2 May 1916 Thomas MacDonagh, who fought alongside Pearce in the IRB, proclaimed:

I go to join the goodly company of the men who died for Ireland, the least of whom was worthier far than I can claim to be, and that noble band are, themselves, but a small section of the great unnumbered army of martyrs whose Captain is the Christ who died on Calvary.[8]

Pearce retained, in Bolt's phrase, the "consummate skill of the communications strategist" right up to the last moment of exposure when he delivered this parting message:

We seem to have lost. We have not lost. To refuse to fight would have been to lose; to fight is to win. We have kept faith with the past, and handed on a tradition to the future. If you strike us down now, we shall rise again and renew the fight. You cannot conquer Ireland. You cannot extinguish the Irish passion for freedom. If our deed has not been sufficient to win freedom, then our children will win it by a better deed.[9]

## Propaganda of the Deed as an Operational Concept

Sixty years later, Pearce's significance to the evolution of insurgency was distilled to a concept by Maurice Tugwell, who, during another iteration of Irish nationalism, had been a British Staff officer at Army HQ in Belfast in the 1970s. Pearce's aim, according to Tugwell, was to mobilise the Catholic Irish population from its quiescent state to provide active support for a revolution against the British. He had exploited the Irish sense of their own misery "to the point where ordinary men and women would take up arms, kill, risk being killed, and give total allegiance to a cause that most had previously ignored or even ridiculed."[10] Pearce's entry points into the target population were the communities that he could exploit because they had kept alive their hatred for the British as a religious duty. The trigger he had been seeking was provided by the British response to the Easter Rising; the behaviour of the troops provided a continuing demonstration of oppression and day-to-day brutality that stretched back over the centuries. Pearce's delivery was deliberately emotional and designed with precision to appeal to well known prejudices.[11] Nothing was left to chance or circumstance.

The importance of Tugwell's forgotten thesis is that it made the connection from the 1916 uprising to the 1970s counter-insurgent campaign in Northern Ireland. From his perspective in the Media

Operations staff in Belfast, Tugwell could see how the propaganda of the deed had become central to the nationalist concept of operations. Faced on the ground by one of the most experienced counter-insurgent armies in the world they found that they were able to make more headway in the virtual dimension. The random act to explode the pent up feelings of the population was superseded by a planned series of emotion-triggering attacks and atrocities. According to Tugwell it seemed as though these had only a passing impact at local level, but their real value to the insurgent side lay in the visibility and drama that was directed towards an internationally influential audience that could only be engaged through news editors around the world.

Tugwell characterised the Provisional IRA campaign under three headings: audiences, narratives and outcomes. There were several quite different audiences or communities in Northern Ireland and winning their support was the top priority for both sides.[12] Within Ulster, every POTD event was complicated by the possible responses of two opposed and well-defined audiences represented by the extremists and activists from both the Protestant and Catholic camps. This created a news environment that eroded the efforts of the British government and security forces which, despite tactical successes on the ground, they could not overcome. News editors were little interested in worthy stories with happy endings.[13] and this put the government at something of a disadvantage. Good news was no news, and this meant there could be no constant stream of images and stories to tell their version of the conflict. Fear of reprisal and the desire to build contacts within the republican movement meant that individual reporters were loath to write bad news stories about the insurgents. Far safer—and, in the heady anti-authoritarian atmosphere of the 1970s, far more hip—to direct your protest against the government

In a propaganda-nourished population the continuous stream of news images and stories had the effect of reinforcing the insurgent narrative and resuscitating hatred. In small static communities which had a self-fertilising habit of continuously rehearsing their own misery, activism became a religious duty. It called on each individual to:

lie and provide false evidence under oath in a court,
hide the tools and weapons used in an unlawful act,
erase evidence,

provide false alibis,
assist in the identification and punishment of backsliders,
and, when called upon, to participate in attacks on the government and security
forces.

By the 1990s, propaganda of the deed had become the principle
tool of an insurgency which arose from or involved a post-modern
society. The randomness of its initiation had been reduced, and the
dramatic event which had once been regarded as a trigger was now
central to the campaign. The IRA (and this was also the case with the
Palestinians at the time) had learned to utilise the energy of the global
media so that the stories and images which they initiated flowed out
across the populations of the world. They achieved their purpose simply by keeping the cause in the public eye. In the Palestinian case for
particularly vulnerable audiences and individuals a routine news clip
showing troops intervening in their distant homeland could inspire
outrage and activism.

This development should have prompted doctrine writers to ask
whether the propaganda of the deed was by now challenging or even
overtaking the Maoist concept of insurgency. But the concept of such
an oblique form of violence was hard to explain and military commanders remained unconvinced about its centrality.[14] The failure—or
rather, the inability—of governments and security forces to respond
to a POTD-led insurgent strategy meant that there were two separate
campaigns taking place simultaneously in the same space. The insurgents waged a virtual offensive through the media on one plane and
the beleaguered governments followed a more kinetic counter-terrorist
strategy on another. For some time, the two campaigns appeared to
be happening on completely different plains, with the government and
security forces seemingly unaware that their body language and total
lack of stage management had in fact become weapons for their
adversary.

## Propaganda

The growing importance and efficacy of propaganda of the deed did
not negate the need for more traditional forms of propaganda. POTD
required degrees of notoriety and desperation that, in principle, could

not be manifested in the government and security forces; it was the preserve of the insurgent. During the IRA and Palestinian campaigns, POTD was characterised by an increasingly cosy relationship between the insurgent and the media that facilitated the mass propagation of shocking images and stories to audiences around the world, to the mutual benefit of both parties. However, this reliance on the global media introduced a high degree of uncertainty into the insurgent's plans. Insurgents could organise a dramatic event but they could not know what news editors would do with it, how it would be presented, where it would be distributed and what its impact might be.

Propaganda in its traditional guise was a more deliberative process. Governments used this type of propaganda in a way that removed the need for a chancy relationship with impetuous news reporters and editors. Its content was carefully contrived and never neutral, it was a deliberate act, something that A did to B. Its could deceive, persuade, demoralise, discredit, or addressed to a friendly audience, it could inspire, encourage, support and promote. A propaganda message could be delivered in many forms—as a symbol or image, embedded in an entertainment, as a mass rally or parade or spectacle, or more prosaically as a broadcast, a rumour spread or a pamphlet printed. Unlike POTD, where the deed itself was the message, a traditional propaganda message was more deliberate and crafted. In common with POTD, propaganda relied on emotions to override facts; the emotional impact of a message had to overwhelm previous certainties and rational judgements.[15] A propaganda strategy set out to foster a willingness to override scepticism and encourage a state of mind in which "a person holds at the same time inconsistent beliefs."[16] The individual's instinct was to regain peace of mind by finding a way to resolve the internal conflict, by allowing both ideas to co-exist and by reducing the insistence on analytical precision. Propaganda was therefore most successful when it engaged emotions rather than in pressing home facts, thriving on what Nicholas O'Shaughnessy calls "multiple exaggerations".[17] It did not ask for belief, it was an invitation to share a fantasy. It tended to know the audience it had in mind, and direct its efforts as precisely as possible in their direction. By contrast, propaganda of the deed was a weapon of desperation, a shotgun blast of violent imagery which indiscriminately hit an array of targets that would react differently according to their previously established prejudices.

## The Concept of Narrative

In plain English a narrative is an account, a narration, a tale. However, this once straightforward word has acquired more complicated meanings in art and strategy. In military doctrine a narrative was "a simple, unifying, easily expressed story or explanation that organises people's experiences and provides a framework for understanding events."[18] In strategic terms a storyline became significant when it was deliberately reshaped to express a sense of identity and communicate a cause and a mission. Narratives framed in this way were not necessarily grounded in fact, they might instead appeal purely to emotion, employing suspect metaphors and dubious history.[19]

Used in its strategic sense in the particular context of an insurgency, the narrative took on a central role.[20] In the 1970s, British troops involved in Northern Ireland often said ruefully of the violence that "a half truth, like a half brick can be thrown a long way and does lots of damage on impact." This referred to the slogans of riot leaders—successful compressions that represented a longer and more elaborate narrative of misery, a sense of injustice and a cause to die for. The opposing narratives of the Catholic and Protestant movements had both been pieced together over a very long period of English occupation, spun together from resuscitated stories and ancient folk heroes, remoulded for the modern age and then reduced into slogans that could turn a sullen crowd into a frenzied riot. To be effective, however, a slogan required a particular audience—one which was familiar with the underlying narrative—so that a few words shouted out in a crowded place could trigger off the entire storyline in the minds of the listeners. This condition was much easier to achieve in a population that was confined to a culturally distinct ghetto where the rehearsal of the narrative was a daily and vigorously self-fertilising process.

The concept of the narrative in strategy is connected to its use in art, where symbols or semiotics also imply the reduction of a more complicated idea into an instantly accessible and recognisable form. This could be a set of initials, a symbol, a colour, a flag. The context is important: a communist star could have a damning association in one scenario but might radiate with inspiration in another. At street level the visual is more compelling than the written. It can be swiftly executed on a prominent building, on the side of a container travelling across continents or on a halted train, it transcends differences of language and culture. These semiotics of insurgency might be a defiant graffiti high on a government building or a huge and elaborate mural proclaiming the edges of the Catholic and Protestant areas of Northern Irish cities. To the initiated, they convey a deeply ingrained, but unspoken, narrative.

Sometimes, trends and major moments in history become reduced to a single iconic image. The war in Vietnam becomes a naked girl screaming after a Napalm attack; protests in Tiananmen Square become the solitary student in front of a tank; the attacks on Washington and New York become the smoke rising from World Trade Centre. Reams of news footage is repeated and repeated, gradually reducing down until one iconic frame can tell the whole story. As the weeks pass, these images come to symbolise not just an incident, but the whole narrative that lies before, below and after it.

The media thus becomes the major participant in a post-modern insurgency. When Taliban fighters attacked Afghanistan's National Day parade in April 2008, the presence of camera crews and reporters ensured that the story and, above all, the images were instantly beamed across the world in all the major languages. The Taliban had already graduated to a much more sophisticated strategic approach in which propaganda was the "key component in their campaign".[21] The attacks in Kabul were part of a sophisticated POTD strategy with the media as the enabling factor. Had Prime Minister Hamid Karzai's parade gone according to plan there would have been no images of the ceremony on any of the international channels or in any newspapers, but a burst of small arms fire and a few mortar bombs transformed the event into a much more interesting spectacle, and the press filed exactly the images and moments that Taliban's own propaganda manager would have chosen. The cameras dwelt on the sense of pantomime, the rout of be-medalled parade soldiers scampering across the parade square before the Taliban fire. They also emphasised a loss of authority showing rows of dignitaries diving for cover behind their

seats on the flag-decked parade stand. This was a classic POTD partnership—the insurgents selecting a media-friendly target in the certain knowledge that this would beam sensational and damning images
into homes around the world. There was no need for the Taliban to
do any translation, provide a subtext or edit the photos; the press had
done the insurgents' job for them and the images were perfect, sending
powerful messages of a stricken regime put to flight in their gilded
uniforms by the daring Taliban.

Altering the narrative of a particular population was becoming a
campaign-winning factor for both sides in an insurgency. Since Mao,
a constant aspect of insurgency and counter-insurgency had been the
competition of different narratives for the same audience. In the world
of postmodern insurgency, POTD and the media have become the
critical devices in this contest, and it is clear that, by their nature, they
instinctively favour the insurgent. However, to what extent do narratives require clear victories on the battlefield for their sustenance?
Freedman argues that, as well as appealing to values, interests and
prejudices in a particular audience, narratives also need to be free from
too much contradicting information—no amount of clever talk can
hide the consequences of a serious defeat.[22] On the other hand, successful strategic narratives, once ingrained in the population can be
powerful enough to blind them to the signs of collapse and ruin. As
Jehane Noujaim's documentary *Control Room* depicts, Al-Jazeera's
newsroom during the early days of the Iraq invasion in 2003, became
so convinced by their own presentation of the Arab narrative that even
when US tanks appeared in the streets of Baghdad they denied the
certainty of Iraqi defeat.[23]

Moreover, in most conflicts, there is very little likelihood of absolute
victory or absolute defeat; there is instead a grey area of insecurity in
which ideas of success and failure are virtual conditions. The crucial
task for the insurgent and the counter-insurgent is therefore to manipulate the attitudes of the population living in this grey area. In the
Balkans, in Iraq, in Afghanistan, Western coalitions went on believing
they could install a new narrative in the minds of the population, one
based on their own brand of liberal democracy and free market economics that they could not imagine anyone would turn down. But
amid the violence of those conflicts, the people withdrew into a sur-

vival mode in which they relied on their own ethnicity, their family and their clan, and it became all but impossible for foreign occupiers to gain access to their innermost beliefs.

## Domestic and Expeditionary Response

A virtual battlefield had existed even before 9/11, but it had an unbalanced configuration in which the insurgent held the best positions. In the 1990s, the overwhelming physical superiority of Western coalitions had compelled insurgents to campaign where they had most chance of succeeding. In developing states, guerrillas chose forests, mountains and deserts as places to engage the stronger opponent on their own terms. But in rich, safe nations, the ravages of urban expansion had closed the wilderness option. Insurgents adapted by adopting POTD as the main component of their *modus operandi*. This choice was instinctive, rather than the result of brilliant strategic thinking. The particular advantage of POTD was that it was highly effective at mobilising supporters and activists who lived beyond the operational space. Its shocking acts had no tactical military value but they kept the insurgents' cause at the centre of public attention. The failure to understand this aspect of POTD led Western governments to mistakenly label them as disembodied acts of terrorism with no intelligent purpose. In reality, they were part of a larger insurgent strategy and could not be dealt with by the crude techniques of counter-terrorism. In the United Kingdom the problem for the counter-insurgents was that successive governments had become entrenched in police-led counter-terrorism which at directorate level did not or could not engage in the creative thinking processes needed for an effective counter strategy.

After 9/11 when the West began to consider its response to post-Maoist insurgency a distinction emerged between the US and the United Kingdom, which reflected their different perspectives towards a counter-insurgent campaign. Although both revised counter-insurgency doctrines were similarly Maoist in approach (in the sense we have been discussing), the US doctrine described what is essentially an expeditionary deployment.[24] Where it concerned the relationships between the counter-insurgent force and the local civilian population, the US doctrine seemed to imply that this contingency was not something that was going to happen in America.[25] Was the reader really to imagine that the attitudes they applied to locals—"learn about the people, know every village, tribal leader"—applied to the streets of New York or Los Angeles?[26] In stark contrast to attitudes in Europe, the Americans did not see insurgency as something that happened at home as well as abroad. Their doctrine was essentially Maoist in tone, emphasising a territorial scenario with anthropological overtones. It stressed the otherness of their operational space. For Europeans, there were domestic ramifications that were more immediately threatening. The connectedness of their own migrant populations to NATO's overseas operational areas meant that a most critical element of the vital ground was on the home front. For the United Kingdom, the vital ground existed in London, Manchester, Birmingham and Glasgow. For Europeans, the insurgency was distinctly post-Maoist.

*The Social Context*

After 9/11 counter-insurgency writers were making a convergence with sociology on the nature of the post-modern population. In 1973 Daniel Bell had suggested three progressive steps by which a society moved from a pre-modern to a post-modern form.[27] His model evolved from agricultural subsistence (pre-modern) to a service employment mode (post-modern) and corresponded interestingly with the parallel progression of the insurgent from rural guerrilla to post-Maoist. It provided an overlapping social terminology associated with that transformation.

The post-Cold War security era had compelled NATO governments and their security forces to change their concept of 'the enemy', to downsize their massive continental structures and engage in a different genre of overseas contingencies. Staff officers and planners had gone white-water rafting into successive conflicts where the stated adversary was more post-Maoist than Maoist. This was unfamiliar territory where society was less formally organised and less easily reduced to a model; where the battle was for the minds of the people and the operational space was dominated by the energy and initiative of global movements. POTD was the offensive instrument to engage constellations of social networks which now made up the vital ground. But there was no interdisciplinary analysis or discussion taking place which could help the counter-insurgent understand this spaghetti tangle of disciplines and ideas or reduce it to a manageable concept. Academics like John Urry had warned that the existing tools for understanding society related to communities defined by the familiar lines of states and borders, and that Western policymakers had not focused enough attention on how post-modern societies had altered the conflict zone. Urry was keen to point out that societies could no longer be defined simply as tangible groups of people on the streets of a particular city; they were part of huge webs of communication that stretched through cyberspace, across borders, and far beyond the state.[28] Governments were still designing a counter-terrorist response for a much more territorially defined form of society. Counter-terrorism tactics of attrition could no longer provide a long-term solution. But Europeans were also wrong to imagine that the campaign could be won in the poppy fields of Helmand province. It was becoming increasingly important for the NATO nations and their coalition partners to understand the entirety of the social context if they were going to design a response to post-modern insurgency.

The sociologist, Manuel Castells, developed Bell's model and incorporated the social impact of mass communications, so as to develop a comprehensive theory of post-modern, post-industrial society, which he described as a "network society".[29] Castells saw the communications revolution as heralding an information-driven society which prized "information labour" and "information capitalism"; a society that was increasingly organised on network flows in less structured, less hierarchical patterns. The important statistics in this theory relate to the expanding virtual ties of the past two decades: the growth of the Internet from ten million users in 1995 to 1.3 billion in 2008; of mobile phone usage from 16 million to 3.6 billion in less than eight years.[30] When a fifth of the world's population is using the Internet, it is no longer just a communication device, it is a social instrument.

In Castells' description societies were shaped by the "traffic" of a network; because networks compressed the space and time between nodes (and therefore individuals) to almost zero, geographical dispersal was no longer an obstacle to organising a movement of like-minded activists. "Flows" described the creative traffic which passed between the nodes and it was this energy that determined the reach and configuration of a network. The path of a flow was determined by the purpose of its traffic. A flow in a financial network might connect banks and corporations to the regulators, a flow in a higher education example might pass through university administrators, academic departments to faculty and students.[31] Networks reorganised themselves continuously and could expand without limit and incorporate any number of new nodes. Employees, consultants and individual business ventures were brought together for a particular project and when the task was completed they dispersed into their original components and would reassemble for another venture in another configuration. The network had become indispensable to young, post-modern individuals and its strands and shapes reflected their social, professional and political energy. In a multi-skilled labour force it allowed small, individually skilled units to associate and move freely from one project to another.

In a post-modern society power was being exercised through networks. They could mobilise a mass of connected individuals towards a desired objective, allowing them to surge together and out-flank the controlling devices of a vertical bureaucracy. Networks were altering the political landscape, simultaneously encouraging autonomy and causing "mass explosions of usage" for social, commercial and political purposes. The Internet and the mobile phone were instruments of an interconnectedness that was decisive in achieving a mass response and the ability to change the values of society.[32] The post-Maoist insurgent understood this intuitively without reading Castells' research, but the government and its security forces were still vertically organised and had little concept of managing or protecting society with these instruments or how to prevent them becoming powerful tools in the hands of subversive movements.[33]

During the late 1990s Castells and his peers had in effect explained the characteristics of the vital ground of the virtual battlefield for the following decade. In the next five years military analysts also addressed the significance of a networked society, but most of them fixated on the network purely as a terrorist weapon rather than as a way of discovering the unique characteristics of the new battlefield. Their approach emphasised the technology rather than its social consequences, it looked at things like cyber warfare and remained fixated on the kinetic 20% of the campaign without engaging the more important ways in which these technologies were altering the nature of the population.[34] As Thompson, Gallula, Templer, Kitson et al might have pointed out, history rarely rewarded an approach that ignored the human dimension of conflict. Targeting individual terrorists was not going to solve the problem; by the time a movement reached the momentum of a juggernaut, individuals were the most easily replaced item in the system.

There were important exceptions to this broad generalisation, for example a 2005 RAND study[35] in which the six authors described what they called a "Federated Insurgency Complex". In effect they had, consciously or unconsciously, reinterpreted Castells' description of social activity in network flows into an insurgent context. The RAND study described uniquely skilled groups convening together to carry out a particular attack and then dispersing into a different configuration for another mission.

After a decade of post-Cold-War upheaval it was a tough proposition for the security forces, whose effect was still essentially physical, to embrace a concept that was almost entirely animated by the virtual. Nevertheless, the young people who constituted their vital audience now lived more and more in a virtual world and through it became exposed to the glittering enticements of the globalised insurgent. Although the insurgents and their supporting constituency might be internationally dispersed, they spent more and more time together on network flows. Whenever and wherever they worked, travelled, exercised, ate or slept, the electronic terminals which connected them to their virtual world were never more than inches from their fingers. By group texting and messaging they could quickly swarm together in a virtual sense or even in a physical sense for recreational purposes but also to carry out acts of extreme violence. By the same process, ideas, statements, proclamations and denunciations could radiate out from a single node. Within such an animated group identifying a leadership structure was problematic; a convincing or commanding message did not reveal the age, experience, determination and gravitas of its sender whereas physical encounter would unmask the lonely obsessive. The anonymity of the net meant that maturity and moderating ideas could be trashed by the unsubstantiated but aggressive response. Freedman suggests that in the virtual dimension, the cautious and the analytical fail to shape the debate because they can be so easily overwhelmed by the dramatic and the sensational.[36] In a network flow there were no badges of authority, it was impossible to say who led any longer. Nevertheless the group had a collective impulse and like a flock of starlings they could rise into the air, turn and land together in breathtaking unison, only it was impossible to say on whose command these things happened. In this way young people on the same network flow could surge and focus their violent emotions on organising instantaneous violence or demonstrations[37] but it was not easy to say what controlled them, except that the message sender had a dramatic message that achieved the desired effect[38].

## A Summary of the Characteristics of the Virtual Battlefield

In a post-industrial or post-modern society where government forces had the physical means to crush a traditional insurgency, POTD was the technique favoured by the weaker challenger. POTD could now be defined as a series of dramatic and visible events staged so that their impact—expressed in images and news stories—would be propagated by the media towards audiences far away from the site of the event that were already predisposed to activism and violence.

POTD was not the same as propaganda; it was essentially deeds and their consequences. It was indiscriminate and risky for the perpetrator because the message and its path to the various audiences could not be controlled. It was an intuitive option for a situation where all other tactical avenues had been blocked by vastly superior forces. The government of an established democratic state would not normally follow a POTD counter-strategy, therefore the contest with the insurgent took place on different operational planes, the insurgent following a POTD strategy and the government following a conventional counter-terrorist or counter-insurgent strategy with associated propaganda campaigns.

The population (as in POP) was still the vital ground, but its constituency had altered. The societies which were now the principal target audience no longer lived together in the same location or had the cohesion of the populations which featured in Part I of this book. They were layered in structures, which overlapped and interconnected, they were an array of audiences in which the individuals were real but the social structures in which they lived were virtual. They did not meet physically in the street, at work or in the club but virtually on mobile phones and the Internet.

In this array the target community, social network or flow became the key objective, both the insurgent and the opposing government needed to dominate its thinking by infiltration and counter-subversive methods. However, a network is an elusive opponent, capable of disintegrating and reconvening in different forms when challenged.[39] Each network had a purpose—perhaps even a well-developed narrative—which held it together. The endless tangle of networks had many overlapping structures so that individuals became members of several flows. The search for a leader or critical point in the structure was, therefore, futile since this was not the vertically organised structure that governments were used to dealing with. Most networks are organically formed, with no formal head or tail, reacting intuitively rather than by a top-down process of command.

Mass communications provide three principal avenues for images of a deed to reach an expectant audience: the deliberate approach, the own-goal and the continuous stream of random news stories. In the deliberate approach terrorists attack a target or an event which already has visibility in the international media so as to ensure that its sensational images are translated into many languages and beamed across the world via every satellite news channel. An own-goal by the opposing government or its armed forces requires an expectant audience but not the organisation of a spectacular event. Examples include the spectacle at Abu Ghraib, Guantanamo Bay or Camp Breadbasket, which were all the result of the government's own institutions and military units, and provided a succession of severely counter-productive stories and iconic images.[40] No planning or action was needed by the insurgent, the event was inherently sensational and its propagation was ensured by the motor reactions of a competitive audience-seeking press. The third route is the stream of random news stories. Although the intent of TV news teams in Afghanistan and Iraq is to convey an ongoing operation to the involved populations of European/NATO states, they have a different impact on each category of audience. To the average white European viewer they bring an apparently neutral account of the campaign, but to expectant and possibly radicalised young individuals living in Muslim communities around the world, they present the unbearable tale of a war against Islam. For them the TV images of beige-coloured armoured vehicles moving through the streets of a Muslim town depict an illegal occupation and an assault on the Ummah.[41] The images of Muslim casualties and uniformed foreign troops are authoritative and so perfectly formed that in some cases they can be transcribed directly into insurgent propaganda videos. In recent years, it has been, above all, the news footage and the endless refrain of occupation, which has turned individual members of migrant communities in Europe from spectators to activists.

# 8

# POST-MAOISM

*Multiple populations, mass communications, the migration factor and the rising significance of the virtual dimension had by the end of the twentieth century vastly complicated the Maoist prototype for popular insurgency. In its post-modern form insurgency had become closer to a social movement and was no longer recognisable to the traditionalist counter-insurgent. However, because they now operated in the same spaces, it became increasingly important to distinguish the Maoist from the post-Maoist.*

As the years passed, interventions into humanitarian emergencies and civil wars got larger, more powerful and more frequent, but not more successful. During the chaotic '90s many international expeditions in the armed category were failures[1] and after each disappointment there tended to be a spectacular discussion ritual to discover the reasons.[2] This process was impeded by its multinational and multidisciplinary nature and the fact that each humanitarian sector or nation had its own criteria for success.[3] From the perspective of a researcher of insurgency, the process was also undercut by the multiple definitions of the adversary. Each sector of the international response tended to take a different view of the opponent and how they should be engaged.[4] There was little attempt made to understand how the adversary had evolved and what were its defining characteristics. In particular, any discussion of the globalised version of insurgency was gridlocked by the absence of common terminology.[5]

Chapter 8 takes a step towards rectifying that situation by summarising the characteristics of a post-Maoist insurgency. The definitions which follow are derived from the preceding chapters of Part II. They rest on two previously made assumptions: firstly that the support of the population is still central to success for both the insurgent and the counter-insurgent forces, and secondly that because of this dependency on the population, an insurgency closely reflects the nature of the people and the community from which it arises. Therefore, insurgents in an undeveloped society are more likely to follow a traditional Maoist strategy while those in a developed or post-modern society will exploit the advantages of post-modernism. Migration and communications technology had vastly altered "the population" (as in POP) and the characterisation of insurgency had to reflect this. Insurgency had to be regarded as a rapidly evolving concept which in a post-modern society became layered, networked, unstructured, organic and without a discernable centre of gravity.

## Multiple Populations

In the equation $I + POP > SF + GOV$ which explained the Maoist prototype, POP was a monolithic concept, relatively static and undifferentiated. This exaggerated the simplicity of the real situation on the ground. The insurgencies in China, and later in Southeast Asia and Africa involved increasingly complex populations, divided along diverse boundaries of politics and ethnicity. When a colonial or Western power was involved, the electorates in their countries also became part of POP, since their votes could determine and influence the counter-insurgent campaign.[6] As with insurgency generally, the characteristics of POP evolved gradually over time, though the pace of change was rapidly increasing in the developed world.

Mao the insurgent, as well as counter-insurgents like Thompson and Galula, recognised the centrality of the population and that its disposition would alter the outcome of the campaign. Successive commanders had declared that the population was their vital ground and that within the operational space it was therefore the centre of gravity. However, by the twenty-first century, in the case of a post-Maoist insurgency this previously unchallenged truth now required so many qualifications that its validity was eroded. Yes, the disposition of the population continued to exercise a pivotal influence but it was becoming increasingly unrealistic to suggest that multiple communities and populations could be managed as part of the counter-insurgent campaign. In reality, only in a pre-modern society was POP still a campaign-winning factor. In a post-modern situation, POP was an unmanageably complex and diffuse entity, its cohesion no longer defined by easily recognisable borders and territories, its structures looking more like those of the Internet than a traditional hierarchical community.

## Different Categories of Population

By the twenty-first Century insurgency and counter-insurgency had become international or global in scope and many populations were directly involved. These fell into several categories which could be explained in generic terms as host populations, frontline state populations, concerned populations and intervening populations.

## Host State Populations

In the operational space there was a host population, which comprised the majority or ruling nation. The host population could itself be subdivided by politics, ethnicity, or religion.[7] The intervention concerned the nature of the host government; the insurgents either had been the former host state government or now sought to overthrow it. The international response sought either to replace, or to secure and strengthen the host government or regime in the operational space.

## Frontline State Populations

A number of frontline states were likely to have borders contiguous to the host state. Frontline state populations could exercise a direct impact on the campaign, supporting the host government, the insurgents or the international response.[8] The interference by frontline states and their populations was usually physical, hugely influential and often critical to the success of either side's campaign.

## Concerned Populations

Beyond the region there existed another category of involved state and its population, whose ideology, religion or ethnicity compelled them to take sides and often an active part. In the twenty-first century insurgencies in Iraq and Afghanistan they could be characterised as the Muslim states, which in both campaigns lay beyond the operational area but nevertheless became involved in the campaign. Some became actively involved with the insurgents[9] and some took a stand with the intervening powers.[10]

## Intervening Populations

Spread further across the globe lay richer and more secure populations whose military and humanitarian assets made up the essential part of an international intervention.[11] They might contribute as members of the military coalition or individually as leaders of a particular development project.[12] In twenty-first century interventions there might be more than 40 contributor states—many representing democratic, politically fickle citizens back home who had the power to end their country's involvement in a coalition. However, the withdrawal of a particular national contingent on its own seldom terminated the collective effort.

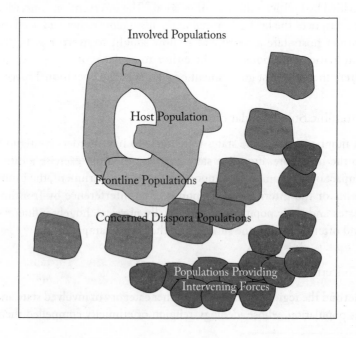

The multiple populations involved in a post-modern insurgency or counter-insurgency campaign can be represented diagrammatically in this way.

In this oversimplified model there could be as many as a hundred involved communities and populations. While POP remains the vital ground, it has become such a complex, incoherent concept that it no longer exercises a decisive leverage on the campaign. Some populations might apply enormous pressure on individual actors, but the POP factor had become like an archipelago surrounding the operational space—still energising the conflict by providing manpower, logistics and ideology, but collectively no longer something that campaign planners could hope to harness for a particular strategic purpose.

## Multiple Populations and the Campaign Centre of Gravity

The European media tended to see the migration of communities narrowly in terms of their own territory but in reality it was a much wider and more comprehensive global process which altered the demography of every region. Migrant labour forces who left their country of origin on a seasonal basis added to the dispersal and intermingling of populations, and still further complicated the concept of POP outlined above. National populations that were once territorially defined could be encountered as communities anywhere in the world.

Before the 1980s, the overseas element of a nation beset by insurgency was seldom critical to the outcome of the campaign. Later, as the urge and opportunity to move abroad increased, the diaspora found itself able to exert increasing leverage as a result of the huge expansion in social communication. Although the four main population categories described above were geographically spread out, and although populations were further dispersed by the movement of labour, all of these peoples now also existed in the same information highways. As a result, the overseas element became a major factor in the insurgent/counter-insurgent campaign. In the twenty-first century insurgency had evolved into something far more complicated and uncontrollable than its predecessors. The concept of the population as the critical point of an insurgency had altered considerably, population now implied an archipelago of different states and communities that were multiple, dispersed, mobile but nevertheless interconnected.

This seriously complicated the picture for the counter-insurgent campaign director. While it remained possible to win over populations living locally in the operational space, they could find the overall campaign fatally undermined by far-away events, such as the disaffection of voters in the "concerned" and "intervening" categories. This had been a possibility for some time, but not to the extent of overwhelming the entire campaign. The disaffection of a wider constituency was a risk, but the campaign focus remained on populations in the operational space. As the effects of globalisation took hold, the relative influence of different populations swung from the national to the international, with consequences not just for theory, but for practical military decision-making. Furthermore, it was doubtful whether the campaign any longer had a genuine centre of gravity in the military sense of that idea. Each category of population seemed to exercise leverage as an independent centre of gravity and this confused an ingrained military mindset that sought to identify clear-cut campaign priorities.[13] Multiple, competing, overlapping centres of gravity provided no simple logic by which to formulate a military plan. The principles articulated by Clausewitz now seemed to be weighed down by exceptions and variables.[14] A population factor that comprised 50 to 100 different states, communities and minority elements living throughout the world was unmanageable; no methodology existed which could turn such a disparate array into a reliable asset. The insurgent could activate tiny, isolated groups living in migrant communities to attack their host states and undermine the counter-insurgent campaign; it was much more difficult for the counter-insurgent to harness a sufficiently united collection of populations to support their intervention.

It is, above all, this expanded, multiplied and unreliable version of POP that distinguishes post-Maoist insurgency from its antecedents. The aspiration to win over POP remained, but it was now almost impossible to achieve. Multiple populations could no longer provide a centre of gravity since there was no instrument or method to harness their collective energy as a reliable factor in the campaign.

## The Insurgent Campaign in the Virtual Dimension

During the Cold War, Maoist insurgency was distinguished by its subversion of the population on an industrial scale. For this to be successful, the insurgents needed secure territory from which to plan, organise and marshal their logistic assets. So although a Maoist campaign set out to alter people's beliefs, it also had to succeed in taking and holding territory.

"Deterritorialisation" is an ugly word, but alas it has come to be very useful in describing aspects of post-modern society. Nations have become deterritorialised, social networks reaching around the world are deterritorialised, the virtual communities which exist only on the Internet are deterritorialised. The global Salafi message was a specific call for Islam to become deterritorialised. It was therefore hardly surprising that the most modern form of insurgency also became deterritorialised, as a response to what was happening on a much larger scale in the world.

The campaign in the virtual dimension was therefore not casually adopted, it was the imperative of their situation. Post-Maoist insurgents still had to subvert people, but the target audience was now dispersed. Their method of subversion could no longer be physical, it could not depend on travelling and meeting people or staging demonstrations and violent events for a live audience to see or hear. Reaching out to their audience indirectly through the media was not just a preference, it was the only option. Their audience was now so huge, so dispersed and culturally so disparate that there was no other way to get to them.

The people they were targeting were not the movement's existing footsoldiers but the vulnerable element of the community from which they emanated. The people they sought out were young men and women, who were often well-educated—not members of a politically downtrodden minority, but those who lived in democratic societies.[15] Although they probably experienced racism, ghetto-isation, discrimination and racial profiling, their disaffection arose more from their own religious fervour, the rage of a resurgent faith and the constant assault of the imagery of what they saw as Mr Bush's war against Islam, rather than real, tangible hardship. The hardened activists attacked their hosts for cultural and ethical reasons and not to redress a physical condition such as poverty, poor housing or a perceived lack of opportunity. They were Europeans and part of Europe's twenty-first century urban society. Some might wear orthodox clothing and arrange their facial hair in a religious-chic manner, but in their persuasive behaviour, use of language and exploitation of communications they were just as cool and savvy as their host peer group. Moreover, they spent much of their day in the virtual domain in the same way as the society within which they lived. News stories, imagery and editorial opinions came to them from a variety of sources. Their social networks of friends, family, and work mates existed in their email address books and mobile phones as much as through physical encounters in the street.

From an insurgent's perspective the transformation of the target audience from an old-fashioned, vertically structured community to informal groups that spent much of the day socialising on a series of leaderless network flows, radically altered the opportunities for subversion. When that subversion took hold, it was able to exercise itself through a new inventory of live audience techniques that gave new meaning to strikes, riots and individual acts of intimidating violence. The physical results, the dollar value of the damage, the casualties, the menace of angry rioters—these things could only be felt by the local audience who were actually there. Unless the attack or the spectacular event could be reduced to a dramatic, media-friendly visual image, its reach was very limited compared to the archipelago of potential supporters. The more important target was now global, and success depended on projecting a virtual message. Having grown up immersed in the media they were trying to appropriate, with the memory of trailblazing movements in Northern Ireland and Palestine in the back of their minds, the organisers of violent deeds had an instinctive understanding of the key objectives on the new battlefield, of how to grab the attention of the press, and what events would filter most vociferously through their network flows.

### The Propaganda of the Deed

During more than sixty years of Maoist-style campaigns the success of the insurgent and the counter-insurgent had been measured in physical quantities—populations, elections, territory and bodies. But by the twenty-first century it was evident that POTD was the operational technique that was central to post-Maoist insurgency. Because the rich, safe nations who are now countering globalised insurgencies have been doctrinally unresponsive to the transition from Maoism to post-Maoism, their politicians and key communicators have failed to absorb the altered dynamics of conflict in the way they measure progress.[16] Meanwhile, their adversary has for some time regarded success as the continued ability to reach a globally dispersed audience, with POTD central to this ambition.

POTD is defined by its violent deeds, not by the promulgation of explanatory texts. As long as the deed is dramatic, after the dust of the explosion has settled and the bodies removed, the insurgents' job is done for them by the media. It is the photographers and their editors who select the most powerful images and propagate them onwards to the intended targets. It is their presentation techniques—not the insurgent's—and the brand aura of their newspapers and satellite TV channels that gives the deed its necessary reach and authority. The impact on those who have already been converted to their cause is not so important, it is the erosive effect on the millions of viewers living in frontline states, concerned states and in the intervening states that matters. In a particular audience, the images arising from the deed reinforces pre-existing animosity, but to a different audience it sows doubts about the utility of the campaign and its cost in blood and national treasure. Day after day, TV news coverage beams scenes of heavily equipped, uniformed troops bringing the ravages of war to Muslim lands, decimating Muslim cities and leaving a trail of grieving families and dead youngsters. It is the insurgent's most effective recruiting sergeant.[17] At the time of writing, no Western government has defined the use of POTD as an operational concept, or recognised that it is quite distinct from the use of propaganda—that it is an act of desperation, something that only insurgents can use and not the governments that oppose them. This has for many years closed off any recognisable avenue for an effective counter strategy.

## Self-subversion

Traditional Maoists had organised subversion and activism in a vertical or top-down manner. Mao's political cadres had moved with his troops and organised meetings and lectures to subvert the local communities. Such methods still exist in the twenty-first century in places like Nepal and Sri Lanka. The defining feature of the post-Maoists is that they are not part of a top-down society and their structures reflect the formations of the Internet and informal social networks. In Europe the first steps towards radicalisation have often been taken in the loneliness of a bedroom, sitting in front of the computer screen.[18] There is no sinister top-down organisation, minder or presence to foster or to compel. The process is organic, arising from a natural convergence of social factors. The relationship to the computer screen is a notoriously solitary affair in which there are no mechanisms to modify or question the dangerous mindset of an extremist, and no ridicule or challenge from a peer group to disarm an egregious ambition.[19] Wild convictions, continuously reinforced by isolation and a self-assuring solitude, become reality. The self-radicalised are sought out by the hardcore activists, putative agents of a formally organised group who encourage and assist the individual on the path to self-detonation. Many of these local talent scouts are themselves "own steam" radicals and only tenuously connected to the hard-wiring of more established global organisations.

The organic nature of the process and the prevailing social environment has generated a social flow that gently pulls together the long-standing activist and the newly converted, so that only a few words of conversation are needed for complete strangers to realise they share the same convictions and follow the same paths.[20] The nature of the Internet society has created an organic form of activism which can lead individuals to committing acts of terrorism on their own initiative. There is no logical organisation chart which security forces can map out and infiltrate and no decision-making process for passing orders downwards from leader to activist which could be interdicted. In the initial stages the activist is impelled from within by a convergence of local and international factors, in a process that is very hard to spot or prevent.

The insurgency in the virtual dimension also has a natural, effortless quality. Post-Maoist insurgents recognise and successfully dominate the virtual battlefield because they are already living in it and using its network flows on a day-to-day basis. Their sustaining populations are large and dispersed and POTD has become essential to their concept of operations. There was no authoritative concept of operations of the stature of Mao's writings which would tell them how to behave or what to do, they are the natives of a very modern space in which they intuitively act out their convictions without the need for formal recruitment procedures or training camps.[21] Individuals seem to decide impulsively to follow radical versions of Islam and even when they move from spectators to activists they come together in isolated groups of similarly self-converted people.

## *The Post-Maoist End State*

A successful Maoist insurgency drew the individual into the mass, a process that became a microcosm of the Maoist state. Their objectives implied tangibility, collective action, territory seized and controlled, regimes overthrown, populations liberated, invaders expelled. During the Cold War it did not matter if insurgencies failed to culminate in a strictly socialist society—it was, after all, possible to borrow the techniques of Maoism without adopting the entire catastrophe of a Maoist state.

But the post-Maoist end state is much less easy to define. In generic terms their objectives seem to be the very antithesis of the Maoist. In the first decade of the twenty-first century the method was still in its infancy, and it was hard to point to a post-Maoist success. Perhaps for this reason, in his study of global movements, Kevin McDonald dwells on their nature and methodology rather than attempting to analyse their objectives.[22] McDonald nevertheless describes three different global movements whose aspirations help to develop a generic end state expectation that distinguishes this form of activism from old-fashioned Maoist subversion.

The first group in his description comprises the series of mass "anti-globalization" movements against the World Trade Organisation that manifested themselves most spectacularly in Seattle 1999, Genoa in 2001, Barcelona in 2002 and in Evian in 2003. These massive demonstrations were organised using the same subversive methodologies and international network communications that are associated with post-Maoism. They relied very much on animating pre-existing passions and on the fact that their international participators lived in a global community than transcended state boundaries. As examples of deployment by swarm on a massive scale they were highly successful, but they could hardly be construed as having a developed or clearly expressed end state. They were remarkable for their size and international organising capabilities but their long-term objectives were disappointing, amounting to nothing much more than impulsive protestations against the G8 and globalisation.

McDonald's second category is illustrated by the Falun Gong which began as a response to the suppression of the pro-democracy movement in China and went on to become a larger global reaction against capitalist modernity.[23] Despite Chinese attempts to suppress the movement, the Falun Gong continued to flourish in the Chinese diaspora and through Internet communities. McDonald avoids identifying any tangible long-term objective beyond the personal and ethical dimensions of the movement. He also points out that we do not yet have the sociological tools by which to understand or conceptualise the phenomenon.[24]

McDonald's third category refers to the new Islamist movements that emerged in the space between diaspora populations and Muslim majority countries. Their generic operational technique was to develop a new concept of public space and establish their autonomy in it, while at the same time building a global identity. Through this process and the spectacular acts of terrorism associated with POTD, their version of Islam became a global issue, a pop culture, a T-shirt design, and a subject that was discussed on multiple news channels every day. The Koran became a bestseller around the world and Osama a favoured name for new born babies. The distance between Islam and Western populations had been removed; it was no longer a subject that needed to be explained by experts, and now took up more than its share of popular religious affairs programming on Western European television and radio.[25]

Were McDonald's global movements embryonic forms of insurgency? Without the familiar military structure of cells and battalions, would political leaders and their counter-insurgent experts recognise them as such? Perhaps they should, for in real terms these movements derive their energy in much the same way as a classic insurgency: they are subversive and their message is highly contagious. In definitional terms, their radicalising or self-radicalising activity can be seen as having the same compelling effect that was experienced in a previous era of insurgency. Post-Maoism is defined by the insurgent's failure to set realistic outcomes, by the uncontrollable nature of the propaganda of the deed, and by the sense that to exist, to belong, to communicate and to generate activism are the insurgent's real objectives far more than the smokescreen of hopeless objectives that have so distracted terrorist experts in the twenty-first century. We still lack the analytical tools by which to understand the nature of social movements that live in network flows. When it was critical that they did, Western leaders and their staff were unwilling to recognise that they were trying to respond to a phenomenon that was riding far beyond the edge of our conceptualised experience. They had characterised their adversary as Maoists, and refused to see that contemporary, global movements did not seek success in the accepted military sense of the word. It was enough for them to exist as social movements and reaffirm their aspirations as a deterritorialised society. Such movements challenge an existing or emerging order. They do not need to find a convincing alternative, for they seek personal rewards that can be satisfied merely by the existence of their movement and their involvement in it, regardless of whether this leads to the construction of some alternative regime. It is reward enough to be part of the creation of a global movement which, from time to time, can utterly dominate the world's headlines in a way that compels governments and populations around the world to sit up and pay attention, to acknowledge their cause and recognise their existence.

## The Military Dimension

It is a strange irony that the analysis of insurgency fixates so much on its tangible military characteristics at the expense of the social and political processes from which its power and energy is actually derived. Although the emphasis of a successful counter-insurgent campaign has historically been on the 80% political-social factors, it is probably true to say that the focus of public attention reverses these figures so that 80% of the reports and news that we read concerns the kinetic, bang-bang stories and individual or organisational conspiracy theories. Clearly, terror sells better than social networking. Having said that, it is important to understand the military context of an insurgency, especially the practicalities of organisation and the capabilities of different kinds of insurgent. However, even in this section of the chapter, which should be the least challenging and most factual part of the discussion, the post-Maoist insurgent presents something of a problem. Instead of being organised in the same reassuring, vertical structures as an infantry battalion or the Roman Catholic Church, when the post-Maoist becomes militarily active, he or she could appear in an infinite number of armed configurations. Not only do the operational structures of an active cell vary from one event to the next, but in recent military experience three or four differently motivated and differently capable insurgent groups might be operating in the same town or even co-operating in the same attack.

Castells provides a researched foundation for the assertion that people existing on a network flow tend to alter their social and professional connections and move freely from one group to another according to their needs. Several analysts of twenty-first century operations find a similarly fluctuating network of insurgent affiliations which alter to suit each operation. Some groups may be vertically controlled and encouraged by a distant organisation; others might be local activists. The picture is still further complicated by the fact that some groups are keen to give the impression of being part of a large and powerful international organisation when in fact they are not. It is this tendency that has led many scattered individuals and small cells to appropriate the Al-Qaeda brand name for particular operations.

## Co-existing Insurgencies

As we saw in Chapter 4, the Maoist formula branched into different forms, ranging in capability from the global insurgent to the feral militias. However, during the 1990s the international forces which intervened in complex emergencies and collapsing states were trained and briefed to anticipate only one of these categories of adversary in each operational space.[26] There was no suggestion in those days that a globalised movement would be likely to operate together with feral

militias and nationalist insurgents in the same place. This perception was changed at a stroke during the 2001-2002 deployments to
Afghanistan where both the initial task force and the NATO troops
of International Security Assistance Force (ISAF) that followed to
maintain security around Kabul encountered a range of adversaries
from global to local within their battalion areas.[27] While sharing much
of the same Islamist rhetoric of Muslim oppression and anti-US outrage, these separate revolutionary movements sprang up from a range
of quarters—be it global, national or local populations. In fact, this
scenario should not have been so surprising, for earlier conflicts in
Northern Africa and the Eastern Mediterranean had similarly been
characterised by the simultaneous presence of different categories of
insurgent.

David Gompert has outlined a scale of ascending sophistication for
insurgent types and located them in their most likely environments.[28]
He names them, rather less controversially than I have, as Type 1, 2,
3,and 4. Type 1 is the local insurgency with parochial goals, normally
found in theatres where outside forces and international security concerns are minimal. His Type 2, the local-international insurgency, is
distinguished from Type 1 by the involvement of substantial outside
interest and support, but nevertheless the outcome of the insurgency
is decided by local factors. Type 3, the global-local insurgency, was
distinguished from Type 2 by its links to a wider regional or global
struggle which moves the centre of gravity away from the local to the
international. Gompert's Type 4 is the global insurgency—empowered
by mass communications, technology and global change and entirely
stateless in that it has no links to any one particular territory. In his
analysis, a purely global insurgency lacks the sanctuary and protection
of a home state, and is therefore vulnerable. This reflected the rather
wishful perspective of the Bush administration. From a European
perspective, where migrant populations are larger and more disaffected
and still able to fly back and forth to their countries of origin, it is
perhaps easier to see how statelessness actually bolsters the insurgency,
providing grievances and opportunities while removing the constraints
and visible target of being linked to a specific territory.[29]

Robert Springborg maintains that the different activist groups in
that region are defined by their relationship to the state.[30] Springborg's

statement to the House of Commons refers specifically to Islamist
political activists and his sample is therefore geographically narrower
than Gompert's. Springborg's National Islamists are, as their name
suggests, strictly national in their objectives. Although some (such as
the Muslim Brotherhood) coordinate and communicate with similar
organisations overseas, their goals are not transnational. Further up
the scale of violent capability there is a second hybrid category of
National Islamists who will use violence more readily to liberate their
country from a despotic regime. Springborg's third category belongs
to National Liberationists, for example Hamas, Hizbollah and the
Sadrist movement in Iraq. They equate to the Popular Insurgents
described in Chapter 2 and Gompert's Type 3 insurgents. They have
serious overseas interests and consort with globally organised insurgents but their distinguishing characteristic is that their goals are primarily national, defined by territory held and regimes overthrown.
Springborg's fourth and, in some respects, most internationally potent,
category is the Transnational Jihadist, which corresponds to Gompert's Type 4 and the Global Insurgent described in Chapter 2.

In Springborg's view the transnational jihadist is "inherently antithetical" to both conventional Islam and the existing structure of Muslim states. In their view the world should consist of a single Ummah,
a united community which is freed from territorial distinctions and
where a uniform system of clerics, officials and teachers replaces the
myriad cultural forms that current exist. Springborg also maintains
that although all four Islamist movements have the same abstract
intent of creating Islamic governments, at a more practical level they
have serious differences which prevent the possibility of a global Islamist revolution. In the context of presenting a conclusive definition
of the post-Maoist insurgent, the interest of Springborg's assessment
is that it adds another perspective on the way in which the monolithic
Maoist concept of insurgency has branched into different forms with
different long-term intentions.

In 2005 Rick Brennan and five colleagues set out a methodology
whereby very differently motivated and organised groups might operate together.[31] From the perspective of an insurgency analyst, Brennan
and his co-writers were explaining a practical concept for the current
chapter in the evolution of insurgency. The central argument of their

report was that insurgent groups were changing the principles on which they organised:

Until recently, most insurgent groups were organised hierarchically, many along the classic Maoist or Leninist model. Internally, insurgent groups have tended to be formally aligned and centralised. Externally, links with other insurgent groups were rare and, where they existed, managed by authorised central administrative bodies in each linked insurgent group. During the last half of the twentieth century, most insurgents' external links tended to be with state sponsors, often with one of the superpowers. With the end of the Cold War, many of these links faded away and insurgents increasingly turned to informal links with other non-state actors. It is the transformation of these links between insurgent groups and related criminals and subversive organizations, and the adoption of advanced information technologies that forms the basis of what we have termed the federated insurgency complex (FIC).[32]

Brennan's paper came to four conclusions. First, that insurgents were increasingly federating with one another, and with other types of subversive groups. Second, that these FICs took the form of multiplex networks which had hub-core-periphery structures. This allowed them to integrate many functions (weapons supply, funding, training, etc) into a single complex. The hub-core structure gave them access to a wider range of technical and professional expertise without compromising their security. As a result the FIC represented a form of insurgent activism that was more dynamic than before and protected its security by its decentralised nature. Third, that the networked structure of the FIC and the minimal and changing linkages between its components ensured that it could resist existing counter-insurgent techniques, including traditional criminal investigation methods and kinetic military operations. Its decentralised nature meant that it did not have a critical point which government and security forces could target in order to disable the entire organisation. Fourth, that FICs were nevertheless vulnerable to factionalism that meant they could be penetrated and degraded.

Brennan's 2005 draft had drawn attention to an extraordinary development. Analysts were accustomed to monolithic insurgent organisations who often treated rival organisations with an even more ruthless hatred than they did the oppressor regime. His proposition was that despite branching out into several different forms, which tended to have very different long-term intentions, it was nevertheless possible for all these categories of insurgency to work together at a local level. In the particular cases of Iraq and Afghanistan, certain factors fostered cooperation between groups and allowed them to override their individual ambitions: their sense of Ummah, their common narrative, their shared outrage against the US and its allies (including the host government) and above all a low resistance to offers of cash. Certain analysts were starting to realise that this federation of insurgent groups was being encouraged by a rhetoric from Washington and London that lumped all resistance groups together under the label "terrorist organisations", when counter-insurgent forces should have been focusing on how to turn one form of insurgent against another.[33] The blanket terrorist label had led to a clumsy, indiscriminate response which had the effect of pushing them together into a federated complex.

Meanwhile, Rabassa and his colleagues described the cooperative strands which ran between the military activists of different Islamist insurgent organisations as the "al-Qaeda nebula".[34] They suggested that after 9/11 US counter-terrorism efforts succeeded in altering al-Qaeda from a vertically structured international organisation which was (at least in principle) centrally controlled, into an array of national and local organisations. These continued to attack local targets—in some cases using the al-Qaeda brand name to boost their international appeal and visibility. The nature of these relationships varied. Some were narrowly practical and ephemeral, lasting through a particular operational phase; others took on the character of a franchise in which local insurgent groups became active supporters on a more reliable, long-term basis. Rabassa tended to agree with Donald that for the national and local insurgent operating on their own territory, the local interest triumphed over the global.[35]

## The Characteristics which Define Post–Maoism

Where does this leave us in trying to define the characteristics of a post-Maoist insurgency? In this description, the global jihadist, the globalised insurgent and the post-Maoist are the same thing. There would be two advantages to achieving a universally acceptable concept and description of post-Maoism. First of all, it would provide a much-needed common language with which to ensure the continuing circus of "global terror" conferences becomes genuinely multi-disciplinary. The current security era, and the universally experienced phenomena that beset it, still have no name. Governments legislate against terrorism and military staff write doctrine to counter insurgency as though they were completely separate things. They are not. Politicians who articulate strategy and the administrations who authorise its realisation must restore the precision and clarity of their vocabulary. Professional communities that deal with the practicalities of these contingencies must develop a terminology which is underwritten by common usage and definitions. The second reason is that post-Maoist insurgent organisations must be distinguished from their Maoist antecedents. They cannot be defeated by the same counter-insurgent methods. Lumping them together as "terrorist organisations" leads to the self-fulfilling disaster of using the same response for both.

The characteristics and descriptions below set out to define a post-Maoist insurgency:

- Post-Maoism refers to an era of insurgency which overlaps the preceding Maoist era.
- Post-Maoist insurgents are likely to arise from a global movement and are therefore part of a global community rather than a population or movement that is defined by territory.
- Post-Maoists strive for long-term objectives which seem to have an unrealistic or intangible character. Their tactical success should not be measured by the achievement of these stated objectives, but by the activation and animation of a huge diversity of supporters. For them, success is continuing to survive, to challenge their adversaries in a violent and highly visible manner, to globalise their campaign and to compel nations and organisations to recognise them.
- Although post-Maoist insurgents are inspired by common narratives, they comprise a global span of cultures and nationalities.
- Popular support is the source of their insurgent energy, however the active supporters have diversified into host populations, frontline populations, concerned populations and intervening populations.
- A post-Maoist insurgency/counter-insurgency campaign has no centre of gravity that can be overwhelmed, protected or managed by either side.

- The insurgent's concept of operations is to activate popular support that is massive and globally dispersed through the propaganda of the deed. The aim of the terrorist attacks mounted for this purpose is not so much to alter the local tactical situation, but to communicate the imagery of the violence to a globally dispersed audience through the efforts of the media.
- Because the post-Maoist insurgent has no territory, their campaign objectives lie in the virtual dimension in the minds of individuals and their consequent activism. The process of subversion may initially be organic, resulting from exposure to propaganda, media stories and imagery, rather than by the efforts of organised subversive structures.
- The post-Maoist insurgent may operate in a federated complex with other forms of insurgency which have territorial or local objectives. Post-Maoists and Maoists can therefore be found working together locally, although this does not mean that they can be dealt with successfully by the same methods.

# PART III

# RESPONDING TO POST-MAOISM

## INTRODUCTION

The first two parts of this book explain how insurgency has become something which now has the capability to invade our lives and threaten our society, our freedom to travel, congregate and celebrate great events. This final part sets out the problems of dealing with that phenomenon. The theme running through the preceding chapters is that insurgency is a continuously evolving concept, its speed of mutation is determined by different societies of which the most dynamic have altered so much that their form and structure are unrecognisable to a developing or modernising nation.

The 1960s generation who began their careers in jobs and industries that were vertically ordered have had to acclimatise to a less structured or in some cases completely unstructured post industrial era. Today individuals who seek to challenge a government or a particular culture have learned how to exploit a deregulated society because they have been moving along in its evolutionary flow. But without the benefit of continuous engagement, the tempo of change makes a networked social group hard to join or penetrate, accounting for the less successful involvement of out of touch individuals, age groups and institutions. Without a continuous engagement with the socialising habits of successive generations of young people, the traditional Maoist would not recognise the post-Maoist form insurgency which can arise from this environment. The evolutionary leap from a 1960s model (I + POP > GOV = SF) would be too great. The need to add a host of additional factors to the equation, which were complicated by globalisation, interconnectedness and their multiplicity, would make this new version unrecognisable as an insurgency.

NATO governments and the majority of their security staff did not recognise post-Maoism as a form of insurgency either. Although they lived in a post industrial era and directly experienced its social consequences, they dealt with the post 9/11 insurgent phenomenon from a Maoist perspective; they neither saw it nor engaged it as a global movement that involved a greater array of dispersed supporters. They also failed to recognise it as insurgency. They had expected insurgency to remain unchanged, something familiar, something that resembled its traditional antecedents and something which only took place in developing nations as opposed their own post modern societies. Because few academics had explained insurgency as a multidisciplinary, as opposed to a narrowly military, process they failed to see how their own populations were vulnerable to insurgent movements, and that when it happened to them it would certainly not look like its classic Maoist antecedent. Countering insurgency required a counter intuitive effort and making this intellectual leap was problematic when military planners had such an idée fixe of insurgency as an eternally Maoist form. Without the benefit of constant engagement and acclimatisation to its changing nature, the modern version of insurgency was unrecognisable to the rich, safe NATO states where it was now beginning to occur. Our security establishment had probably moved in social terms into the post-industrial era but their perception of insurgency had not.

By 2008 the most up-to-date doctrine was still stuck in an expeditionary form[1], in other words focused on a campaign epicentre that lay in a particular overseas territory and its traditional, or at best modernising, society. The following characteristics that distinguished post-Maoism had not been engaged:

- The involvement of multiple populations which challenged the concept of a campaign centre of gravity

- Mass communications and connectivity
- The migration factor
- The virtual factor
- The centrality of the propaganda of the deed in the insurgent's concept of operations
- The bottom-up direction of activist energy
- Absence of plausible end-state objectives in the insurgent's manifesto.

Certainly it was possible to point chapter and verse to where some of these ideas were mentioned in a catch-all fashion in the US FM 3-24, but that did not save the US doctrine from being essentially Maoist. If it was really a response to a new security era as opposed to the tactical particularities of Anbar province, the 2006 version needed to explain and address the fact that the seven characteristics above had moved the campaign into a completely different space. To be relevant a doctrine had to provide an operational concept for the evolutionary stage we had now reached, it had to address a form of insurgency which now beset the NATO nations, not the modernising states of the Middle East and South Asia. It had to provide a concept of operations to contain a movement which survived and grew through the constant use of propaganda of the deed, lived beyond the concept of territory and had no tangible end-state that could be negotiated or interfered with by kinetic means. In truth it was not the doctrine writers who had failed for it is not their job to design new operational concepts. First there needed to be a genuine strategy and a palpably successful concept of operations, only when that succeeded could a doctrine writer capture its lessons for future generations. In 2008 British doctrine writers were striving to capture something that had not succeeded; there was no genuine strategy and no campaign plan that brought together the different disciplines of the competing government departments. Whitehall was neither determined nor politically configured to run a twenty-first century counter-insurgent campaign. It was hardly surprising therefore that for much of this decade British doctrine writers have been fruitlessly searching for a "new" doctrine for countering insurgency.

The consequences of being collectively unable to recognise an insurgency except when it presented itself in a familiar Maoist form, was that the global war against terror was fought on separate planes; the US and its allies focused on the tangible military dimension and the jihadi adversary on a virtual battleground.

Although US coalitions deployed to Afghanistan and Iraq ostensibly to counter a globally organised adversary they spent most of their energy engaging national and regional insurgents that had a distinctly territorial agenda. However in both of these places they did also encounter the tentacles of a much more modern and internationalised insurgency. But to all these different forms they applied the same generic approach. Their territorial boundaries ensured that the US coalitions could only engage a traditional adversary. When insurgent groups presented themselves in the coalition's operational space they could be successfully destroyed by ground forces using a kinetic approach. But when the globalised insurgent movement (which ostensibly they had come to crush) became established on a different plane and in a different way it was relatively invulnerable. The insurgent constituency ranged beyond the territorial boundaries of the coalition forces; their vague long-term aspirations could not be reduced to realistic objectives that were negotiable or even kinetically vulnerable. The insurgents' aim was to stay in the headlines and to keep "scoring goals" in a highly visible and dramatic manner. They fought for attention and recognition, and they struggled to increase and animate and embolden an archipelago of followers which lay far beyond the borders of Iraq and Afghanistan. They were a movement without a need for territory whose informal networks could not be easily interdicted by the old fashioned vertically structured institutions that set out to quell them. Their organising energy was generated organically; their initiatives were bottom–up[2]. Their potential foot soldiers lived for most of the day in the virtual domain, connected to an array of followers who existed in the hubs and chains and network flows of the Internet system. They acted impulsively; they had no effective command structure or centre of gravity that could be smashed by an effects-based operation. So, the campaign against globalised insurgency was being conducted on different planes, the coalition expeditions followed a Maoist style counter-insurgency limited by territory and meanwhile the globalised movement described above operated in a different space using the techniques of a different era.

*Different US and European Priorities*

Prior to the 2001 attacks on New York and Washington, the US and its NATO allies in Europe were already aware of the threat from al Qaeda. The scale and visibility and drama of 9/11 forced NATO countries to address the prospect of continuing terrorist attacks from globally established movements with greater resolve. It was no longer possible even for the most inert government to ignore a problem which took up so much space in every discourse. The possibility of more attacks troubled every part of society, the millions of commuters, transportation terminals and great events when people would congregate to celebrate, mourn or relax. No government could ignore a movement which had demonstrated that it desired to attack these things with such ferocity.

The US counter strategy was inspired by its own dramatic experience. In their view an extremely complex terrorist attack such as 9/11 could only be mounted from a foreign sanctuary or safe haven. Without the security of a physical base it would have been impossible for an international terrorist operation to:

- Plan and do the necessary staff work
- Create an international infrastructure to support the attackers
- Select, train and mould the attackers into a coherent team
- Obtain specialist technology and equipment
- Test the practicability of the plan[3]

In their view the most likely sanctuaries were in Pakistan, South Western Afghanistan, the Arabian peninsula, the Horn of Africa, Southeast Asia from Thailand to Indonesia, West Africa and European cities with expatriate Muslim communities.[4]

The concept for the "war on terrorism" assumed that a future attack would come from a foreign sanctuary or safe haven, similar to Afghanistan, where a complicated project could be put together and tested in a secure environment. The US concept was therefore to anticipate and interdict possible foreign safe havens. It was this fundamentally expeditionary approach that was reflected in the US National Strategy, in the land forces doctrine and in presidential declarations.

It is understandable why, for political and emotional reasons the European NATO allies enthusiastically supported the initial 2001 intervention in Afghanistan with their troops and humanitarian assets. However it seemed to take the Europeans, particularly the British, several years to understand that although they shared with the US the possibility of being attacked, in their case the most likely source of the attackers was not from an overseas sanctuary but from within their own migrant communities. Deploying expensive military contingents to Afghanistan and Iraq did not reduce that threat, it exacerbated it by providing European-based jihadi recruiters with a cause. Although the US Muslim population was estimated by PEW as 2.35 million[5], its social characteristics were different in several important ways to the European Muslim communities. The European migrants typically had settled together in large socially isolated communities whereas the US Muslims tended to be more evenly dispersed, more heterogeneous and more ambitious. America was itself a migrant society its creative energy had been refuelled by successive waves of migrants; no doubt Muslims encountered racism and hostility in the same way as their European counter parts, but in the US there was an overriding national compulsion for individual opportunity which helped to assimilate the stranger. European society was more stagnant, less promiscuous and absorbed its immigrant waves with less enthusiasm.

According to the 1990s version of al Qaeda's capabilities, described prescriptively in the US 9/11 Commission, there was an obvious logic for the US to prioritise its expeditionary campaign over its domestic security measures. And if the strident promotion of the US invasions in newspapers, TV stations and in every government building across the land offended US Muslims, they had to accept it. However by July 2005 after the bombs in Madrid and London, it should have been increasingly obvious to the Europeans that the US logic for the "war against terror" could not be applied so comfortably to them. It was a narrowly national-US perspective and its consequences were forcing the Europeans down an unsafe path. The US model still assumed a net flow of attackers originating from sanctuaries around the world and heading for the US. But the Europeans were already aware that in their case the threat lay in their own population. Yes, the aspiring bomber might leave the United Kingdom for a final training experience in Pakistan and then return to detonate himself in the streets of London, but the process started and ended in Britain. In his 2003 assessment of the US—European relationship, Jonathan Eyal pointed out that the US assumption that European nations would support the US intervention in Iraq was based on an outdated view of the transatlantic relationship. The longstanding US-European operational linkages had grown from three successive global confrontations in the preceding century when both sides faced a common enemy, it could no longer "be maintained at a time when the US has different strategic priorities and a radically different perspective on new threats".[6]

## The Logic of Part III

In the scale of military threats against a state, post-Maoism has the status of a virus or an aggressive parasite rather than a terminal act of military violence. However, that is not to say that any state should accept the presence of a growing global movement within its population seeking to attack its host. Across the world, two different categories of response to post-Maoist insurgency had emerged— expeditionary and domestic. Part III sets out to describe these two different forms of campaign with a view to assessing how far they actually engage the insurgency that should be their primary concern.

The assessment of the expeditionary campaign is based on recent studies of Afghanistan rather than Iraq. The response to Afghanistan has engaged the military support of a majority of European states under US leadership and exhibits the problems of a genuinely global response more faithfully than the more unipolar campaign in Iraq. Furthermore Afghanistan's connectedness to globalised insurgents and to the migrant populations in Europe is also well established. The assessment of the domestic campaign is based on the United Kingdom. Although Chapter 10 uses a European collateral in some cases to support its propositions, this is essentially an analysis of how the British government has in practical and operational terms responded to a post Maoist insurgency within elements of the British population.

Both chapters reach the broadly similar conclusion that the globalised insurgent is conceptually ahead of the response. Paradoxically it is the post Maoists (stateless, extra territorial and living for most of the day in a virtual dimension) rather than the government institutions that seek to destroy them, who represent the *modus vivendi* of a post modern society. The response to them is essentially nineteenth century in its organisational characteristics (vertical, ponderously authoritarian and with a top-down management style). Governments and military formations proclaim that technically speaking they are networked, interneted and multi-taskable, but their manpower and assets are still vertically commanded in stark contrast to their adversary which is impulsive and unstructured.

Although governments and their military contingents overseas appear to be addressing the problem, a much more precise understanding of the problem reveals that they have concentrated on the familiar parts, the visible terrorist, the tangible assets and the targets they traditionally associated with the known form of insurgency. Chapter 11 argues that when governments present statistics of elections held, territory secured and terrorists killed these industrial measurements do not show that they have addressed their adversaries' sources of energy or their ability to animate a global constituency through a propaganda of the deed campaign. Nor does it imply that they have a strategy to reduce or remove the social conditions that foment disaffection within their own populations. If we genuinely wish to regain our sense of security and individual freedom to travel and associate in face of a post Maoist insurgency, we need to overtake the insurgent conceptually. This would entail first of all reactivating the principle of political leadership. But that is not enough. At a practical level the counter insurgents needs to have instruments and structures which match those of their opponents. The authoritarian instinct of government may have to adapt to a new era of countering insurgency which could be politically defined by its devolved style, microscopic in scale, involving a multitude of local campaigns, a swarm of local organisations which surge towards their targets in a spontaneous and loosely controlled offensive, organisations which individually are just as impulsive and as inspired as the adversary, but above all are acceptable to the disaffected because they visibly belong to the same culture and live in the same network flows.

9

# THE EXPEDITIONARY APPROACH

*In the Global War on Terror, the main operational emphasis was placed on expeditionary operations in Iraq and Afghanistan. However it is doubtful whether the counter-insurgency campaigns in those places, which were essentially Maoist in concept and territorial in their conduct, addressed the post-Maoist adversary that they had come to engage. It was also doubtful whether an international expedition with multiple actors from every discipline would have the coherence or the determination to succeed in a counter-insurgent mission.*

Although by the new millennium post-Maoist movements had been growing like a cancer for some time, the response to them was a sudden convulsion rather than a gradually escalating counter-insurgency. In the 2001 and 2003 invasions, the US decision-making processes were suffused by passion rather than sober analysis. In both cases there was a tremendous pressure to get out on to the ground fast and the implications of being occupiers as well as invaders was missing from the planning discussion. In his stark narrative of the Iraq invasion, Thomas Ricks depicts a political stampede in Washington in which emotional statements steamrolled over the complexities which lay beneath the surface.[1]

Each deployment set out with the aspiration that speed and the magic of effects-based warfare would ensure a swift conclusion. "You pay attention to the day after," wrote General Franks to Rumsfeld's staff "and I'll pay attention to the day of."[2] In the event these expectations were disappointed. The idea that the regime could be speedily changed and the 'day after' problems handed over to a new set of civil agencies was never realised. Instead, the complexities which had been steamed out of the discussion in the planning stages began to assert themselves with exponential vigour. After the military intervention phase, the invaders found themselves enmeshed; both campaigns had acquired an open-ended list of drag factors and an extended cast of actors.

This chapter asks whether the expeditionary approach can in principle reach and win the heartlands of a post-Maoist insurgency. It is not a case study or a lessons learned analysis of Afghanistan and Iraq. Its purpose is to question the utility of responding to post-Maoism through an expeditionary approach. However in the post-9/11 environment, the question was complicated by the ambiguity of the motives for intervening in Afghanistan and Iraq. Although each intervention set out with objectives, some of which lay within the overall intent of the campaign of Global War on Terror, as they became more and more enmeshed in their particular territory, the missions were enlarged and complicated by the behaviour of other actors. These revised missions raised questions as to whether the campaigns in Afghanistan and Iraq had taken on a new direction which was no longer focused on a global adversary. The security situation on the ground changed so quickly as a result of the overwhelming military build-up that new adversaries, which had never been considered as part of the original objectives, appeared almost immediately.[3] As time wore on the US campaigns moved away from addressing a global movement and found themselves engaging old-fashioned territorial/nationalist insurgencies.[4] This was particularly true in Afghanistan where the global jihadist organisations that had been the primary objective of the invasion swiftly dispersed into other regions. The local insurgency took priority over the global movement. This change of emphasis was accompanied by an Orwellian newspeak which evolved as the Bush administration altered its approach to the problem; the language of counter–terrorism which so characterised the US policy documents of 2003[5] gave way to the language of counter–insurgency.[6] President Bush and his staff began to speak of a long war and less about the techniques of counter-terrorism.[7] From the perspective of achieving a more directed campaign, this was a welcome change of conceptual approach; the new security era was at last being understood through the prism of insurgency. However, down on the ground in Afghanistan and Iraq it turned out to be a very twentieth century counter-insurgency, which in many respects failed to engage its twenty-first century adversary. Both campaigns were grappling with locally established insurgents whose only global dimension was provided by the transient presence of the foreign jihadist.

Although the security era after the Cold War had no name, it was distinguished by the frequent interventions of rich, secure states into the territories of poor and less successful ones. These expeditions ranged from the strictly humanitarian to the predominately military. The multinational interventions were variously led by the UN, NATO and the regional security organisations; the more unilateral interventions were led by military framework providers which included France, India, Nigeria, Russia, the United Kingdom and the US.

Multinational forces were viewed differently by each involved population, who criticised or applauded in such unpredictable combinations that it was extremely difficult to measure success. However, judged by the stated objectives, many failed in the long-term to achieve the peace-building goals that were either expressed in their intent or came with the obligations of intervention.

## The Concept of an Expeditionary Approach

Although titled the 'National Strategy for Combating Terrorism' the US response to al Qaeda (and therefore to post-Maoism) did not amount to a strategy; it was more accurately a concept of operations. In its opening pages it depicted an adversary that was essentially kinetic and territorial, which existed in tangible hard-wired structures. The word "insurgency" was never used. The terrorists were, according to this assessment, vertically organised with a terrorist leader at the top of the structure who provided overall direction, breathed life into the campaign and became the catalyst for action.[8] Consistent with the prevailing logic that this was not an insurgency, almost no mention was made of the possibility of popular support. These were socially disembodied terrorists. They operated at three levels—state, regional and global, the last category being the most hostile to US interests.[9] The US strategy for combating terrorism was to attack its sanctuaries and leadership, and disrupt its communications and material support including financial networks.[10]

In the executive part of the document there were a number of goals to be achieved. Under the first goal (defeating the enemy), the operational objectives were to identify individual terrorists and terrorist organisations, locate them and destroy them. Under the second goal (to deny sponsorship, support and sanctuary), the operational objectives were to end state sponsorship for terrorism and maintain international standards of accountability in the combating of terrorism. Under the goal to strengthen and sustain the international effort to fight terrorism the objectives were to:

> Work with willing states
> Enable weak states
> Persuade reluctant states
> And compel unwilling states.

The goal which might have saved the 2003 US strategy from being an entirely kinetic response was "to diminish the underlying conditions which terrorists seek to exploit."[11] However, there was only one objective under this heading—to "win the war of ideas", which could have acknowledged the crucial part of the problem specifically that global jihad had for some time enjoyed rapidly expanding grassroots support around the world. Instead this section mainly described the physical arrangements for defending US citizens and their property at home and abroad and failed to recognise the nature of popular support.

In view of the drama and proximity of 9/11 and the inherent distaste in Washington for the subject of countering insurgency, the 2003 strategy was not a surprising document. By 2006, almost three years later, there was a tacit acceptance of the realities of a counter-insurgent campaign on a global scale.[12] The US Department of Defense's Quadrennial Review spoke of a long war against objectives that lay beyond Iraq and Afghanistan. In this perspective US forces would be required to work with other governments to achieve an indirect approach that would unbalance the terrorists physically and psychologically. The operational concept was to be similar to that of TE Lawrence's seizure of Aqaba at the beginning of the previous century.[13] However, several levels of command below the White House, US Army Brigadier Kimmit's 21 February 2006 briefing to the foreign press on CENTCOM's current objectives reflected a somewhat different view of the adversary to that of the 2003 National Strategy. CENTCOM's counter-insurgent interest stretched from Kenya to Kyrgyzstan and their adversary in CENTCOM's estimation, was no longer a vertically structured terrorist organisation with a hard-wired leadership. In his short statement Brigadier Kimmit set out this rather different version:

If you look at the long war through the narrow lens of Iraq and Afghanistan, you're going to get the problems set wrong and possibly the solutions wrong as well…

What is remarkable about these organizations, even though they are not tightly bound together, they are put together much like a cellular network telephone. There is a network out there. There's no doubt about it. And this network manifests itself not simply in the normal ways that the military would view it, with fighters, leaders, training camps, so on and so forth, but this is also a movement that makes tremendous use of what we call the "virtual domain." Not simply the geographic domain of land and space and terrain, but it is also the virtual domain of the Internet.

So within the framework of the Global War on Terror, there were different types of US military commitment. The most intensive was the possibility of full military invasion as demonstrated in Afghanistan and Iraq, and further down the scale of commitment were the US training and assistance missions in every region of the world. Using its global reach and military command structures the US was resolved to disrupt the conditions for potential terrorist safe havens to become established in weak states. In regions where the opportunities for terrorist activities were high the US sent military task forces which had the military capability to alter the tactical situation on the ground. In places where local government was able to exercise its authority the US supported them with training missions and military equipment. At the higher level of military commitment, US Combined Joint Task Force in the Horn of Africa (CJTF HOA) was based in Djibouti where it acted as a stepping off point from which a larger force could be swiftly built up. Within the region CJTF HOA also had the capability to intervene if necessary in low-level violence. Still further down the scale of military commitment lay the US-European Command's Counter-Terrorism Initiative in the Trans-Saharan region. Its tasks were to improve and support the indigenous security forces in North Africa and the Sahel areas with a view to countering emerging extremism.[14]

The British efforts in this vein were less focused on the Global War on Terror. In the wake of the Cold War, small military missions conducting what the British called Defence Diplomacy, were used for a wide variety of purposes which included assisting in the restructuring of the massive continental armies that were formerly part of the Warsaw Pact.[15] More recently, overseas military missions provided training and counter-insurgency expertise to failing governments of countries which might be construed as being on the frontlines of the Global War on Terror. Although these isolated training teams and the British officials who served their respective foreign governments so loyally were in some cases disproportionately influential in the restructuring of military forces, they were never designed to directly address what was happening in the breeding grounds of post-Maoist insurgency.

The expeditionary approach therefore comprised a range of fairly visible and invisible initiatives largely orchestrated by the US DoD, Department of State, and USAID.[16] This chapter is concerned with the efforts that fell within the aegis of US Operations Enduring Freedom and Iraqi Freedom. This includes not just the invasions of Afghanistan and Iraq invasions at the top end of the scale, but also the training and assistance missions to individual states further down. Running simultaneously there were additional operations to achieve intelligence penetration, interdict drugs traffic, prevent illegal money transfers, monitor the movement of ships, aircraft and people, and also departments dedicated to strengthen information management and attempt to construct a positive public image for the Coalition's activities.[17] This chapter sets out to understand the strategic effect of these operations.

## Motives for Intervention

Although the 2001 and 2003 US invasions deployed under different political pressures, each had objectives which fell within the intent of the Global War on Terror. Both forces were deployed on the assumption that a group of terrorists arising from globally established insurgent communities still needed territorial bases from which to strike targets in America and Europe. Moreover, the place where they could prepare in safety and receive visiting jihadist groups had to be beyond the reach of any states which might seek to destroy it. The ideal spot was in what were referred to as the "black hole" areas in the international state system. These lay within a dysfunctional state where, because of a complete absence of governance, territory could be taken over by local war leaders who would fiercely protect their fiefdoms against all comers. Successful war leaders, however, needed cash in order to survive and therefore attracted every kind of lucrative wickedness from the trading of humans and pirated cargos through to the sharp-suited money launderers, arms traders and mercenary security agencies. Defined in this way the black holes in the international system acted as industrial parks, places where international actors, criminals and all their associated activities could traffic illegally. But to be viable and attractive, the war leader/entrepreneur had to maintain a level of anarchy than ensured they remained beyond the reach of any national or international system of retribution. And somewhere in this lawless jungle the international criminal or terrorist would find a space and buy the required protection to set up and carry on business.

Every democratic, free trading state had reasons to destroy the regimes in the black hole territories of the international system,[18] but very few had the military reach and the political determination to do it. The motivation for the US to invade a country was therefore strengthened when it could be shown to comprise lawless territories that were effectively black holes in the international system. At the time of writing there are approximately twenty five states where ongoing insurgencies enclose small parcels of territory in which local war leaders have both the motive and the capability to create black holes of varying sizes in the international system which could be exploited by a globalised insurgent movement.[19] For the US to select one of these as the objective of a military invasion required a convergence of several other pressing circumstances.

Unfortunately in the history of recent military interventions there is usually a serious disparity between the stated reason to intervene and the actual intent of the state leading the force. At the operational level the foremost gripe of every international force commander since

1948 has been that the politically acceptable version of the mission failed to relate to operational realities on the ground. This has been the case for traditional UN peacekeepers as well as for the multinational forces in the Balkans. In the international community of the UN General Assembly the invasion of a sovereign state has been regarded as an intensely provocative act, forbidden except in the very particular circumstances set out by the UN Charter, which did not reflect the objectives of the Global War on Terror.[20] After 9/11 the conditions set out in the Charter were not designed to accommodate Global War on Terror objectives, and this has forced countries to mask the real intentions for invading a foreign country behind diplomatically acceptable language. The disparity between political intent and military realities complicated the process of identifying the motives of an expeditionary approach. Beyond the strategic intent spelled out in the National Strategy, US actions post-9/11 were also determined by the public need for a very tangible form of retribution, a political desire to project themselves as the world's leading military power and to project this image both domestically and to the rest of the world.[21]

For all these reasons it is not easy to set out the motives of the US-led expeditionary approach. But when the operational concept was stripped of the language of diplomacy, an invading force commander in the Global War on Terror might have to address these objectives:

- Secure the territory specified with a view to destroying or capturing the assets of the globalised insurgency based in that area.
- Subdue the national political elements and their forces which had previously created a favourable environment for these insurgents and their facilities to exist.
- Restore the monopoly of violence within the state into the hands of an interim administration.
- In the long-term, help to create the political and social conditions within the state for an elected government to be established.

## Characteristics of a Military Intervention

A military intervention at the highest end of the scale of expeditionary commitments in the Global War on Terror has several generic characteristics, the foremost of which is that it is invasive. Although the US counter-insurgency manual is a competent document, it fails to engage with the idea that a counter-insurgent campaign conducted on someone else's territory is per se an invasion of that territory. It may be possible to put a legal gloss on its status, but the reality on the ground is that the arrival of an overwhelming foreign military force has the effect of an invasion. This suggests that the invader therefore holds the initiative and should dictate the path of the campaign. However, experience since the 1990s demonstrates that after their sudden arrival, the foreign troops only retain the initiative for a limited period of time. There is a honeymoon interlude in which the invading troops are largely welcomed and when this mood passes the nature and condition of the host state and the actors therein will reassert themselves and begin to influence the nature of the campaign. The near-certainty that the realities of the host state will overwhelm the aspirations of the invader[22] overturns the political assumption that a force can arrive, alter the regime of a state and then swiftly depart. This is a planner's expectation; in every recent case it has been severely dented by contact with reality. In the twenty-first century context, what starts as a precisely controlled military affair degenerates into a multinational, multidisciplinary event that has little chance of achieving the conflicting aims of a growing swarm of participants.

A description of the characteristics of a military expedition therefore has to reflect what it will probably become *after* the honeymoon, rather than what the planners hoped for prior to contact. Despite the presence of powerful US forces in Iraq and Afghanistan, local factors and the independent behaviour of the civil agencies has introduced an unmanageable characteristic that is similar to a 1990s humanitarian intervention. Beyond the precision of the military component there has been a consistent lack of coherence in which the tensions between actors are exacerbated by the challenges of the operational area. This was also the reality of the 1990s multi-disciplinary, multi-sectoral intervention. So despite the best intentions of its planners, a future military expedition with objectives that fall within the framework of the Global War on Terror may assume the characteristics described below.

## The Status of Occupier

Although planners wish that their troops will be continuously show-
ered with rose petals and scented water by the local population, after
the honeymoon period is over they will be stigmatised with the
responsibilities of being occupiers. This characterisation of them will
survive long after they have installed some form of legitimate government. Being an occupation force carries obvious penalties of international condemnation and negative association, but more significantly
the occupier becomes the target for national or local forms of insurgency that have very little to do with the Global War on Terror. There
is a long-established norm that intervention forces, no matter how
carefully they behave, are very quickly seen as occupiers. This has also
been experienced by UN and multinational forces, particularly when
they assume responsibility for law and order and come into abrasive
contact with the host population. For understandable reasons no doctrine writers have so far written a twenty-first century manual or
guidelines for occupying forces, and although coalition politicians are
reluctant to accept that their contingents are occupiers that is how
they will be seen by the local people. In its twenty-first century context, occupation is the longest and most important part of intervention; furthermore it implies serious responsibilities under the Geneva
Conventions and can only be achieved humanely and effectively by a
top class professional army.

## Unilateral versus multinational

It is possible that a future military expedition within the framework
of the Global War on Terror could be a multinational intervention
authorised by the UN. The advantages of the UN option are that,
empowered by a Security Council mandate, it has some legitimacy in
the international domain and by achieving a careful East-West balance
of contingents it is more able to disarm the accusation of being a
Western-, NATO- or Christian-motivated invasion. The major disadvantage of a UN force or genuinely multinational force is that militarily it will be insufficiently competent to achieve a re-monopolisation
of violence, which is its foremost objective. An intervention might also

be organised and provided entirely by the US. The obvious advantage of a unilateral invasion is that it retains its military effectiveness and in a strictly kinetic manner will achieve a monopoly of violence to a much greater degree than the multinational option. However, its bristling muscularity, strident national identity, and antagonising cultural presence may become the recruiting sergeants for every form of local insurgency and resistance. So although in military terms it is the most effective solution, after the honeymoon the strong unilateral invasion also attracts the strongest forms of local resistance. The best option for a future military intervention is therefore likely to be a US led coalition, but it is questionable how far the overwhelmingly powerful US framework provider will allow its military force on the ground to be genuinely multinational in composition.[23]

## The influence of the host nation

The results of international interventions since the 1990s show that regardless of being multi-national or US-led, after the honeymoon is over, conditions in the host state will determine the outcome of the mission rather than the assertive powers of the invader. Although each host state is unique, there are several conditions which are common to most intervention scenarios. Whether the host state has endured an absence of governance (as in the case of Afghanistan) or an excess of despotic power (as in the case of Iraq), in most cases the intervention will encounter a traumatised population. At a very visible level there may be displaced communities and refugees to relocate and the probability that the population is already close to the edge of survival. But there will also be long-term obstacles to the concept of a quick regime change. Populations that have been traumatised by decades of despotic abuse or civil war tend to shrink into small, essential structures for survival based on the family and the clan.[24] The act of invasion requires the occupation force to become responsible for the traumatised populations they find in the operational space. Invaders from democratic states do not have the option of dealing with them in a decisive, authoritarian manner. The occupiers are accountable to the humanitarian aspirations of their own electorates and in time they also become more and more responsive to the populations in the host

state.[25] Furthermore, a population that has for several generations survived in clan and family structures will not instantly embrace a democratic form of government. They may rush to the polls and display
their inky fingers to the credulous press, but that does not mean they
accept the implications of statehood or the impositions of democratic
provincial government. The genuine social changes that go hand in
hand with the acceptance of democracy imply a multi-disciplinary
process of rebuilding that requires decades to succeed and is deeply
antithetical to the suppositions of a quick regime change.

*The responsibilities of the intervening forces.*

In two decades of serial interventions, multinational and unilateral
forces have arrived in capital cities to find a state that is flat on its
back. Whether Baghdad, Kabul, Mogadishu, Sarajevo or Pristina, in
each case the interveners became inexorably responsible for the survival needs of the urban population. By virtue of being the only viable
organisation in the area with powerful transport, communications,
logistics and engineering assets, the intervening military becomes the
de facto city manager and soon after its arrival will be consulted on a
day-to-day basis on the running of urban areas and aspects of the
state. Regardless of whether the interveners are UN peace forces or a
US-led coalition, in both cases they will continue to find them selves
looking after:

- Imposition of law and order;
- Provision of immediate humanitarian survival needs;
- Burial of remains and immediate damage clearance;
- Custody of prisoners;
- Restoration of civil amenities (water, power, refuse collection and
  hospitals);
- Security of state borders.

In order to secure the host state as a viable democracy in the international system, the intervening force will also have to establish a
monopoly of violence. This is an inescapable requirement of regime
change and failure invites a reinstatement of the previous regime. In
unadorned army language, achieving a monopoly of violence means

countering insurgents and their terrorist factions until all the armed bands within the state are either crushed or have been persuaded to become part of the government's military forces. It means that the populations and militias that oppose the peace-building or nation-building processes have been won over to the government's side and there is now a workable level of security for the rebuilding process to begin. The campaign to achieve this level of security will involve the intervening forces in the following tasks hand-in-hand with the independent civilian agencies:

- Reconciliation between the factions of the population;
- Resuscitation of the economy;
- Rebuilding the essential infrastructure;
- Restoration of governance;
- Restoration of the institutions for a civil society;
- Reconstitution of state security forces;
- Rebuilding the state's pool of skilled professionals.

## Ownership

Throughout the period of intervention there have been continuous transfers of ownership of the peace-building and state-building processes. When the intervention force arrived in the capital of the host state, generally the only other foreign actors were the international organisations that had bravely remained in the city through the worst moments of the previous regime. Despite the presence of civil agencies, the military invaders would find themselves leading the initial efforts to secure the population, not because they were searching for a post-Cold War raison d'être but because at this stage they would be the largest and most effectively organised body in the state. However, when more and more civil agencies received funding and built up their presence, they also began to assert their expertise and authority. In most cases (except for Iraq where the US military presence was overwhelming), force commanders were happy to accede to a division of responsibilities with the humanitarian and development sectors. Unfortunately, this introduced the complication of a multidisciplinary decision-making process which became an added drag factor on the military campaign. Very few civil agencies saw themselves as assets or force multipliers in a counter-insurgency campaign. As the international presence built up in the operational space, the rebuilding process dominated the operational agenda. But its direction and ownership were further complicated by the resuscitation of the host state government who needed to have more and more responsibility for the control of the various sectors in the rebuilding process.

## Cost

The penalties of intervention had to be measured in human terms as well as in the cash price of restoring an ailing state and keeping a large expeditionary force in the field. In 2003, the invasion of Iraq was trailed as a low-cost operation.[26] By using an effects-based tactical approach, the public was assured that surrender would be followed so swiftly by the transfer of power that there would be hardly any casualties, at least to the invaders. And in Iraq the rebuilding costs would be found from increased oil revenues. However, five years later the military and civilian casualty figures for Iraq and Afghanistan exceeded planning expectations.

| Iraq | | | Afghanistan | | |
|---|---|---|---|---|---|
| Coalition | Killed:  4456 | | Killed: 907 | | CNN[27] |
| US | Killed: 3978 | Wounded: 29,379 | Killed; 482 | Wounded: 1894 | CRS |
| UK | Killed: 221 | Wounded: 3082 | Killed: 176 | Wounded | UK MoD |
| Civilians | Killed: 100,000 86,6000–94,5000 | | | | Lancet Iraq body count |

In the US an optimistic prediction was reinforced by a deferential press which in the crucial first months of the campaigns on the ground failed to challenge the absence of strategy in the Global War on Terror and was also reluctant to publish footage that showed the real cost of invasion in terms of civilian casualties and destruction during the initial advance into Iraq. It was Al Jazeera, in their determination to present the true picture to the archipelago of Muslim communities around the world, who published images of the dead and spectacles of gory chaos in Baghdad's hospitals.

By 2007 organised public pressure in Britain prevented the government spin machinery from continuing to evade questions about the real cost of the war, especially in terms of casualties and the large numbers of very seriously injured soldiers who would need long-term care.[28] It was clear by now that the casualty figures had exceeded the British government's expectations and that ad hoc arrangements to treat large numbers of war wounded in a near-dysfunctional health system had exposed both the inadequacy of hospital care for the severely injured and the planning failures of the MoD.[29] There were also the looming consequences of post-combat stress which were better understood in the US than in Britain.[30]

In both the US and the United Kingdom the main question was how much the voters would bear. Both countries had professional volunteer forces and paradoxically in political terms their troops were becoming more expendable as a consequence of their increasing disengagement from the population. In the US, Bacevich has argued that although politicians continuously praised the high moral standards and determined efficiency of their armed forces, the continuous US casualties were calmly absorbed and did not animate the voting public sufficiently to call for a termination or reduction of military effort. In Britain, where politicians and their information managers were even more distanced from and less aware of their armed forces, there were ritual photo opportunities and speeches about the bravery and excellence of the 'lads on the frontline' but also a sense of relief among the political advocates of Blair's wars that the general public was so indifferent to their cost. Only a handful of politicians on either side of the British Parliament had any family connections or knowledge of the armed forces. The British Army was particularly isolated and their failure to engage public attention was reinforced by the extinction of a generic British war correspondent who in a previous century might have provided a tougher cost-benefit analysis of British participation in the 'war on terror'. In the US and in the United Kingdom there was a lack of awareness amongst the uninvolved element of the population of the enormous strain that maintaining two long-term campaigns had put on the regular armed forces. This situation was altered in the summer of 2009 by media and public interest in casualties arising from Operation Panther's Claw; TV coverage of the operations, the UK military and the impact of casualties began to increase.

In addition to the problem of human casualties, Rumsfeld and his staff had hugely underestimated the dollar cost of Operation Enduring Freedom. The official assessment was challenged by Joseph Stiglitz, who, in stark contrast to the Congressional Budget Office estimate of $500 billion, argued that the war might cost between $1 and $2 trillion US dollars.[31] In 2008 Stiglitz and Bilmes revised their figures to $3 trillion without including the individual costs borne by the coalition partners.[32] They accused the US government of wilfully confusing the true nature of the war expenditure and of fiscal mismanagement. The actual cost of the operations in Iraq and Afghanistan was, in their estimation, in the region of $16 billion a month. The gap between the official figures and their own was explained by budgeting failures, and serial miscalculations of the cost of future operations and of borrowing. They successfully ferreted out additional lists of troops killed and injured in the margins of the operation, while on training and while they took part in logistic operations and supporting activities around the world. The government had vastly underestimated the cost of rehabilitation and the long-term support of those with seriously injured limbs and the brain damaged. Using large numbers of contractors had also been very costly, especially their death and injury benefits which were considerably more expensive than that of a regular soldier. The US voter had yet to bear the burden of these costs as they had been financed by borrowing. The UK faced the same problems on a commensurately smaller scale. At the outset Chancellor Gordon Brown had set aside £1 billion in additional funds to pay for operational expenses. However, in 2007 Stiglitz and Bilmes, having encountered similar problems of obfuscation and opaque accounting by Whitehall officials had estimated that the war was already costing the United Kingdom in the region of £7 billion. Both the US and Britain had yet to calculate and reveal the long-term burden of the Global War on Terror, especially the interest to be paid on loans and the individual benefits to a host of seriously disabled veterans.

*The Utility of Military Intervention*

Despite the visibility of the multinational interventions by the UN and regional forces during the post-Cold War period there was an analytical failure to understand that the US military interventions in Afghanistan and Iraq were part of the same genre and would therefore encounter the same generic problems. Whether an intervention was led by the most powerful nation in the world or arranged in an ad hoc manner by the UN, it had to have a viable strategy as well as an effective set of instruments by which to achieve its aim. Post-Cold War experience showed that the chief instrument, the military expedition or multilateral intervention, had a bad record of success. There were known reasons why so often this turned out to be an unsuccessful option, and this applied even when the US with all its horses and men intervened in a sickly collapsing state. These inherent penalties could be summarised as:

- The disadvantages of occupation
- The unintended consequences of antagonising local resistance.
- The appalling conditions in the host state and the consequent need for massive state-building efforts in addition to the military objectives of the intervention
- The likelihood of cultural rejection and armed resistance to the rebuilding programmes
- The loss of control as more and more states and international organisations become involved
- The need to allow the host state to have ownership of the campaign within the operational space
- The extended duration of the campaign
- The cost of the campaign in lives and dollars.

*The US Perspective*

Politicians were nevertheless bound to present military intervention as having a demonstrable utility. The Bush administration had staunchly maintained its version of the threat since the 2003 National Strategy. Their resolve could be applauded for its consistency, as the logical consequence of conviction politics and for providing the leadership and the security that was required by a nervous American population. However from the margins of the debate, Frank Furedi advanced a somewhat different interpretation.[33] In his view, the actual statistics of death by terrorism showed that the government and the population should have been more prepared to absorb a degree of terrorism as an acceptable risk.[34] Instead, US and British leaders had told their voting populations since 2001 that terrorism was an unacceptable absolute, presenting scenarios of mass casualties, implying there were 'known unknowns' regarding the potential use of nuclear and chemical weapons. Furedi's accusation was that fostering this level of uncertainty and anxiety created a dependency on strong leadership and the demand for a continuing Global War on Terror. It also created large public meetings thirsting for presidential and government reassurances such as this:

...our most important job in government—whether it be the federal government, state government, or local government—is to protect you. And remember the lessons of September the 11th: that oceans cannot protect us, that we face cold-blooded killers who, in our case, resorted to mass murder to send a message.

President George W Bush, Las Vegas, Nevada, 31 January 2008.

Politically, it was possible to show that the expeditionary approach was successful and that the intervention instrument had been effective. By deed and declaration the federal government had protected the US populations from a serious overseas threat that had been incubating in terrorist organisations scattered from Northern Africa to Southeast Asia. Al Qaeda was still, according to this view, the primary threat to the international community.[35] The White House argued that the US expeditionary approach had greatly reduced al Qaeda's ability to plan elaborate mass casualty attacks which would require the coordination of their franchised or allied organisations.

With the capture of Hambali[36] linkages with South Asia had been reduced and the capture of Abu Faraj-al-Liki[37] had effectively severed the planning and communication linkages between the Middle East and the Horn of Africa. The death of Abu Musab al-Zarqawi, head of al Qaeda in Iraq, and the elimination of his senior activists in Pakistan further isolated al Qaeda from its network of subsidiary organisations. These reversals now prevented al Qaeda—the number one enemy—from exercising its leadership over the global network of terrorist organisations. US expeditionary operations had also succeeded in removing the facility of the safe haven. According to Ambassador Crumpton, the US Coordinator for Counter-Terrorism, safe havens had great strategic importance. Without them al Qaeda was no longer able to plan and prepare a sophisticated attack on the scale of 9/11. In his valedictory January 2007 interview, Crumpton confirmed that US operations had reduced al Qaeda's operational elements into less secure sub-units. In place of the massive bomb blasts in high-density areas, NATO states should expect smaller, less carefully planned local attacks. The US' kinetic success had shattered al Qaeda's coherence and turned it from a global terrorist organiser of attacks into a Cheshire Cat organisation, appearing and disappearing, reactive and constantly on the run. Without the security of a place in which to regroup it could not mount major attacks on the US mainland or on the its overseas assets. These kinetic successes were reinforced by the ideological rejection of al Qaeda's use of indiscriminate violence by respected Islamist thinkers such as Nuiman bin Othman, Said Iman (otherwise known as Doctor Fadl) and Abu Baseer al Tartisi.[38] Although these figures were unknown to the majority of the US and British populations they nevertheless actively influenced the radicalised and vulnerable individuals in the isolated Muslim communities. In contradiction to al Qaeda's previous directives, Abu Baseer had told a British audience that they should not commit acts of violence on British territory because "by living here and interacting with society you're effectively agreeing to be bound by the (British ) laws."[39]

Presented as a list of successful actions against 'terror' the US expeditionary approach seemed to be succeeding. From the perspective of the Bush administration, Operation Enduring Freedom in all its forms seemed to address a domestically accepted version of the adversary. A strong Republican government had smashed al Qaeda's structures abroad and established an impressive Homeland Security shield to defend US territory. But this was an exclusively American approach to overseas contingencies; in this view, as long these actions served a domestic political purpose and satisfied the American audience, they succeeded. The White House was far less concerned about how this looked from the perspective of an international audience.

The problem was that in strategic terms the US expeditionary approach set out to address a 1990s version of the adversary. Even as the US National Strategy was being drafted, the real-life global movement which threatened NATO nations had changed. By the twenty-first century it did not resemble the demonised versions of terrorism that was being presented to the US population. The expeditionary campaign had evidently succeeded in domestic terms, but as an international strategy it did not touch or influence the forces which lay at the heart of the problem.

In Frank Gardner's August 2008 BBC Radio 4 broadcast there was a seminal moment when, having convincingly shown that al Qaeda's manifesto was now seriously challenged on all sides against a background of tactical setbacks, he asked his interviewee Hanif Qadir: "So does all this mean that al Qaeda is finished? Can the West start to breath easy?"[40] And from the perspective of the exponents of the expeditionary approach to the Global War on Terror, Qadir gave completely the wrong answer: "The number of young people getting involved in violent extremism and who are prepared to go to Afghanistan and Iraq to fight the jihad is growing.".

The expeditions of the Global War on Terror had addressed the mosquitoes but not the swamp; in Europe the processes of subversion and activism were being intensified not reduced by the campaigns in Iraq and Afghanistan. The US National Strategy had depicted its adversary not as an insurgency but as a terrorist organisation that was politically isolated—as a set of techniques that were static, inert, stagnant—at a time when real-life society, technology and the entire global environment around them were fizzing with change. It seemed that leaders on both sides of the Atlantic lacked the political determination to address an adversary which had post-Maoist characteristics. Instead they had recreated it as something familiar, something that they could destroy with weapons and ideas they already possessed; something with vertical structures, hard-wired organisation charts and a need for territory. In fact, the insurgent movement that now beset the West had very quickly moved beyond these limitations. Post-Maoism was evolving with post-modern society at the speed of an express train into something far more complicated and at the time of writing only partially understood. It could not be reduced to fit the language of political leaders and their information managers. Post-Maoism referred to a global movement, which was de-territorialised, which had no real long-term aims, which far from being socially disembodied probably had millions of followers, which was impulsive and organic and revitalised by propaganda of the deed. In seven years of expeditionary operations the Global War on Terror had not recognised or addressed these characteristics.

At the operational level the US and its NATO allies had not won over the populations in the host nations in a strategically significant manner. The opinion polls reflected a degree of support that was ephemeral, which depended on presence and short-term successes. The coalition would have had greater impact in the host nations if they had behaved more like an imperial power, but they were prevented by their own history and their sense of themselves as spreaders of democratic liberalism. The contradiction of being a politically correct invader meant that there always had to be a visible withdrawal strategy. This proclaimed to the international community, to the members of the US General Assembly, to the voters at home and, above all, to the populations in the operational space, that once stability had been achieved and the operational area was no longer in danger of becoming a future safe haven, the major league armies would leave. For millions of families at the edge of survival in the operational space, the certainty of the US' eventual withdrawal and therefore the uncertainty of their presence, sent a disturbing message. If the invaders were sure to withdraw, who would be the final inheritor of the host state? Although the newly elected governments in both Afghanistan and Iraq were presented to the local people as guarantors of a better future, neither was sufficiently strong to convince the vulnerable masses to commit their support. What if they committed themselves to supporting the new government, only for the insurgents to seize control of the state again and carry out a ruthless revenge on those who had opposed them? Instead of a politically correct withdrawal strategy the coalition forces needed to build up the infrastructure of occupation, huge barracks with swimming pools, sports clubs and palatial air conditioned shopping centres for generations of future occupiers, as the Romans and the British had in their successful conquests; these things would have sent a message of long-term commitment that might have compelled the support of a wavering population.[41] And of course, these things were out of the question.

## The European Perspective

After the 2003 EU-US spat prior to the invasion of Iraq, British and to a lesser extent European politicians seemed more determined to work in a US-European partnership against global terror. The British in particular were resolved to bury differences over foreign policy and concentrate on working with the US Global War on Terror initiatives.[42] Although the post-Cold War era now presented a hugely altered European political landscape, the British Foreign and Commonwealth Office still appeared to be following its longstanding mantra for regional security on the lines of 'Russians out, Americans in' with a variable position for dealing with French and German ascendancy in Europe. But in the twenty-first century the Cold War imperative for European-US unity had also altered. Despite the political sweet-talking and the undignified stampede to support US operations, there were many reasons why the Europeans and particularly the British, at the most fundamental level—in their own domestic populations, faced a completely different situation to the US and therefore needed to be more careful and qualified about the utility of the expeditionary approach.

For centuries, Europeans had been conditioned by the probability that their wars would in the end be fought in their own sovereign space, across their own arable lands, through their cities and among their own populations. Going to war therefore had very palpable and immediate consequences and was usually not something that happened on someone else's territory. As a result, and more so than the British, continental Europeans took a more consensual approach towards dealing with adversaries. According to Jonathan Eyal, small vulnerable countries which lived in close proximity had "grown accustomed to believing that managing, rather than eliminating, security risks" was a better policy for damage control and survival. On the other hand, US geography and its historical experience of continental wars and allies was completely the opposite. For them national interests took first priority: the US population was habitually suspicious of the consensual approach of international alliances, and organisations like the UN were of no use to them if they required that US national interests should be compromised.[43] Conversely, twenty-first century Europeans could not afford to ignore the realities of their interconnectedness with the rest of the world; they therefore could not take comfort in the same versions of the adversary and the war on terror that the US administration presented to its population. Faced by their more direct access and closer ethnic connection (through their migrant communities) to the Iraq and Afghanistan war zones, they were much more vulnerable to the ramifications of the violence.

The US National Strategy was absolute, it failed to recognise that by the twenty-first century most terrorists were the visible part of larger insurgent movements. By insisting that all terrorism should be the target of the Global War on Terror, the US had mixed together insurgent movements that were potentially extremely dangerous to their interests with the ones which were not. To be fair, in 2002 when the strategy documents were being written, doctrinal thinkers had been surprised by the sudden revival of interest in insurgency and there were no supporting research programmes looking beyond the limited horizon of counter-terrorist thinking. However, this situation quickly rectified itself and from 2003 onwards academic initiatives and funding focused on these issues. The US produced by far the most powerful group of writers in this respect including many names whose works have been reverentially cited in earlier chapters. The US also led the way in producing the up-to-date doctrine for expeditionary forces. It was a sad irony that although it possessed so much analytical talent and initiative, its expeditionary strategy was nevertheless indiscriminate and, from the European perspective, self defeating.

The US campaigns in Iraq and Afghanistan and beyond had got bogged down with insurgencies that were irrelevant to their efforts to eradicate the globalised movement which threatened them. Individual writers had identified many forms of nationalist insurgency which they had variously referred to as popular, feral, national liberationists, national Islamists (the hybrid variety), global-local, local-international and local. What is most significant about these categories was that very few of them presented a serious risk to the homelands of the coalition nations or their assets. They were intensely national and narrowly territorial in their ambitions, and they were therefore largely antithetical to a pushy, franchised insurgent movement with a genuinely global manifesto such as al Qaeda. But beyond Iraq and Afghanistan, the images of US invasion, occupation, collateral civilian casualties, over-zealous confrontations with the local population, the use of torture—all of that bad body language and bad news imagery—had transformed these nationalist movements from potentially useful instruments in the efforts to counter globalised insurgency into adversaries.

The US seemed to shrug off the consequences of its international unpopularity in a way that the interconnected Europeans could not. Crucially, America's Muslim communities appeared to accept the ramifications of the Global War on Terror in a way that Europeans Muslims were far less prepared to do. Guantanamo Bay, rendition and the triumphal images of beige-coloured armoured vehicles grinding through the streets of Muslim cities had antagonised young Muslims in Europe. In jihadist propaganda, European hostages were photographed in the same Guantanamo style orange-coloured prison suits before being executed. Whereas huge spending on homeland security had made fortress America more and more impenetrable to foreign visitors of every category, Europe's open frontiers could not be secured in the same way. Operational experience showed that even the most developed border obstacles did not prevent massive illegal immigration.[44]

Above all, the entire concept of the adversary in the US' Global War on Terror did not fit the European reality. Europe's Muslim communities were less well integrated, and more antagonised by the Global War on Terror.[45] Europe was less threatened by a net flow of terrorists entering its territory from the overseas sanctuaries than by terrorist attacks arising from within their own population. By the 1990s the security problem for Europe was already the antithesis of the model presented by the Bush administration. Europe's bombers and their supporting infrastructure came from the second or third generations of migrant families. They were Europeans; they were not being subverted from an overseas sanctuary, they were the product of a home-grown, organic process. This left European security forces fighting on two different fronts, the domestic and the expeditionary. They might have had political reasons to support the US expeditionary campaign against overseas sanctuaries, but they had to reconcile that commitment with rising disaffection within their own migrant population. Their problem was that the two fronts were not mutually exclusive and it quickly became apparent that it was impossible to win over their own disaffected domestic populations against the tide of images and reverberations from the overseas campaign. It was the continuous traffic of routine news and commentary regarding the occupation of Iraq and Afghanistan, rather than jihadist propaganda, which antagonised the disaffected element of the population, especially those who saw their faith as the target of the war on terror.

With the benefit of hindsight and objectivity, the Europeans needed to give their domestic campaign priority over the expeditionary. The net flow of potential terrorist attackers was *not* from an overseas sanctuary into Europe, it arose in their midst. The home-grown activists were more immediate and dangerous than the possibility of attack by foreign or foreign-domiciled terrorists. The overseas sanctuaries that harboured training camps had been regarded as an essential stage for an attack on the European population, but in fact they were merely desirable not critical to its success. It seemed as if the Europeans continued to accept the primacy of expeditionary operations because the logic of this prioritisation had never been politically challenged.

With hindsight it becomes increasingly possible to argue that the military campaigns in Iraq and Afghanistan were not configured to engage a post-Maoist movement, but that in the emotional aftermath of 9/11 it would have required a political leader of superhuman qualities to have addressed that particular truth. After several years of expeditionary experiences the immediate threat to the European populations was a form of insurgency that had crossed an evolutionary threshold from Maoism to post-Maoism, and the practical response was far more complicated than the average politician cared to explain, especially to an audience accustomed to sound bites. In the first decade of the twenty-first century Europe politicians had barely engaged with the idea that the population existed for most of the day in network flows and the uncharted archipelagos of the Internet and that these structures were altering at the speed of a train with the communications revolution. They barely understood that within their own populations thousands of vulnerable and disaffected individuals could be subverted by insurgent organisations who freely exploited that same virtual dimension. Not only had no operational concept emerged by which to defeat this insurgent activity, no government had recognised the full extent of its political nature. The possibility of insurgency arising from a global movement had emerged at least a decade ahead of our ability to recognise to it. At the beginning of the twenty-first century the traditional expeditionary approach was held out as the only possible response, it served the political ability of the moment even as it had spectacularly failed to engage the real adversary.

# 10

# THE DOMESTIC APPROACH

*For more than a century the British experience of insurgency had been mainly expeditionary. But after 9/11 when a domestic adversary threatened them, the British responded with police, security services and an array of government departments. Although these collective efforts were presented as counter-terrorism they had the architecture and operational characteristics of countering insurgency. Because political violence in Europe now had post-Maoist characteristics, this unique operation could become the prototype for the next chapter of countering insurgency.*

After 9/11 al Qaeda and its subsidiaries continued their offensive against NATO nations, targeting their populations, cities and overseas assets. Although the Western media emphasised the sensational nature of these attacks, the political response was becoming more measured and less emotional so that by 2005 when bombers assaulted the London commuters and once again commandeered public attention, there was already a better understanding of the adversary. By 2006 government departments and security staff were acknowledging by deed and by declaration that the post-modern insurgent (they tended to say "terrorist") had some distinctly twenty-first century characteristics and had exploited the communications revolution with great success.

Meanwhile sociologists had by now explained how post-modern societies (in the sense established in Chapter 8) were being altered by the communications and information revolution. The discussion of insurgency was becoming more multi-disciplined as academics were increasingly included in the efforts to define the insurgent forms that now beset us.[1]

This chapter describes an emerging concept to counter post-Maoist insurgency—the domestic campaign. In 2008 there was no proven method for dealing with political violence which arose from a global movement and the overseas expedition did not engage the communities which were the source of insurgent energy that afflicted so many European states. In 2008 the internal security campaign in the United Kingdom was by now so large and elaborate that it could no longer be described as a counter terrorist operation; its significance was that it represented a genre of similar initiatives in other European countries. If these were successful they seemed to be a more logical basis for future operations than the large expeditionary forces in Iraq and Afghanistan. It made sense to secure the home populations in European states before attempting large-scale counter insurgency offensives in distant regions, especially when overseas operations so exacerbated the very communities they sought to engage. From this perspective the Global War on Terror had been a distraction, far from addressing the movements that were now growing within NATO countries, the expeditions to Afghanistan and Iraq had acted as their recruiting sergeant. Furthermore by 2008 even the most forward looking research had so far failed to point with any conviction to where the adversary's heartland lay, or how a deterritorialised society could be measured or understood. When the essential nature of the target population and its vital ground were so poorly understood, it was hard to design a concept of operations that addressed the insurgent energy that was the source of our insecurity. Despite these handicaps, Britain's domestic counterterrorism operation was a promising place to start looking. Its focus was more relevant to the nature of post-Maoism than the military expeditions in Iraq and Afghanistan. The United Kingdom had become an obvious place for a counter-insurgent approach at the domestic level; within its coastal boundary lay a vulnerable and radicalising Muslim minority which was being subverted both internally and by externally based organisations; furthermore its host population, police and security forces had a previous experience of countering terrorism. Surely in these circumstances the British could, after the initial bungling which characterised their counter-insurgency operations, eventually find a successful concept by which to turn the situation around?

Although British officials and the media steadfastly referred to it as "counter-terrorism", the campaign organisation, when drawn out on a single sheet of paper with the full panoply of Whitehall departments, local government, security services, police units and non government agencies, bore far more resemblance to countering an insurgency than to countering terrorism. However, calling it terrorism served a political purpose. No sensible government would allow its domestic troubles to be described as an insurgency even if, according to its own doctrine, it had all the defining characteristics.[2] In previous campaigns when politicians and officials used counter-terrorist labels, those involved at the operational level had understood the separation between the rhetoric and the reality. So, despite the political preference for calling insurgency terrorism, the campaign on the ground had followed an essentially counter-insurgent concept, which in addition to the kinetic business of counter-terrorism had focused on a political strategy for winning the population in the vital ground.

The counter-terrorist campaign in Britain which developed between 2000 and 2003 was organised and implemented by the Home Office and the mainland police forces. Neither had organised a counterinsurgent campaign or had much experience with the political business of winning over the communities at the heart of the problem to the government side. Blair-era politicians and communicators had instinctively adopted the language of counter-terrorism in their presentational approach, and while this meant the Cabinet Office at least had a plan to protect the state from terrorist attack, it was less certain how they could engage the population in the vital ground politically.

For several centuries, a very small cast of actors had dealt with British small wars and insurgencies in foreign places.[3] Now the nation faced an evolved, post-Maoist version of insurgency with a very differently constituted team. It was certainly true that there were elements and agencies in the Home Office which had formidable reputations in the tracking and capturing terrorists, but there was no department and very few individuals that had experience of undoing the subversive effects of a long-term insurgency or running a major campaign involving the entire national government machinery right down to local level[4]. By 2000 the adversary in Britain was identifiably post-Maoist consequently the counter strategy had to be something more than a traditional counter-insurgent or counter-terrorist operation. In this case the involvement of a much wider span of government departments and civilian actors guaranteed a different style of campaign. The domination of the Home Office and the police and the absence of any military influence brought a new generation of operational talent into the campaign process.

Sadly, from the perspective of the impartial observer, it was a very opaque process. Senior policemen, counter-terrorist experts and Home Office officials were naturally secretive, nothing in their experience prepared them for the public exposure involved in mounting a political campaign rather than a police operation. In the hierarchy of their operational leadership there were no outstanding key communicators who could explain what was happening with the conviction and authority that the situation demanded. This was not just a matter of being inherently secretive, many in the Home Office simply did not understand the entirety of the operation or felt too restricted by the Official Secrets Act to explain it in unclassified terms. This gave the campaign a closed, slightly sinister personality that was alien to British counter-insurgency. There was no police or Home Office version of the bluff military figure who could appear before the public in the manner of General Jackson or General Richards to explain the commander's perspective. Attempts by Labour politicians and sponsored figures to fill this gap were quickly trashed at public meetings and also on the networks that were trusted by the target audience.

This chapter sets out to describe the unique character of the British domestic campaign, the particular nature of the jihadist adversary in the United Kingdom and the practicalities of the extremely complicated response.

*The "insurgency" in the United Kingdom*

The British counter-terrorist campaign was shaped by an evolving perception of their domestic adversary. During the 1990s the nationalist Islamist resurgence in some Muslim states had developed into threatening insurgencies. When these governments reacted against their dissident communities, in some cases with great brutality, it sent a stream of political refugees into the prevailing torrent of migrants already heading for Europe. These more recent asylum seekers represented a wide range of unrelated cultures and causes mainly from the Gulf States, North Africa and eastwards as far as Kashmir. When they arrived, the British government did not set conditions for their entry and temporary residence; their nuanced response was to welcome, exploit and discourage according to the nature of each exiled movement. For their part, the members of these movements regarded the United Kingdom with indifference but also recognised that it provided a useful base from which they could continue fund-raising, recruiting, proselytising and even some outdoor training. In some cases they also used Britain as a mounting base for overseas operations.

Two simultaneously developing strands of activity soured this considerate relationship. Towards the end of the 1990s al Qaeda had succeeded in increasing the scale and ferocity of its attacks against the United States and its overseas presence, culminating in 2001 with the attacks on New York and Washington. These events electrified the communities of Islamist activists who, regardless of their disparate causes and cultures, began to coalesce as a federation of global movements. Their connectedness was reinforced by the US strategy for the Global War on Terror which rashly included most forms of insurgency and terrorism in its arc of retribution.[5] Besides confronting insurgent organisations that were irrelevant to its mission, the rhetoric accompanying the GWOT had the effect of demonising the exiled movements in the United Kingdom, which previously had no reason to become the adversaries of the British. As a result the main direction of the jihad and its subversive efforts was reversed so that they now menaced their adopted host. It was no longer possible for Britain to imagine that it could benignly accommodate Islamist revolutionaries.

Like many other European nations, the United Kingdom was now part of an insurgent archipelago that stretched from Jakarta to Stockholm. When the Islamist movements with asylum status began to turn against Britain, the threat of their redirected hostility was exacerbated by the "atomisation" of British-based terrorist structures.[6] Instead of belonging to an old-fashioned terrorist organisation with a vertical structure and formal overseas linkages, the British Islamist activists were disappearing into the British communities to which they now belonged, and without a structure they were much less easy to trace. According to British counter-terrorist officials,[7] their *modus operandi* was for local and international insurgents to come together for a particular project and when that was completed or the group was penetrated by the security services, they dispersed and then reconfigured with new partners.[8]

Meanwhile, a completely different form of violence was beginning to manifest itself in the urban areas, which involved not the recent asylum seekers but the Britain's long established Muslim communities. The 2001 riots by young Muslims in the Midlands (described in Chapter 6) represented an organic form of disaffection which arose from communities that two or three generations ago had migrated to the United Kingdom. According to Professor Ted Cantle's 2001 report for the Home Office, their sense of outrage and acts of violence resulted from the effects of enclosure, separation and a mutual ignorance of the host and migrant community's cultures.[9] The significance of the 2001 riots and the continuing urban tension was that it emanated from a completely different sector of Britain's Muslim communities and for reasons that had nothing to do with global jihad or Salafi extremism.

In the late 1990s British security services were still looking outwards at the overseas Islamist connections to recently arrived Muslim asylum seekers and the increasing need to look inwards at Britain's disaffected Muslim communities was not given the same priority. Radicalisation within established Muslim second and third-generation communities was not a subject of interest for the intelligence services unless it became connected to an external Islamist organisation. This outward-facing intelligence posture was encouraged by the American counter-terrorism strategy and Mr Bush's characterisation of the threat as coming from overseas. The Britain's domestic security apparatus had been facing in the wrong direction for several years focusing its main energy on attacks mounted from abroad, when its more immediate problem turned out to be from the self-radicalised elements of its own population.

After the electrifying effect of 9/11, the manner of disaffection among migrant communities in Europe moved resolutely towards a post-Maoist paradigm. In principle, many young British Muslims became radicalised through a process, which took place locally without the knowledge or oversight of any organised network. Subversion was more likely to be initiated by a disaffected friend, or in a group, or sitting alone in front of the Internet screen, and not by some top-down, highly structured overseas movement. The glittering prizes that drew individuals towards extremism were ostensibly religious, but security officials in the United Kingdom were pointing out that for many second- and third-generation adolescents, their confused identity was a greater source of insecurity. They felt they could never be part of what they saw as a traditional British culture and many did not in any case wish to be part of it. But nor did they wish to follow the local customs of their parent's country of origin.[10] Participating in a global movement seemed to solve their problem of identity. It did not matter that the movement they aspired to join had no realistic objectives, the attraction was the social sense of belonging, the shared outrage, the momentum of a movement, proselytising a cause, surviving as a group, growing in numbers, challenging authority and compelling nations and international organisations to recognise them.[11] There was also for some an overpowering ethical imperative to set right the offences to Islam by Western culture generally, and by the host state in particular.[12]

Government security agencies struggled to find a model that could explain the process of subversion and radicalisation, a generic description of what caused an individual to become a bomber. As the list of British terrorist convictions grew, so did the number of variables and it became increasingly difficult to establish a useful stereotype. However, it was important for the authorities to share their understanding of the generic stages of subversion, and so a restricted version of an MI5 research document found its way into the hands of *The Guardian* newspaper, setting out the basis for understanding radicalisation in Britain.[13] This concluded that although there was no authoritative way to profile a "British Terrorist" it was nevertheless possible to say that the majority of the disaffected were British nationals or lived in Britain legally. Many lacked religious literacy and probably did not live in orthodox Muslim families. MI5's main findings from hundreds of cases studies concluded that:

- The majority of terrorists were British, around half were born in the United Kingdom, others had migrated later in life. Some of these fled traumatic experiences and oppressive regimes and claimed asylum, but more came to Britain to study or for family or economic reasons and become radicalised many years after arriving.

- Far from being religious zealots, a large number of those involved in terrorism did not practise their faith regularly. Many could be regarded as religious novices, few had been brought up in strongly religious households, and there was a higher than average proportion of converts. Some were involved in drug-taking, drinking alcohol and visiting prostitutes.
- There was no more evidence of mental illness or pathological personality traits found among British terrorists than normally found in the general population.
- British-based terrorists were as ethnically diverse as the British Muslim population, with individuals from Pakistani, Middle Eastern and Caucasian backgrounds and assumptions could not be made about suspects skin colour, ethnic heritage or nationality.
- Most British terrorists were male, but women also played an important role, sometimes tacitly condoning their husbands', brothers' or sons' activities.
- While the majority were in their early to mid-20s when they become radicalised, a minority first became involved in violent extremism at 30 or more.
- There were few lone individuals with no ties. The majority of those over 30 had steady relationships, and most had children, which challenged the idea that terrorists were young men or that someone with a wife and children was less likely to commit acts of terrorism.
- They were not unintelligent or gullible, but nor were they more likely to be well-educated; their educational achievement ranged from total lack of qualifications to degree-level education. However, they were almost all employed in low-grade jobs.[14]

MI5 concluded that most were "demographically unremarkable" and simply reflected the communities in which they lived. Contrary to popular opinion, the radicalising influence of extremist clerics diminished after 2004, having reached a peak in the 1990s. The terrorist groups operating in Britain were different in many important respects both from Islamist extremist activity in other parts of the world and from historical terrorist movements such as the IRA or the Red Army Faction. Unless the government understood the varied backgrounds of those drawn to terrorism in Britain, it might not prevent violent radicalisation continuing in the long-term. Without "attractive alternatives" to terrorist involvement traditional law enforcement tactics could backfire if handled badly or used against people who were not seen as legitimate targets.[15]

The model below shows in broad terms the different stages of disaffection in Britain and emphasizes at which point an individual or group becomes extremely dangerous. In this chart there are six categories of radicalisation and subversion from Uncommitted to Operationally Ready. Although the insurgent energy of the movement tends to move from left to right, the chart does not intend to convey the sense of a fixed progression leading towards extremism and violence. Some violent extremists have moved swiftly and directly from being uncommitted to operationally ready in a matter of weeks, and very many individuals remain disaffected activists without becoming violent in any way. The chart intends to convey that it is nevertheless probable that a small but constant stream of individuals move from left to right at different speeds, passing from one category to another until they are operationally ready.[16]

The Process of Subversion and Grooming Leading to a Terrorist Attack

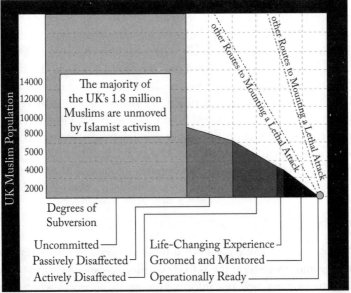

*Uncommitted*

For many reasons the vast majority of Britain's 1.6 to 1.8 million Muslims fall into the uncommitted category mainly because they are socially secure and follow an Islamic faith which is not politicised. In addition they may be relatively prosperous, securely employed and successfully established members of society, with a realistic sense of their identity in the United Kingdom.

*Passively Disaffected*

Individuals, groups of friends and entire families may become passively disaffected because they no longer accept the conditions in which they live and are affected by the continuous news and imagery of NATO expeditions and the Global War on Terror. In a temporal sense they resent living in a badly housed community; being insufficiently educated and therefore unable to get a better job; being racially profiled by police and government officials and actively discriminated against in the streets, at work and at school. As Muslims they feel that the Global War on Terror, British society and British foreign policy is confrontational towards Islam and they are angered by the inconsistencies of the British government in its efforts to counter terrorism in their local community. There are no accurate figures to show precisely what proportion of the British Muslim population is passively disaffected. Officials interviewed to research this chart felt it could be between 6,000 and 8,000. However, some felt that the number of passively disaffected Muslims in the United Kingdom could be very much higher and that almost any orthodox Muslim living in Britain who monitored the British media would be angered in some degree by the news and imagery of the Global War on Terror and Britain's counter-terrorist operations. This assertion was supported by Pew, who in July 2006 found that 47% of UK Muslims in the United Kingdom felt that "there was a conflict in being a devout Muslim and living in a Western society."[17]

*Actively Disaffected*

Whereas the passively disaffected tend to internalise their sense of outrage and misfortune, the actively disaffected category do not. They may attend meetings, join informal groups or networks where their sense of injustice and the challenges of an apparently hostile British society are discussed in a more angry and vituperative fashion. They may also demonstrate and join local action groups.

## The Life-Changing Experience

A violent physical encounter, the trauma of a close friend, a news story or an image may affect an individual so strongly that they are resolved to take action or by their behaviour become highly vulnerable to talent spotters and recruiters that belong to formally structured subversive organisations. Individuals who are completely uncommitted, as well as individuals who are already disaffected, can have a life-changing experience in this context. For example, an uncommitted British Muslim who is a respected member of British society with a successful career may become deeply disaffected in a matter of days by the public humiliation of a racial profiling experience at an airport, on the street, or by a disturbing news image from the front lines of the war on terror. Whether the individual is previously uncommitted or already actively disaffected, the life-changing experience tends to lead to the next stage in the process of subversion.

## Groomed and Mentored

Many actively disaffected groups and individuals do not have a formal contact with a genuine terrorist organisation. They might encounter individuals who were previously mujahadeen or had been to a training venue overseas, but so far their exposure to subversion was largely organic, arising from the realities around them rather than from the efforts of a cadre of locally based terrorists. However, at this point in the subversion process they might actively seek these linkages or encounter a cell or an individual that is genuinely connected to a formally organized terrorist group based in the United Kingdom. In this more pressured relationship the individual might be groomed and incited to commit an act of terrorism against the British host.

## Operationally Ready

In the final stage of the process the individual may travel overseas to learn the techniques of bomb making and the tactics of detonation as well as taking part in theatrical initiation ceremonies. On return to Britain the mentoring organization might have selected a target, organised accomplices and prepared a methodology for an attack.

The model above does not set out to be definitive. Operational staff have commented that in their experience the relationship between the stages is more chaotic and the numbers are constantly changing.[18] Riding beyond the six categories or stages of subversion that it suggests, there are other paths which an extremist may follow to achieve a successful attack.[19] The number of people in each category also varies. When Muslim outrage is running high, perhaps after some specific event in Afghanistan or Iraq has been splashed across the world's media, the numbers of disaffected also rise. But during times of distraction (major sporting events) or when public sympathy is mobilised in favour of the host state and the global media condemns a particular act of extremism, they reduce. Regardless of these fluctuations, year by year the sum of those actively mentored and becoming operationally ready has increased.[20]

The model's aim is to explain a trend rather than to record every individual peculiarity encountered over several hundred cases. It strives to show the different stages of disaffection; it is not a profiling system of likely terrorist characteristics. Although the process moves from left to right, from the Uncommitted to the Operationally Ready, the majority of individuals will remain in the same category without necessarily moving to the right. Individuals may move directly into a category rather than following the progression implied by the chart. Individuals are more open minded and receptive to a political counter strategy at the outset of the process on the left of the chart. By the time they reach stages five and six, they have a fixation and self-sustaining momentum that may only be interrupted physically and almost certainly not by the political overtures of a local government official.

The main conclusion is that the degree of disaffection depicted above had to be viewed as something more dangerous than just terrorism; it had insurgent energy, which attracted support and gained momentum and an ability to regenerate itself. In principle the weight of a counter-effort needed to be focused on the left of the chart, and less on the culminating end of the process. The government had to be politically strong enough to absorb casualties and bear the loss of credibility and popular support. What was certain is that it would never be able to anticipate, disarm and contain every lethal attack at the sixth stage of the process. By the time an individual was operationally ready the level of fanaticism was usually so intense that it could only be arrested by physical intervention and by the attritional processes of counter-terrorism. The security services could only react—the terrorist had become a missile fixed on an unalterable course; the preventive dimension of the campaign had to take place at a previous stage and lay completely beyond the kinetic processes of countering terrorism. In the British experience, the key to shutting off the flow of attackers lay in altering the situation earlier when the insurgent was still in a formative state. That was when the campaign was still dynamic, when the disaffected individual might still be indecisive, when the government could be manoeuvrist, and therefore when the insurgent banners could be seized and a political strategy could engage minds, undermine loyalties and successfully challenge the newly acquired convictions.

## Plans to Counter Terrorism in the United Kingdom

Because it seemed to have no tangible or realistic purpose, key communicators on both sides of the Atlantic saw international Islamist terrorism as something that could not be engaged politically and as something that "could only be destroyed or utterly isolated."[21] This view tended to miss an important practicality: it was not their fixed and unrealistic aspirations which were the deciding factor, it was the extent to which their activism was contagious and had succeeded in disaffecting and radicalising future generations of activists. It was ill-judged to see the task of undoing this damage merely as a counter-terrorist operation. Simply because the adversary's aims failed to meet a twentieth-century notion of insurgency at a political level, it did not follow that the principles of countering insurgency, which had been tested in previous campaigns could be ignored at the operational level. We were still dealing with a movement that had the characteristics of a dangerous insurgency. British society was in the throes of change; it was possible that in a post-industrial context, insurgency no longer looked anything like its twentieth century antecedents. By 2002 the

United Kingdom was threatened by a global movement, which had succeeded in establishing itself in the minds of an element of migrant communities in Britain and had subverted them to such a degree that it now had momentum. Calling it terrorism and organising a narrowly focused manhunt would not shut it down. The actual name given to Britain's response scarcely mattered, what mattered enormously was that the counter operation had to be focused on the insurgent energy and the subversive nature of the disaffected element of a population. This was the crucible for a succession of terrorist plots.

By the end of 2001 the instigators of violence in Britain were increasingly connected to Islamist extremism. 9/11 had succeeded beyond all expectations as an awakening call. Edited, dramatised and broadcasted over and over again, its images had electrifying effects on the already disaffected element of the Muslim community. Increased activism in Britain encouraged a stronger sense of identity, an awareness of the Ummah and of the interconnectedness of Islamic movements which were now residing in the United Kingdom. The foreign strand of Islamist extremism and subversion was becoming increasingly merged with the British strand of domestic disaffection.

In the months directly after 9/11, government ministries, police and security services reacted energetically to the prospect of a similar terrorist attack in the United Kingdom and further disturbances in their mainland cities. But without a co-ordinated plan, national efforts to anticipate these attacks were destined to be less than effective and in some cases counteracted each other. During the 1990s when the tempo of events was slower and the threat of terrorist attack seemed less immediate, a degree of police and government incoherence had been acceptable. But by 2001 the disaffection of Britain's migrant communities and their global connectedness compelled security officials to see that the country had become unusually vulnerable. A more unified and convincing national strategy was needed.

As permanent secretary to the Home Office, Sir David Omand had been the most senior civil servant in that Whitehall Department and therefore well briefed on the domestic disturbances among Britain's Muslim communities and also on the threat the country faced from externally based terrorist organisations. When he moved to the Cabinet Office as Security and Intelligence Coordinator in 2002, Sir David was therefore more keenly aware than most of Britain's vulnerability and of the need for a coherent national campaign. Individually government departments had been working to anticipate events within their own area of responsibility, but now they faced a coherence between organised terrorism from overseas and disaffection at home. Sensational and visible attacks in one part of the world were animating disaffected communities in another. The challenge facing Sir David Omand was to draw together an array of government departments, security services and police which had a long established habit of working independently.

On the 22nd October 2002 he achieved his first organisational objective by convening a meeting of all the involved departments and agencies. His critical mass included parts of the Cabinet Office, Home Office, Treasury, Foreign Office, Ministry of Defence, the Security Services as well as the Metropolitan Police. There were so many attendees that, rather than use the conference facilities in Whitehall, the meeting had to be held in the more spacious rooms of the Civil Service Sports club. In his opening brief he established himself as national co-ordinator and called on the participants to engage as a whole in helping to construct a national strategy rather than by simply following their departmental priorities. He urged them to cross departmental boundaries and to think nationally. His plan was to create a national structure to address Britain's vulnerability to attack, improve its ability to respond to an attack and to counter growing disaffection or 'radicalisation' of Muslim communities, in addition to supporting the pursuit of the existing terrorist networks at home and overseas. It was intended as an immediate response, a five-year plan, but not as a long-term operation that could support a widely advocated political narrative.

Omand's overall aim was to merge the individual operations represented in his Sports Club audience into a single national instrument to counter terrorism in the United Kingdom. In the short term his objectives were to address Britain's vulnerability, prevent attacks, and in the event that an attack should nonetheless succeed, to create a response system that could minimize damage and restore the essential services very quickly after the dust had settled. Once there was a workable level of security in Britain, attention could be turned to confronting the root causes of disaffection by building healthier, more integrated migrant communities at home, and stronger international security alliances to counter the threat from abroad.

Although Sir David's ambition was to create a cross-government instrument, it was probable that departmental interests would reassert themselves at the operational level beyond Whitehall's oversight so new Cabinet machinery under the Home Secretary was created. Moreover, his initiative was taking place at a time when parliament, the media and a significant sector of the population was buzzing with resistance to the British's military expedition to Iraq. For this reason the government seemed chary of exposing this initiative to create a national instrument to counter terrorism to public scrutiny or debate. The government were no doubt striving to avoid a connection being made between the intervention in Iraq and a rising sense of domestic insecurity in the United Kingdom.

## The Architecture of CONTEST

In stark contrast to the campaigns of ENDURING FREEDOM, CONTEST was a strictly domestic affair and took place almost entirely on British territory; it was also very complicated. Its embryo could already be discerned at Sir David Omand's Sports Club meeting in October 2002. Although politicians and civil servants insisted on calling it counter-terrorism, the span of its participants, the nature of the objectives and the scale of the campaign placed CONTEST far beyond this narrow categorisation. The purpose here is not to argue about definitions but to understand the entirety of its secretive and complicated nature.

The 2002 meeting at the Civil Service Sports Club had launched a critical mass of British police and government departments towards a series of operational objectives. But in political terms it was not easy to connect the government's public statements with the emerging campaign. Blair's political efforts in 2002-03 did not explain or advance the complex aspirations of Home Office campaign. This was partly because the government's information managers were anxious to separate counter-terrorism and CONTEST in particular, from the public debate on Britain's deployment to Iraq; making a direct connection between a domestic initiative and the escalating counter-terrorism campaign had become politically unsound. The Education, Local Government and Community Cohesion departments of Whitehall rightly did not want their programmes to be linked to counter-terrorism. Subtlety was important, and the campaign became shrouded in secrecy. The early stages by which the Sports Club initiative grew into a national campaign progressed as a series of classified Cabinet papers which evaded public scrutiny and debate until 2006.[22] CONTEST had become a very British affair, secretive, understated and without any dramatic calls for national support or mobilisation. But without the prime minister's public authority it did not benefit from the positive media exposure and the public support that may have come with it. CONTEST was a civil servants' operation with convoluted lines of control which allowed each department to move in its own direction and at its own pace, there was no white-hot melting pot in which departmental interests could be merged.

In Whitehall the Office of Security Counter Terrorism (OSCT) was designed as the hub around which government departments, intelligence and the police coalesced and co-operated. The OSCT's achievement was to reconcile the actions of a very disparate array of actors and to keep them fixed on the objectives of CONTEST. In the Whitehall hierarchy the OSCT was a subordinate part of the Home Office, but in the context of the operation it was required to reach far beyond its normal boundaries and draw together officials from the allied departments of Transport, Education, Local Government, Energy and Rural Affairs. The OSCT also had a co-ordinating function for the Foreign and Commonwealth Office, Ministry of Defence and the Security Services.

## Operations at a Regional Level

Although the organisational cement had been drying in Whitehall for some time, at a regional level the interdepartmental linkages, especially between the police, local government and the national intelligence services were still in a formative state in spring 2009. What the operation seemed to lack was a single controlling instrument. Had a campaign of such scale and complexity been organised by the military, there would have been an operational order, a single document which set out the commander's intent showing the participating agencies and units the extent of their subordination and their individual tasks. In military thinking an operation order would be essential because it gives the authority to task subordinate units and spell out the actions required of them. But CONTEST was not a military operation; not only was no such order likely to be made, but from the perspective of the police and the civil authorities such an instrument would have been intrusive and unconstitutional, and would have interfered with a pre-existing *modus operandi*. So from the Prime Minister's office down to the borough council of a town the size of Oldham, the operation had to be managed through the existing provisions for government and law enforcement. [23] Although this arrangement skilfully avoided the confrontation of departmental interests at the local level, it failed to establish the degree of coherence that had been regarded as essential to previous British counter-insurgent operations. If the OSCT in Whitehall was in the driving seat, it didn't seem to be able to steer its efforts at a local level. In the absence of anything resembling an operation order[24], each department at regional and local level was individually making its own way into an uncharted area. CONTEST was "brand new"[25]. Without a command and control instrument similar to an operation order, the Prevent strategy had started a gold rush of government departments, police and NGOs at the local level racing each other to claim new operational areas for themselves.

At borough council level—the front lines of the government campaign, the generalities of the Prevent strategy translate into a more immediate relationship between the officials and police and the population. Although senior police officers are careful to stress that they do not specifically target the geographically defined Muslim communities, that nevertheless is where activism tends to originate. The December 2008 to January 2009 Israeli bombing of Gaza and the continuous television images of the damage and casualties outraged some elements of the Muslim population in Britain. The violation of Gaza aroused people who were normally "uncommitted" ( referring to the Stages of Subversion Chart on page ... ) so that they became "actively disaffected", many uncharacteristically taking part in noisy local meetings and travelling to city centres to march in demonstrations which resulted in TV coverage that was transmitted around the

world. The meetings and demonstrations were monitored and sometimes successfully exploited by individuals and organisations, which
in some cases may have had hard-wired connections to international
terrorism.

The bombing of Gaza and the local response to it represent a process in which a distant but highly visible event incites an already tense
domestic audience. The animated response of the Muslim communities in the United Kingdom was probably also a Europe-wide phenomenon. From the perspective of the town hall and the local police
the demonstrations, the uncharacteristic surge in the number of
excited meetings and even the wildly seditious proposals made by particular individuals were accepted as being more or less lawful. In most
cases the majority of participants returns to normal life and no arrests
are made. However after the streets are cleared and the community
resumes a calmer tempo, questions remain over the extent to which
this event and many others like it initiate a longer term radicalising
effect in certain individuals who, as a result of this experience have
embarked on a path that is set to culminate in violent extremism.

At a local level the effects of the Gaza bombing and incidents like
it impact on a second or third generation of migrant youths who do
not see themselves as guests in a European country, who speak English as natives speak it, and identify with British fashions, cultural
icons, sports teams and pop music. But unlike their parents they are
also aware of the ambiguity of their identity and politically watchful
of injustices done to Islam and Muslim communities world-wide.
Within the local community the activism, which arises from the process described above may be focused in particular places and among
specific social categories including:

- Young people who are unemployed, dabbling in drugs and crime
  and generally becoming distanced from the state and its local
  institutions,
- Radicalised women who influence their peers, relatives and children
  and distribute extremist materials,
- Meeting places within the community where events are held and
  organised which are also frequented by talent scouts and activists
  from more sinister organisations.
- Educational establishments.

At town hall level the operational concept of the Prevent strategy is to identify individuals and groups emerging from this continual process (dramatic event—local reaction) bent on violent extremism. However Prevent also means taking measures and creating structures that will disrupt the process, especially where it is subverting vulnerable elements of the community. The concept is also to re-engage the isolated and the violent back into mainstream society.

Where elements of the local population have become disaffected and may be heading towards violent extremism then a division of labour occurs between the preventers and the pursuers. The Prevent strategy is focused primarily on stages 1, 2, 3 and 5 and the Pursue strategy concentrates on 5 and 6 (see chart "Stages of Subversion" on page …). From the perspective of the forces engaged in prevention, a point is reached in stage 5 when an individual or group becomes so isolated and dangerous that it has to be the responsibility of the more kinetic Pursue programme. The division can be represented like this:

| | | |
|---|---|---|
| | 1 | Uncommitted |
| PREVENT | 2 | Passively disaffected |
| | 3 | Actively disaffected |
| | 5 | Being groomed and mentored |
| PURSUE | 6 | Operationally ready |

The execution of the Prevent strategy at a local level falls to an array of government actors which includes: police forces, social services, cultural services (libraries etc) sports and leisure services, children's services, youth offending teams, youth inclusion services, probation, local prisons, health authorities, primary care trusts, border agencies and many other government offices and departments. In addition the programmes seek to involve local community leaders and local schools, colleges and universities.[26] Most agencies were already established before the Prevent strategy and are already organised into operational partnerships such as: Local Strategic Partnerships, Crime and Disorder Reduction Partnerships (CDRP) and Children's Trusts.

CDRPs were organised prior to the full deployment of the Prevent strategy, chaired by the commander of the police Basic Command

Unit they became a crucially important interface between the police, government services and the local community as a matter of necessity. A CDRP might consist of representatives of the local authorities such as Community Safety, Education, local authority area managers, and officers from the police Basic Command Unit, the neighbourhood Inspector and representatives of the regional Counter Terrorist Intelligence Unit. Initially these monthly meetings were essentially operational to share information and co-ordinate the Prevent effect locally. By 2008 the CDRP reverted to its original function of crime prevention and tackling extremism is now lead by the Preventing Violent Extremism initiative within the local authority, who will inform the CDRP of their needs.[27]

Returning for a moment to the first chapters of this book and in particular to the operations in Malaysia, there is a striking similarity of purpose between the loosely convened police–civil authority meetings in Greater Manchester region (spring 2009) and the District Officer's Security Executive meetings that have been an organisational characteristic of every British counter-insurgent operation since the 1960s. In both cases the aim has been to draw together the different actors—police, local government, intelligence and civil community representatives, to keep reviewing their operational plans and to achieve a coherent effort that above all, was politically led. The BCU commander's monthly meeting at the borough council level not only has an evolutionary relationship to the District Officer's security committee, but is also an indicator that although this phenomenon is not called insurgency, the response to it seems to have adopted a familiar organising instrument that would not be necessary in a strictly kinetic operation.

Although the execution of the Prevent concept is well thought out and enthusiastically conducted at local level, there are obstacles to its success which may compel a change of approach. The tangle of local managers, who all seem to have a say but not an overall responsibility, is a recipe for muddled and counteracting efforts between different agencies even with the same borough. But above all, the fundamental difference between the District Officer's committee in Malaya and the BCU commander's monthly meetings in twenty-first century Britain is that the latter is not politically led. Consequently there is a tension between the aspirations of Prevent, which are essentially political and the police role which is essentially law enforcement. For example when police stop a convoy of relief supplies heading for Gaza in the Greater Manchester region and detain three suspected violent extremists, the law has been successfully enforced. However if the communities who organised and gave to the convoy are then stirred up by images of its interdiction, and their outrage and demonstrations are exploited by the media and local agitators, then the political objectives of Prevent have been reversed and the campaign has tactically failed. The obvious question is whether this a police-led or politically-led operation? In previous British experience it must be politically led, but at ground level Prevent is led by the police and the absence of political oversight ensures that law enforcement takes priority. These contradictions impose a need for a more developed police-government relationship. However politically decided police operations would have sinister consequences for our civil liberties in the longer term.

In other British counter insurgencies there has been a relaxed and collegial relationship between intelligence services and the military and police units however in the Prevent deployment, MI5 and GCHQ it is said[28], participate diffidently at the regional level. Instinctively they do not foster open hearted working relationships with local officials and participants from non-government agencies who are close to or, worse still, may even become, their intelligence targets. An additional problem is that British police forces do not accept the military definition of intelligence. The concept of intelligence–led operations is hard to reconcile with law enforcement where information is also evidence, and a long-term strategy that delays arrests may be challenged by the public. The corollary to the Gaza convoy story is that had the police failed to act, other elements of society might have protested just as vociferously against their apparent inaction. Unlike the military units in Northern Ireland in the 1970s and 80s, the police have many other tasks involving the greater public which must take priority over the political campaign to win over an insurgent minority.

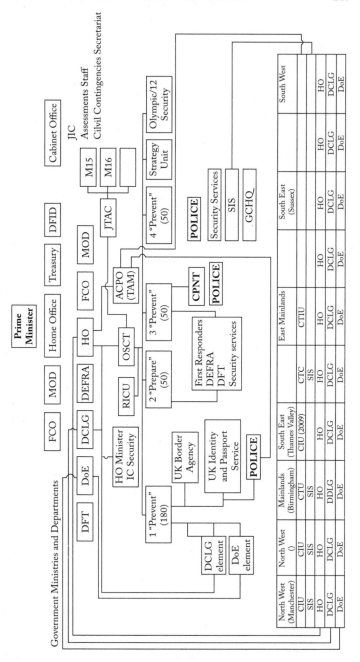

The UK Home Office CONTEST Strategy

# 11

# THE INSURGENT ARCHIPELAGO

*The practicalities of insurgency were transformed by information-age societies. The newest forms of insurgency were unrecognisably different, and as a result NATO states were slow to adapt to the task of protecting their domestic populations from political violence; most anticipated a more familiar adversary based on their previous expeditionary experiences. In the event they were surprised by the nature of post Maoism, and in future may continue to be surprised by the swiftly altering nature of insurgency.*

In every human group there is the capacity to rebel and in the post-9/11 world it is probably easier to initiate and spread disaffection than in any previous security era. Migration, climate change, population displacement and unbearable disparities between rich and poor, ensure that each state has within it an element that is disaffected. In the past, insurrection was a national affair; populations were defined by territory and it was unusual to find parts of the same population distributed across the face of the entire world. Consequently insurgent movements were nationally focused; revolutionaries from different nations and cultures might write to each other and visit each other but their rebellions were geographically limited.

## The Insurgent Archipelago

The insurgent archipelago refers to these elements or nodes of outraged and disaffected people who existed in their territorially separated places across the world but are now connected by proliferating communications and therefore part of the same global movements. In this context a node might be an individual activist, an outraged group or an entire community. Before the onslaught of mass communications a disaffected node within a population was isolated by geography and by the efforts of oppressive regimes. However in the information age, particularly in the twenty-first century it becomes more and more possible for a dissident to make linkages across the world with a host of other similarly motivated dissidents. However this development is not peculiar to the disaffected nodes in the insurgent archipelago, a much larger element of each nation's mobile phone and Internet-using population is already linked to global networks through their work and their individual interests. This interconnectedness also has huge significance for the insurgents; it strengthens them and protects them from hostile governments and security services. The disaffected node that was previously kept down and out of sight by its isolation is now visible to the rest of the world, supported by international networks and linked to the information highways. By joining a global movement of likeminded activists, the insurgent node gains access to Internet meetings and the opportunity to put their case to powerful organisations where they were previously unknown. By developing into an extended network, the movement acquires a personality both in the international system and in law; it can no longer be so easily suppressed by extrajudicial methods.

Collectively the individual nodes spread across the world make up an insurgent archipelago which flourishes in a space that is not territorially defined; this distinguishes it as a very modern form of insurgency. This space is not the cyber equivalent of the Maoists wilderness where extremists fled for safety, it is a space that is already crowded by an established host of Internet and cellphone-using populations around the world. In this space, the aim for both the insurgent and the counter-insurgent is to win the minds and beliefs of the involved populations. Although winning their support remains a primary objective, just as it was in Jiangxi province in 1929, the methodology is quite different. The disaffected who exist in the archipelago can only be reached and animated indirectly, through TV images, newspaper reports and materials conveyed by the Internet, and much less often through the tangible presence of a leader and his enforcers.

## *The Nature of the Evolution of Insurgency*

This book makes a number of propositions about insurgency. First, that it is essentially a political activity and not a form of warfare. Insurgency, from the Latin word to insurge, refers to the act of rising up against a stronger authority. It is not a method of fighting, it cannot be used to defeat armies or invade territory. Certainly the military forces which emerge at the final stages of an insurgency to fight civil wars can do these things, but insurgency, the act of rising up against a stronger authority, refers to the stages of activism and subversion that precede this development. After Mao devised a process to subvert populations on an industrial scale, the military dimension on both sides of the insurgent—counter-insurgent equation certainly grew larger, but the instruments and strategies that were central to success were political rather than military.

Second, insurgency evolves at the same speed as the society from which it arises. However individual societies evolve at very different speeds according to their prosperity, security and enterprise. It is therefore possible that starkly different forms of insurgency can occur during the same period and within the same region where rich and advanced societies coexist with very poor traditional ones. Insurgency evolves more swiftly than governments and their security forces can conceive operational responses. At the operational level, counter-insurgents should assume that they will start a campaign using the operational concept of the previous one and that it will certainly need to be altered. Political leaders and their security advisers are often unable or unwilling to see that the nature of the insurgency has moved on from their previous experience and understanding of it.

Third, as populations become more globally connected, particularly urban populations, so does the insurgency which arises from them. Migration and the establishment of minority communities within the framework of a host nation give an insurgency greater depth and an extraterritorial dimension. Globalised insurgents, which occupy the archipelago of scattered communities around the world tend to attract globalised responses. These characteristics make it hard to identify a campaign centre of gravity for either the insurgents or the counter-insurgents.

Fourth, the operational nature of globalised insurgency is becoming increasingly informal. Although insurgencies have in the past been regarded as an irregular activity, nevertheless they still had a formal leadership and a top-down controlling structure. Now globalised insurgencies are more and more informally fastened together, following the patterns imposed on them by the Internet. They can be regarded as movements rather than formal organisations, they are without a defined leadership, held together by horizontally ordered networks and animated by collectively addressed messages. Their rebellious energy is almost unmanageable, subversion may be organic, activists may react individually to images and news stories, becoming self radicalised and self recruited in what the British Home Office describes as "self starting" networks. There can also be an informal or disengaged relationship between the apparent long-term objectives of a movement and its day to day tactical actions. It is now easier to understand these individually motivated attacks as being ethically inspired at an intensely personal level or as part of a propaganda of the deed campaign rather than as directly contributing to the achievement of a vague strategic aim.

Fifth, the nature of an insurgent archipelago dictates an unusually different operational approach which is hard to understand from a structured, military perspective. It is probably incorrect to imagine that there is any longer a formally conceived and widely promulgated concept of operations emanating from a recognised leadership. It may be more likely that individual cells intuitively aim to conduct propaganda of the deed attacks, which have a re-energising and re-generating effect on the wider movement.

Sixth, the propaganda of the deed, as defined in Chapter 7, plays a central role in the globalised insurgent's instinctive operational approach. Whether it is a spectacular attack, a news story arising from an expeditionary operation by NATO nations or the dramatisation of a local issue, the media version of these events energises and unifies the insurgent archipelago. This effect is an essential condition for the continued animation, growth and survival of a global movement and is greatly facilitated by the continuing proliferation of communications.

## Maoist and Post Maoist Structures

The operational differences between the traditional Maoist and the twenty-first century post Maoist can be explained in the following charts.

In the chart below, the early Maoist insurgency was distinguished by several strands of insurgent activity which all contributed to its success. The direction of the organising energy was from the top downwards. A Maoist uprising was also defined by its dependence on a particular territory and by the labour intensive nature of its activities. The need to influence and to organise people on the ground and the constant presence of the leadership and their enforcement cadres meant that the style of command was physical. Maoist insurgencies are very labour intensive. Even a terrorist attack involving the use of high explosives has to involve a number of different actors and planners, and a small military attack may require several hundred participants[1]. To succeed the insurgent leaders had to be constantly present, working among the people, subverting, animating and organising activism at the tactical level. Because the linkages depicted below were carefully organised, clandestine, fragile and linear, the structure was vulnerable and could be interdicted. The Maoist has been a jealous insurgent and has not tolerated competing movements. Tactical alliances against a common oppressor tended to collapse in unforgiving violence. This discouraged a federated approach to organising operations

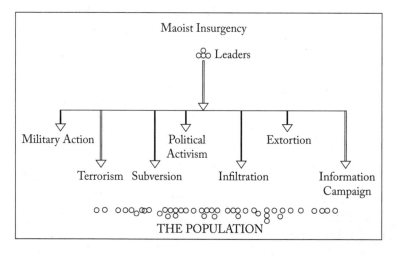

that included several different insurgent movements that existed in the same national territory, which might co-operate for a particular operation and then disperse.

The post Maoist model is more informal, almost chaotic and conveys the bare outline of a *modus operandi* rather than an organisation. Because the movement draws its energy from an archipelago of supporters, it is unrecognisably different to its Maoist predecessor. The collective aim to engage and subvert a target population is in principle the same as the Maoists, but the operational space and the objectives within that space are entirely different. The post Maoist needs to be understood as a form of political violence, as a globalised insurgent movement but not simply as international terrorism or as a hybrid type of warfare.

In the chart below, each disaffected community or node that makes up the archipelago has within it a continuous cycle of activism, subversion and preparation for a terrorist attack which is energised from time to time by a sensational (POTD) event. This can take place in another continent or locally; but in both cases its impact is transmitted through the media and is not achieved because it was physically witnessed by thousands of disaffected individuals. At grass roots level the process is largely self-sustaining and leaderless. In the insurgent stage it relies on personal disaffection and self-recruitment and not on the constant *modus operandi* presence of revolutionary leaders. It is globally influenced and connected, but the process is above all determined by

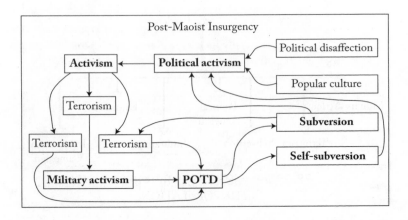

local circumstances such as peer group pressure and alienation. Presented in this way the two models emphasise the extent to which evolutionary forces have transformed the familiar organisational structures of an early Maoist insurgency into a seemingly chaotic activity that is largely self sustaining.

## A Clash of nineteenth and twenty-first Century Organisations

The charts above show how the evolutionary process had transformed Maoism into something that was unrecognisable as insurgency. As a result European governments were surprised by its unfamiliar appearance as well as by the speed at which the techniques of political violence had evolved. It took several years for them to acknowledge its insurgent characteristics, and even longer to abandon the Global War Against Terror nomenclature and its associated mindset. Governments were habitually unprepared for emerging insurgencies, but in the transition from Maoism to post-Maoism their surprise was particularly intense. The default response was to explain it as terrorism and react in a narrowly kinetic manner. This tendency was reinforced by a mental unwillingness to move on from the last contingency. In British experience each campaign seemed to begin with the field manuals and mind set of the previous one[2]. After 9/11 the doctrinal catch up was taking longer than ever. By 2009, except for the British policing operation CONTEST, no political concept had emerged by which to secure a national population through winning over its disaffected migrant communities. It was completely wrong to think of General Petraeus's 2006 field manual as the blue print for engaging a twenty-first century globalised insurgency, especially its manifestation in Europe.

Domestic security had to take primacy over international commitments. The protection of the home population had to be prioritised over coalition expeditions which tended to jeopardise the campaign on the home front. But even in the unlikely event of a new era of clarity in strategic thinking, national governments in Europe were still structurally disadvantaged when campaigning against globalised insurgents. Their ministries were still organised in the vertically subordinated manner of their nineteenth-century antecedents and the controlling energy still flowed from the top downwards in the same authoritarian manner as before. In stark contrast, the globalised insurgents were true manifestations of a twenty-first century society, they could out-manoeuvre and out-communicate the government, especially when both sides sought to win over the same populations. Although the British government's CONTEST operations represented the first steps in the right direction, lines of direction were excessively ponderous and unwieldy. There was too much Clausewitzian friction between Whitehall's intent and its manifestation at borough council level, too many different actors, too many conflicting interests, too many levels of command. The white Anglo-Saxon talking heads who represented Whitehall policies were culturally and physically too removed from street level. The response of the target community was therefore generally negative.

"You had Jack Straw's (Foreign Secretary) comments about the veil worn by a small percentage of Muslim women, you had Ruth Kelly (Secretary for Communities and Local Government) attacking Muslim schools saying they're a breeding ground for extremists, you had the Prime Minister saying they want to destroy what we hold dear to us, and calling the caliphate a barbaric system, and you also had John Reid ( Home Secretary) urging parents to spy on their children."[3]

The communities they were trying to win over were culturally distinct, and the disaffected groups and individuals within them were more readily accessed through the network flows on which they lived. They belonged to the Facebook generation and their key communicators were definitely not the ageing, orthodox first generation migrants picked out by the Home office as the community interlocutors. Young British Muslims fizzing with indignation were more likely to be animated by iconic figures from their own society and life style. For these reasons there was never a balanced discussion, and when the sensational images of terrorist attacks, local tensions and upsetting news stories from Afghanistan continued to inundate them day after day, there was nothing to challenge the subversive interpretation of these events.

However this situation began to change when a swarm of local organisations and NGOs deployed at street level into the most disaffected areas of the United Kingdom. Although many appeared to have no government strings attached, they were nevertheless indirectly sustained by various British government departments. Due to their energy, their apparent independence and their credibility the successful ones managed to establish some very valuable communicating relationships where before there had been none. Their successes were patchy, very local and personality dependant, nevertheless it was a move in the right direction. The operational principle was for government departments to fund individuals and organisations, sometimes through an intermediary NGO; despite this official support they had the independence and informality of independent organisations. Broadly speaking their purpose was to divert disaffected young Muslims away from dangerous militancy[4]. These initiatives showed that local Muslims, in particular people who were credible and in communication with the community at risk, made the most successful entry into a disaffected group. Being credible was a matter of living in the same town, using the same mosque, school and shopping centres, having the same accent and appearance, messaging on the same network flow and having an equally committed and convincing approach as the subversive voice.

Although the participants in this swarm would have vigorously denied it, their efforts were having a counter-insurgent effect and their success, although limited, should have drawn attention to a small but significant salient where the government was beginning to regain territory in the struggle for Muslim minds. They were being successful because they were responding in an unconventional way to an unconventional adversary. Political figures and Whitehall officials had failed to embrace or communicate effectively with these alienated communities; to the white British population they were unapproachable, in each borough they existed in social networks which lay beyond the understanding and reach of the Anglo-Saxon establishment and the police. The advantage of employing a chaotic swarm of barely controlled individuals and agencies was that they were convincing and credible and their apparently disorganised and intuitive efforts reflected the informal structures of the adversary. They were genuinely from the same background as the people they sought to influence. Their largely freelance efforts had intentionally or unintentionally hit on a remarkably original concept which might become the basis of a new approach. If disaffected young people responded to local and familiar communicators, the concept was to saturate their environment with individuals and agencies who would challenge the subversive discourse and provide an alternative.

Needless to say this concept involved political risks and attracted powerful criticism. From the perspective of the top down, authoritarian structures of the British Home Office, a swarm of individuals moving along in a loose crowd became an uncomfortable partner, a barely controllable dimension of an otherwise vertically managed operation. Moreover it was probable that a number of these individuals and agencies had abused the government's patronage and through inertia or misspending had failed to deliver a counter-insurgent effect. Policy Exchange an apparently independent think-tank, articulated these doubts and their views were endorsed by Ruth Kelly (Britain's Secretary of State for Communities and Local Government). They argued that a swarm of local actors (they did not use these words), deployed with government support, could not succeed because it relied on "non-violent extremists" to engage with violent extremists. The problem in their view was that non-violent extremists were themselves at the forefront of stoking up local grievances therefore propagating the same extremist Islamist ideology that fostered intolerant, anti-Western disaffection[5].

Although accused of tampering with their evidence in a previous paper on the same theme, in this case their objections were well argued and convincing.[6] But disappointingly, both the 2009 Policy Exchange paper and Ruth Kelly in her fulsome endorsement of it, failed to see that the road to success was not so much about the absolute correctness of the messengers as the ability of the government side to engage with the communities at risk. It was extraordinary that the same government, which had so laudably put aside its disgust for the murderous nature of the IRA and its derivatives in order to press ahead with 1990s peace process and engage with the dissident communities in Ulster, could not apply the same thinking on the British mainland. Yes of course powerful Muslim organisations such as the Muslim Council of Britain had articulated inflammatory views about the activities of British Army and British foreign policy, but in that respect they were no different to the former terrorists and political agitators associated with the IRA who as a result of the peace process now sat in the British parliament and held office in the Northern Ireland executive. Sadly the Policy Exchange paper and the general endorsement it received from the British establishment indicated a staggering disability, almost a national failure, to understand the negotiating processes and principles that have been habitually used to bring a long festering insurgency towards termination. It also showed how few political figures really understood what animated political violence within their own community.

## *The Future*

Despite the criticisms of the British government's domestic counter terrorism campaign, the Whitehall machine and its structures will eventually stumble onto a workable concept of operations. Historically, after a bungled start, British counter-insurgency operations have usually succeeded in finding a way to restore peace to a troubled population. In that happy event a concept for success should emerge that would have application in many other countries where migration and mass turbulence encourage similar forms of political violence that are sustained by a wider global movement. When it finally emerges, this counter-insurgent doctrine will be distinguished from its military antecedents in the US and the United Kingdom in several important ways. It will have to address insurgency as political violence and not as a form of warfare in which the military have primacy; the principles and procedures it suggests therefore have to include an array of government departments and non-government agencies which are also involved. Above all it must recognise the centrality of communications and the propaganda of the deed for both the insurgent and the counter-insurgent. Rather than confronting the dissident narrative head on by challenging it in the same networks and news propagation systems where it has already become established, future operations will have to engage disaffection on the ground at a very local level. The emerging theme would be that local beats global.

Looking ahead, in these terms it is possible to predict a strategic era in which globalised insurgency grows out of its strictly Islamist interpretation to become a generic instrument utilised by other insurgent archipelagos. As before, the movements which exploit this instrument may represent stressed ethnicities or cultures that have spread around the world but also movements with a global cause perhaps arising from collapsing environments, increasing migration or the growing number of populations at the edge of survival. And hopefully by this time NATO countries will have eventually developed a concept of operations to deal with post-Maoism, rather than Maoism.

In these circumstances it might be possible to anticipate a future era beset by rapidly evolving forms of globalised insurgency but nevertheless contained by governments and their security forces who have successfully transitioned into the twenty-first century and are now able to exploit its information dimension and are able to engage its social characteristics. However this fairly rosy picture of the future decade as a dangerous but manageable era is likely to be completely upset by much more menacing developments.

Climate change, rising sea levels and desertification resulting in mass migration seem to be distant scenarios, but in 2009 their harbingers have already arrived. Worldwide government intervention may no longer be able to halt or significantly alter the long-term rate of climate change and increasing green house gasses are forecast to raise the global temperature by between 1.7 and 2.4 degrees. Melting glaciers and polar ice caps have already changed precipitation patterns bringing intensive rainfall to some regions and drought to others. As a consequence of reduced rainfall, China anticipates a one-third decrease of crop yield by 2030. In the near and medium future the receding Himalayan glaciers may reduce the Indus, Ganges and Bramaputra to seasonal rivers inflicting a massive reduction in agricultural food production on the Indian subcontinent. By 2020 up to 250 million people, mainly in North and East Africa, will find themselves under severe water stress. In the West African region by 2020 it is estimated that as a result of desertification 50 million will have migrated into a conurbation stretching from Ghana to the Niger delta. Some countries are likely to escape the worst effects of climate change and the northern fringes of civilisation in Canada, Scandinavia and Siberia may begin to take on a greater significance as safe havens for the survivors from less fortunate regions. In particular, the island nations of Japan, New Zealand and the United Kingdom will continue to receive regular rainfall which combined with warmer temperatures will ensure that these countries become increasingly abundant food producers. However the island states, in particular the United Kingdom, will also be the destination of the bottom billion, referring to the migrating survivors from the poorest countries in the world. According to Anthony Giddens, affluent nations, which see themselves as safe from the effects of environmental collapse in equatorial regions, can no longer imagine they are not involved.

"The pressures created by climate change and increasing energy scarcity .... could cause the problems of the bottom billion to be dispersed around the world as a whole. What has happened in Sudan is an awful reminder of how global struggles may play out if ways are not found to contain and reshape them".[7]

In 2009 the leading edge of these conditions has already begun to manifest themselves at a time when global governance and international organisations are not sufficiently effective to police the conditions that would achieve a convincing survival strategy. Britain the destination for many populations in the bottom billion will become an overcrowded life boat and

"in the human world of life boat islands, constrained by limited food, energy and living space, the ethos will be wholly different from the cosy self-indulgent twentieth century".[8]

In a future security era dominated by the effects of climate change, the nature of insurgency will once again alter unrecognisably along with stressed populations from which it arises. It is possible that as Britain begins to move towards its grim task as a lifeboat island, future governments will increasingly abandon consensual and persuasive methods of maintaining internal security in favour of the imposition of emergency regulations on a scale not experienced since 1945. These may well remove the freedoms of movement, speech, association and access to information networks as well as imposing rationing on food and energy. In these circumstances the urge for insurgency will still exist but will have mutated so vigorously that once again, it will present itself in a completely unrecognisable form, much to the surprise of the beleaguered government.

## Conclusions

In the context of countering political violence, the Britain is a uniquely challenging operational space. In contrast to much of Britain's previous counter-insurgent experience, the post 9/11 domestic campaign took place in a highly developed state with a population that was multi-cultured, relatively rich, informed, politically sophisticated and highly demanding. The government faced tough constraints as a result of its democratic accountability and a vituperative press which has habitually acted in place of the elected opposition. The target in the United Kingdom was a very contemporary movement, energised from the bottom-up and able to survive decapitations and the severance of links to overseas terrorist organisations. There appeared to be no strategic centre of gravity, no defined leadership, no credible manifesto, no tangible or believable end-state and no obvious or proclaimed concept on which its tactics could have been based. The entire insurgent process had no definition and no name by which it could be recognised. It was a very twenty-first century affair, thriving on social energy that arose from network flows and a constantly fluctuating mass of interconnected individuals whose community was more virtual than territorial.

For many European states the interconnectedness of the global and the national compelled a reassessment of the campaign relationship between the expeditionary and the domestic. Europeans were rightly sceptical about the value of expeditionary military forces which were seeking to stabilise a hostile foreign country, particularly while migration from the same region into their own homelands continued unabated, bringing with it disaffection at home. With the growing recognition that the security of Europe's home populations had to take operational precedence, there was a pressing requirement for a more relevant concept to deal with a twenty-first century insurgency.

In operational terms CONTEST responded to this need. Despite its secretive and understated nature, as an operational model CONTEST had application not just in Europe but farther afield in the richer and democratically inclined Asian and Middle Eastern states. As an instrument CONTEST had the possibility of providing a pathway into the next security era. It could become an operational concept which genuinely engaged a twenty-first century adversary in a way that the military expeditions of the Operation Enduring Freedom genre had not. CONTEST was a different sort of campaign involving unfamiliar actors; if successful, it could be a prototype for homeland operations to deal with disaffected and insurgent communities in other European states and beyond.

However the British version also had some very serious defects. First of all it could not be regarded as a substitute for a political strategy. At the outset the Blair government failed to articulate or establish a convincing narrative that answered the strategic questions: why was Britain compelled to do this? What would our multicultural population and our constitutional freedoms look like when we got to the end of this process? The proclaimed strategy was CONTEST itself, but in definitional terms, CONTEST was no more than a concept of operations, a series of practical aims; the strategy, in the correct meaning of that word, was completely missing. There was no vision, no compelling reason for a migrant community to embrace the British state.

Furthermore the operation had been conceived in an evolutionary vacuum, without the willingness to recognise any of its antecedents. The government continued to think of CONTEST as counter-terrorist operation and superficially it had the appearance of a counter-terrorism operation. But when all its parts were plotted on to a single sheet of paper it also had a much larger counter-subversion dimension than any previous British campaign. Nevertheless in April 2009, the British government still seemed to be in denial as to the true nature of the domestic adversary. Its March 2009 CONTEST 2 publication continued to prioritise the threat from foreign terrorist organisations over the growing volume of home-grown activism within the United Kingdom.[9] This created an unresolved tension between the government's narrowly counter-terrorist oriented briefing line on CONTEST and the reality that their response was increasingly counter-subversive, and therefore according to Britain's own institutional and academic definitions—counter-insurgent. As the grandees of previous counter-insurgent campaigns would put it—the nature of the adversary was often defined by the nature of the response.[10] Unfortunately the officials directly involved in the United Kingdom did not have the experience to understand that a campaign, which narrowly focuses on the terrorist, tends to obstruct the engagement of the population who are probably supporting the adversary and are therefore the main source of their regenerating capability.

In organisational terms Home Office officials and their staff had marshalled an array of actors into a single operation without sufficient planning or campaign experience for such a scale of activities. The actors had coalesced without the benefit of an explicit operational order or a properly authorised director. The operational liability of each participating element was unclear, and the aspirations of White-hall could be disregarded by the fiefdoms at the borough level.

CONTEST should also have acted as a harbinger for the British military. There was no visible military presence and although that was logical enough in a British domestic setting, it raised the possibility of a new era in which the military would have very little part to play in countering insurgent organisations. The operational problem for the Civil Service was not the physical absence of the military, but the vacuum left by the removal of the military's supporting institutions—its planning, operational learning and doctrine-development functions. Military campaign planning expertise was not intuitive, it was the product of an outstanding staff system, with its own professional col-leges, training facilities and doctrine development teams, which had played a key part in Britain's expeditionary forces. These capabilities were still needed whether the campaign was conducted by the police or by the military. In 2009 it remained to be seen whether CONTEST could succeed as a Home Office-run operation and whether it would become a prototype for a new era of national security.

# NOTES

## PART I: MAOISM

### INTRODUCTION

1. Referring principally to the post-colonial experiences of Britain, France, Spain and Portugal whose armies and colonial services were variously engaged from 1948 until the late 1960s.
2. For example Hezbollah, a major political party in Lebanon with hundreds of thousands of political supporters is still sometimes called a terrorist organisation.
3. "Many nations don't really have counter-insurgency doctrines, as far as I could tell, and as for the Alliance itself, I must confess to not knowing if a NATO Counter-Insurgency doctrine actually exists!" General Richards, Commander of the largely NATO International Security Assistance Force in Afghanistan, interviewed for *RUSI*, April 2007.
4. "Manoeuvre" is used throughout in its military sense of "an approach to operations in which shattering the enemy's overall cohesion and will to fight is paramount; it also refers to an attitude of mind in which doing the unexpected, using initiative and seeking originality is combined with ruthless determination to succeed." 'UK Army (Directorate General Development and Doctrine) Land Operations', MoD UK, May 2005.

### 1. MAO THE PROTOTYPE

1. Referring to the revolution of 1911, which effectively ended the Qing dynasty but failed to replace it with a viable alternative so that the country continued to slide into a period of warlordism. See Peter Zarrow, *China In War And Revolution 1895-1949*, London: Routledge, 2005.
2. Maurice Meisner, *Mao Zedong*, Cambridge: Polity Press, 2007, Chapter. 3.
3. Ibid.

4. The fact that not much actually changed for the peasantry in this brave new world does not alter the attraction of these promises or their validity as part of the process of subversion.

5. "For God and his Maid! To Orleans!" Joan of Arc was characterised as a charismatic but rash peasant girl inspired by a vision from God, who succeeded in defeating the English armies in the Hundred Years War. George Bernard Shaw, *Saint Joan*, London: Penguin, 1960.

6. Stuart Schram, *Mao Tse-Tung Basic Tactics*, New York: Praeger, 1961, p. 134.

7. Ibid.

8. This is an expression coined by Peter Zarrow to describe the process of establishing the communist structures in a community in such a way that it became an absolute lifestyle that could not be casually discarded. Peter Zarrow, *China In War And Revolution, 1895-1949*.

9. Mao's Selected Works constitute the main part of these publications. However, more interesting from the perspective of this study were the later translations by Sam Griffith and Stuart Schram which, besides being precise and informative, were derived from Mao's lectures to his cadres during the revolutionary war and therefore more relevant to this study. See Mao Tse-Tung, *Selected Works*, London: Lawrence and Wishart, 1958; Sam Griffith, *Mao Tse-Tung On Guerrilla Warfare*, New York: Praeger, 1961; and Stuart Schram, *Mao Tse-Tung Basic Tactics*.

10. This extended to Thailand, the Philippines, Sri Lanka and Peru. See Thomas Marks, *Maoist Insurgency Since Vietnam*, London: Cass, 1996.

11. In Mao's words: "No force can stop a tide such as this … those who go against it will die." From Mao's manifesto on establishing the Xiang River Review in 1919, cited in Maurice Meisner, *Mao Zedong*.

12. This refers to the *UK Keeping the Peace* series, published in 1957 and revised in 1963.

13. "Counter-Revolutionary Operations Part I: General Principles", UK MoD, 1977.

14. Ibid., pp. 15-16.

15. This definition was inspired by Dr John Pimlott of the War Studies Department of Sandhurst and published as an official definition in 'Operations Other Than War—Counter-insurgency Operations', *UK Army Field Manual*, Vol 5, 1995.

16. This view is emphasised by the publication of the *UK Army Field Manual* version of 'Counter-insurgency Operations' in 2001, which was essentially Maoist in approach.

17. For example, see in the recent edition—'Counter-insurgency Operations', *UK Army Field Manual*, Vol 1, Part 10, pp. A-3-4.

18. According to Paul Wilkinson writing in 2001, "if we examine the world map of organisations involved in terrorism, we find that the majority are very small groups, ranging from a few dozen to a few hundred activists.

Only a minority, approximately 25 per cent, number their members in thousands. The tiny groups simply lack the critical mass necessary for launching an insurgency." From Paul Wilkinson, *Terrorism Versus Democracy: The Liberal State Response*, London: Routledge, 2006, pp. 18-19.

19. During the Cold War, Mao's lectures became the basis for the handbooks that reached the insurgent leaders in Europe, sub-Saharan Africa and Southeast Asia. In the 1960s, translated versions by Griffiths and Schram were widely published and became directly relevant to counter-insurgency doctrine writers who were by then grappling with the conceptual problem of rural uprisings in Vietnam and Malaya. They document the military and political techniques, which were developed in the period of his early success. *Basic Tactics* is derived from his lectures that were compiled and printed in 1938. Sam Griffith, *Mao Tse-Tung On Guerrilla Warfare*, New York: Praeger, 1961 and Stuart Schram, *Mao Tse-Tung Basic Tactics*, London: Pall Mall Press, 1967.

20. "When the enemy advances we retreat … when the enemy retreats, we pursue … when the enemy halts, we harass." Stuart Schram, *Mao Tse-Tung Basic Tactics*, pp. 62-65.

21. Mao's lectures on military techniques for attacking these targets included the following injunctions (Stuart Schram, *Mao Tse-Tung Basic Tactics*, pp. 126-7):

- do not attack strong positions,
- do not fight hard battles unless there is a 100 per cent guarantee of victory,
- use deception ("uproar in the East, strike in the West"),
- attack an enemy that is following by ambushing from the line of march,
- ambush a known enemy route,
- empty the country side in the path of an advancing enemy.

22. Stuart Schram, *Mao Tse-Tung Basic Tactics*, p. 134.

23. Subversion by violence included intimidation, selective assassination and the organisation of menacing riots, which might incite the security forces to respond with firearms. Targets included political parties, lawful meetings and rallies, government structures including the police and military forces, strikes and meetings for the purposes of fomenting disorder. Taken from 'British Doctrine of the Cold War Period', *UK MoD Counter-Revolutionary Operations*, Land Operations, Vol 3, Part 1, 1977, pp. 17-18.

## 2. EVOLUTION

1. The explanation of global change and the associated research was completed by the author in 2002 and some aspects of it were published in John

Mackinlay, 'Globalisation and Insurgency', *Adelphi Paper* 352, Oxford: International Institute for Strategic Studies, 2002.

2. David Held, Anthony McGrew, with David Goldblatt and Jonathan Perraton, *Globalisation*, Global Governance 5, 1999, pp. 483—496.

3. Mark Duffield is not alone in arguing that the "exclusion of the south" can be traced to the events of the 1970s. Mark Duffield, *Global Governance And The New Wars*. London: Zed Books, 2001, Chapter 1.

4. Jean-Christophe Rufin, *The Economics of War: A New Theory for Armed Conflicts*, Forum: International Committee of the Red Cross (Geneva), Series 2, (2000).

5. Ibid.

6. From information supplied by Paul Molinaro, *Department of Defence Management and Security Analysis*, Cranfield University, 6 August 2001.

7. The popular models were the small 10-seaters, which had ever-improving short take-off capability, such as the Cessna series. The lighter Antonovs were also popular, especially among small entrepreneurs flying into the remotest areas from very primitive airfields.

8. The cost of container traffic is dictated by the popularity of the route so that a "heavy leg", for example exporting Western goods to the Gulf and sub-Saharan Africa is heavily subscribed and therefore operating at cost, whereas the returning leg or the "light leg" in which many containers would have to be empty, would offer transportation at less than cost. This favoured small entrepreneurs seeking to export on the light legs.

9. In case of West African crisis zones small foreign traders, who in some cases have been operating in the region for several decades acted as intermediaries between the international market and local dealers, exploiting the proliferation of communications and transport as well as the deregulation of local resource markets, which like the diamond market could not be controlled by international sanctions. From the author's research visit to Freetown, Sierra Leone, September 2001.

10. Frances Cairncross, *The Death Of Distance 2.0: How The Communications Revolution Will Change Our Lives*, London: TEXERE Publishing Limited, 2001.

11. International Telecommunication Union, cited in Ibid., p. 3.

12. Ibid., p. 215.

13. In sub-Saharan African nations, gross domestic product decreased from an average of 14 per cent of that enjoyed by most industrialised states to between five and eight per cent.

14. In Harvey's description of hedge fund dealing, the tiny profits in each transaction would not in normal circumstances have been worth picking up, but with computer assisted data processing, money could now be made from "gathering up infinitesimally fractional differences in the movement in prices". David Harvey, *Conditions Of Post Modernity*, Ox-

ford: Blackwell, 1989. Cited in Ed Hoogvelt *Globalisation And The Post Colonial World 2ⁿᵈ Edition*, Basingstoke: Palgrave, 2001.

15. Ed Hoogvelt *Globalisation And The Post Colonial World 2ⁿᵈ Edition*, p. 88

16. Anthony Sampson *The Midas Touch: Money People And Power From The East To The West*, London: Hodder and Stoughton, 1989. Cited in Ibid.

17. Ed Hoogvelt, *Globalisation and the Post Colonial World 2ⁿᵈ Edition*, p. 175.

18. *The Observer*, Editorial, 2 Jan 2000, p. 24.

19. Paul Kennedy 'Preparing for the 21st Century: Winners and Losers', *The New York Review of Books*, Feb 11 1993. Cited in Patrick O'Meara, Howard Mehliinger and Matthew Krain (eds), *Globalization And The Challenges Of A New Century: A Reader*, Bloomington: Indiana University Press, 2000.

20. Eugene Linden, 'Exploding Cities of the Developing World' *Foreign Affairs*, 75, 1 (1996), cited in O'Meara, Mehliinger and Krain (eds). *Globalization And The Challenges Of A New Century: A Reader.*

21. Ibid.

22. Peter Marcuse and Ronals van Kempen, *Globalising Cities, A New Spatial Order*, Blackwell: Oxford, 2000, p. 271.

23. Eugene Linden, 'Exploding Cities Of The Developing World'.

24. Held and McGrew, *Globalisation*, Global Governance 5, p. 486.

25. Benjamin Barber, 'Jihad vs McWorld', *Atlantic Monthly*, (March 1992). Cited in O'Meara, Mehliinger and Krain (eds), *Globalization And The Challenges Of A New Century: A Reader.*

26. David Keen, 'The Economic Functions of Violence in Civil Wars', *Adelphi Paper*, 320, New York: Oxford University Press, 1998.

27. Che Guevarra, *Guerrilla Warfare*, Harmondsworth: Penguin, 1969, p. 13.

28. Anthony Clapham, *African Guerrillas*, Bloomington: Indiana University Press, 1998, pp. 6-7.

29. Bard O'Neill, *Insurgency And Terrorism: Inside Modern Revolutionary Warfare*, Washington: Brassey's, 1990.

30. David Keen, 'The Economic Functions of Violence in Civil Wars'.

31. Martin Oppenheimer, *Urban Guerrilla*. Chicago: Quadrangle Books, 1969, p. 42. See also David Keen, 'The Economic Functions of Violence in Civil Wars', p. 48.

32. Martin Oppenheimer, *Urban Guerrilla*, p. 42.

33. Ibid.

34. Dennis Bright, *Commission for Conciliation and Peace.* Interviewed by the author in Freetown in September 2001.

35. The tactics were simple. Women and children from the "battalion" moved ahead to search for armed men from the opposing forces. Combat during an attack had a ritualistic quality. The attackers were unlikely to be carrying much ammunition, and therefore hoped that, at the sound of gun-

fire, the armed defenders would flee without forcing a contest. There were
unlikely to be many casualties caused by warriors firing on opposing warriors. If the attackers ran out of ammunition before the defenders they
would have to withdraw in a weakened and vulnerable state, without
small-arms ammunition or food. From the Author's research in Sierra
Leone and Liberia published in John Mackinlay, 'Globalisation and Insurgency'.

36. The important exception to this are the urban lumpens particularly the
*mooryan* in Mogadishu who are described by Roland Marchal, 'Forms of
violence and ways to control it in an urban war zone: The *Mooryan* in
Mogadishu' in Hussein Adam and Richard Clark (eds), *Mending Rips In
The Sky: Options For Somali Communities In The 21st Century*, New Jersey:
Red Sea Press, pp. 193-208.

37. Crystal Procyshen, 'Islam, Institutions and Insurgency', in *Conflict, Security, and Development*, Vol 1, No 3, (2001), pp. 43–50.

38. Bhupendra Jasani, 'Orbiting Spies: Opportunities and Challenges', in
*Space Policy*, No 18 (2002), pp. 9–13.

## 3. GAPS IN OUR KNOWLEDGE

1. In General Rupert Smith's account of the campaign in Ulster, after an
unsuccessful phase of attrition against the armed element of the Provisional Irish Republican Army, the British adopted a policy of creating a
more economically viable community or "middle-classing" the troublesome
areas of Belfast and Londonderry. This required them to admit that these
places had been considerably neglected and discriminated against and also
that the initial military phase of attrition had been wrongly conceived.

2. See General Richards RUSI interview in Chapter 1.

3. Martin Van Creveld, *The Transformation Of War*, New York: Free Press,
1991.

4. This refers to the very detailed general deployment plan during the 1960s,
1970s and 1980s, which was constantly practised and revised for the three
NATO armies (North, Central and South) and comprised army corps of
member states.

5. Parts of this section were researched and previously published in John
Mackinlay and Alison Badawi, *Re thinking Counter-insurgency*, RAND,
2006.

6. After the interventions in Afghanistan and Iraq there was a brief but intense
stampede to rediscover the British and French experience in counter-
insurgency which led to a number of anthologies and research projects
in which these twentieth-century counter-insurgent campaigns were
revisited.

7. The British have been continuously engaged in the containment of low
level violence in civil communities since 1945. It is possible to argue that
for some of this time there were spells of tranquillity with very few casu-

alties, but nevertheless British units were officially on active service for an almost unbroken period.

8. This is a fairly widely articulated view at the Major/Lieutenant Colonel level, encountered personally when supervising the MA theses of British officers at the British Joint Services Command and Staff College 2005/6 who had recently served in Iraq.

9. By the 1820s many British regiments had already organised themselves into linked battalions which provided for "service companies" to deploy overseas and "depot companies" to remain at home where they could recruit and train with a view to replacing their linked partners. The purpose of the "Localised and Linked Battalion Scheme" was to keep one battalion in its local recruiting area in Britain and a sister battalion stationed in the colonies where most of them had direct experience of low-level conflict. See Correlli Barnett, *Britain And Her Army*, London: Penguin Press, 1972.

10. John Nagl, (1996) *Counter Insurgency Lessons From Malaya And Vietnam.*

11. Mao Tse-Tung, *Selected Works.*

12. This constantly used metaphor originates from General Sir Harold Briggs' description of his Malayan concept of operations in which he described the futility of pumping the flit canister at an endlessly regenerating cloud of mosquitoes rather taking a manoeuvrist approach and draining the swamp from which they emanated.

13. Implying that the techniques used to suppress the Warsaw uprising or the city of Grozny, in which the population had overwhelmingly sided with the insurgent force, were unlawful and would not be considered by the British even though they might be initially successful.

14. See under "Westmoreland" in John Nagl, *Counter Insurgency Lessons From Malaya And Vietnam.* Also General Sir Mike Jackson's dictum on the "cost benefit" principle of intrusive patrolling so as to make personal contact with the local population. Interview with the author, September 1999.

15. The insurgents of Vietnam, Columbia, Northern Ireland, and the Basques and Tamils may have given and received support from their respective international diaspora and financial systems, but fundamentally they were concerned with the overthrow of a particular government of a particular state by a population of that state.

16. As a battalion staff officer of the 6th. Gurkhas the author attended the District Security Executive Committees in 1966 in Kenningau, Sabah chaired by the District Officer who was by then a Malaysian.

17. Versions of this system continued long after the countries had ceased to be colonies. As late as the 1960s British battalions despatched to restore law and order, would arrive in these wild places and subordinate their

staff officers to district and state level meetings where a security agenda would be decided.

18. "Bremer, by all accounts a smart and diligent man, but not the right person for the job—that is, someone who could provide strategic leadership and inspire a diverse collection of people suddenly brought together to handle an ill-defined, difficult and expanding mission." Thomas Ricks, *Fiasco: The American Military Adventure In Iraq*, Washington: Penguin, 2006, chapter 10.

19. See Mark Etherington's descriptions of British Foreign Office officials in Iraq and their (feeble) approach to the practicalities of organising a counter-insurgency campaign in Mark Etherington, *Revolt On The Tigris*, London: Hurst, 2005.

20. Rory Stewart, *Occupational Hazards: My Time Governing In Iraq*. London: Picador, 2006, p. 69.

21. Rajiv Chandrasekaran, *Imperial Life In The Emerald City* London: Vintage, 2006, and Thomas Ricks, *Fiasco: The American Military Adventure In Iraq*.

22. Reminiscent of *Apocalypse Now* Do Long, the last outpost on the river, where the front line is nothing but abandoned men—drugged, leaderless and morally destroyed by the senselessness and horror of their mission. Francis Ford Coppola, *Apocalypse Now*, Hollywood: Paramount, 1979.

23. The international response now represented a huge array of different actors. But the continuous tension between the humanitarians, developers, human rights agencies, the political negotiators and the international military forces was never resolved and disabled the strategy to stabilise the state. The completely anodyne nature of British doctrine reflects this. Joint Warfare Publication, 'The Military Contribution to Peace Support Operations', *Joint Doctrine and Concepts Centre*, 2004, Swindon.

24. Interview with General Sir Mike Jackson, 1996.

25. Bakunin M., 'Letters to a Frenchman on the Present Crisis', 1870.

26. Maurice Tugwell, *Revolutionary Propaganda And Possible Counter Measures*, PhD Thesis at King's College London, 1979, p. 111.

27. Ibid.

28. The disaffected nationalist in Northern Ireland had firm beliefs of reuniting Ireland (in face of one million Protestants living in Ulster) and the dispossessed Palestinians of retaking Palestine (in face of the Israel Defence Forces and all the attendant problems of the existence of an Israeli state).

29. Represented by the contemporary writings of Bard O'Neill of the US National War College who has been an influential figure in US and British doctrine development, his contribution to the UK Armed Forces Manual, 'Counter-insurgency Operations' is acknowledged in the *UK Army Field Manual*, 1995, pp. 1-9.

30. Bard O'Neill, *Insurgency And Terrorism: Inside Modern Revolutionary Warfare*, p. 97.
31. Barry Rubin, 'The Origins of the PLO's Terrorism' in *Terrorism and Politics*, Barry Rubin (ed.), London: Macmillan, 1991; Martin Kramer, 'The Moral Logic of Hizbullah' in *Origins Of Terrorism: Psychologies, Ideologies, Theologies, States Of Mind*, W. Reich (ed.), Cambridge: Cambridge University Press, 1990; George Gerbner, 'Symbolic Functions Of Violence And Terror', in *The Camera's Eye: News Coverage Of Terrorist Events*, Yonah Alexander & R. G. Picard, Washington: Brassey's, 1990.
32. Attempts to publish a new British doctrine in 1995 were postponed due to the prioritisation given to peace support operations. See Chapter 4.
33. In the mid-1970s the IRA successfully manipulated the domestic press using a "propaganda of the deed" campaign, but in concept and reach it was a very minor aspect of their overall campaign, a fact reflected in the British counter-strategy.
34. Interestingly this was the same draft that was "postponed" in 1995.
35. *UK Army Field Manual*, 2001, pp. A-3-13.
36. Ibid.

## 4. THE CHRONOLOGY OF NEGLECT

1. Maurice Tugwell, *Revolutionary Propaganda and Possible Counter Measures*; Maurice Tugwell, 'Terrorism and Propaganda' in Paul Wilkinson and Alasdair Stewart (eds), *Contemporary Research On Terrorism*, Aberdeen: Aberdeen University Press, 1989.
2. This refers to the NATO based coalitions in former Yugoslavia and Somalia, Commonwealth of Independent States-based coalitions in Moldova, Georgia and Tajikistan and Economic Community Of West African States-based coalitions in West Africa.
3. Complex emergencies were defined by the international community in 1994 as "a humanitarian crisis in a country, region, or society where there is a total or considerable breakdown of authority resulting from internal or external conflict which requires an international response that goes beyond the mandate or capacity of any single agency and/or the ongoing UN country programme", from the Inter-Agency Standing Committee (IASC), 10th meeting, December 1994.
4. Both as student and later as an instructor at the Royal Military Academy Sandhurst, the author was frequently involved in organising exercises in this vein.
5. British Army Staff College, *Counter Revolutionary Warfare Handbook*, Camberley, 1989.
6. The Staff College handbook was updated each year; in 1989 it was edited by a team of officers led by Lieutenant Colonel ASH Irwin who later became Lieutenant General Sir Alistair Irwin.

7. British Army Staff College, pp. 1-5.

8. Ibid.

9. Staff College 1989, pp. 4-2, 4-3 and chapter 4.

10. According to General Irwin's retrospective analysis, the Staff College's position accurately reflected the position of the average field commander: "Whether he likes it or not the commander simply does not have the freedom of action to put PSY-OPS (as it was then described) at the heart of his plan. When I was GOC Northern Ireland I had frequent discussions with John Reid the Secretary of State for Northern Ireland on this very subject and if I had proceeded to take this aspect of the campaign into my own hands I would quickly have been shown the door." Correspondence with General Alastair Irwin, 17 April 2009.

11. Staff College Handbook, 1989, p. 1A-1, citing Christopher Dobson and Robert Payne, *War Without End*, London: Harrap, 1986.

12. Staff College Handbook, p. 1-12

13. Correspondence with General Alastair Irwin, 16 April 2009.

14. The relevant team was led by Colonel Alan Mallinson, but greatly influenced by Lieutenant Colonel Charles Dobbie, an officer with strong convictions, who left the army to become a priest.

15. In 1997 Clare Short was the British Secretary of State for International Development and the post was elevated to Cabinet Level which gave her department a greater influence on the conduct of British operations in that period.

16. Several iterations of peace operations doctrine emerged from this process. Despite their wide distribution, in the author's experience, at battalion level, British unit commanders fell back on their Northern Ireland experience rather than the UN's prescriptions for peacekeeping. *HMSO, UK Army Field Manual*, Vol 5, Part 2, (interim version), Wider Peacekeeping, 1994. *HMSO, Peace Support Operations*, (JWP 3-50), 1996. HMSO, *The Military Contribution to Peace Support Operations*, (JWP 3-50, Second Edition), 2004.

17. Interview with the senior British doctrine writer involved, June 2009.

18. This refers to a list of roles: peace-building, peacekeeping, peace-enforcing, peace-making, peace-monitoring, peace-maintaining—that were constantly recited like a mantra when discussing the practicalities of restoring order in the style advocated by the UN.

19. General Sir Rupert Smith, General Sir Mike Jackson and General David Richards all made similar statements to this effect.

20. The full title to this publication is *Director General Doctrine and Development Tactical Handbook for Operations other than War*, UK MoD, 1998.

21. *Land Operations Vol III, Counter Revolutionary Operations Part 1*. UK MoD, 1977, paragraphs 0326-0329

22. Paul Wilkinson, *Contemporary Research on Terrorism*, p. 18.

23. Ibid., p. 19.

24. It is true that the animal rights groups have a continuing source of energy. Nevertheless because they are not nationally threatening, they and similar "lunatic" groups are classified as terrorists or criminals.

25. For example granting independence to Malaya during the early stages of the insurgency succeeded in isolating the Chinese insurgent movement from the likely inheritors of the independent state.

26. Referring to people-based movements such as the Liberation Tigers of Tamil Eelam (LTTE) in Sri Lanka and the Maoists in Nepal.

27. Referring to, for example, the National Patriotic Front of Liberia and the Revolutionary United Front in Sierra Leone.

28. It is arguable that *any* criminal band to some extent is the consequence of degenerating social conditions. The line which separates the feral militia from the road bandit is therefore fairly subjective and relies on a local judgement on the extent to which the social environment which gives rise to the criminal activity can only be addressed by a major political/internal security campaign.

29. Sarah Sewall's introduction to *US Army/Marine Corps Counterinsurgency Field Manual*, Chicago: University of Chicago Press, 2007.

30. This situation became clear to the author and to others attending the French Institute of International Relations meeting in Paris 3-4 June 2007 'Counter insurgency and Stability Operations US, French, British and German Approaches'.

## 5. MULTIPLE POPULATIONS AND MASS COMMUNICATIONS: THE INTERNATIONALISATION OF INSURGENCIES

1. This was the assessment, for example, of a British general returning from command in Basra speaking at RUSI in 2005. See *Conference Synopsis: Transformation of Operations on the Cusp*, Royal United Services Institute and US Joint Forces Command, 14-16 March 2005.

2. Eugene Linden, 'Exploding Cities of the Developing World', *Foreign Affairs*, Vol 75, No 1, 1996.

3. Joshua Forrest, 'State Inversion and Non-state Politics', in Leonardo Villalonand, Phillip Huxtable (eds), *The African State At A Critical Juncture*, Boulder: Lynne Reinner, 1998, p. 45.

4. This refers to the UN presence and interventions in Angola, Afghanistan, Namibia, Nicaragua, Mozambique and Sudan during this period.

5. There are many illustrative campaigns from former Yugoslavia to Cambodia to choose from; see for example General Lewis McKenzie's hilarious but tragic account of the fighting in Sarajevo. McKenzie L., *Peacekeeper: The Road To Sarajevo*, Douglas and McIntyre Ltd, 1993. Also General

Romeo Dallaire's description of being abandoned by officials in New York in Romeo Dallaire, *Shake Hands With The Devil*, Knopf: Canada, September 2003.

6. The official definition of a complex emergency was then "a humanitarian crisis in a country, region or society where there is total or considerable breakdown of authority resulting from internal or external conflict and which requires an international response that goes beyond the mandate or capacity of any single agency and/or the ongoing United Nations country program." See *OCHA Orientation Handbook on Complex Emergencies*, Office for the Coordination of Humanitarian Affairs. August 1999, http://www.reliefweb.int/library/documents/ocha__orientation__handbook_on__.htm.

7. There is no coherent explanation of the security dimension of this problem in the latest manual published by the UN's Office for the Coordination of Humanitarian Affairs, http://www.reliefweb.int/library/documents/ocha__orientation__handbook.

8. This is tacitly acknowledged in the IASC 2004 'Civil Military Relationships', *IASC Reference Paper*, 28 June 2004, http://www.humanitarian-info.org/iasc/content/products/docs.

9. 'Wider Peacekeeping', *HMSO*, AFM Vol 5, Part II, 1994 (Interim).

10. "Local forces" refers principally to the militias challenging the government, but could also include government forces, whose loyalty was not always reliable.

11. At the time of writing the new British Army draft, *Countering Insurgency—A Handbook for Commanders* (UK Army draft—Army Code 71749), has taken a robust line.

12. Despite committing mass murders and sundry war crimes these forces were labelled "spoilers" by the civilian agencies, no doubt to preserve their special neutral status in the humanitarian space. See for example Marie-Joelle Zahar, 'Reframing the Spoiler Debate in Peace Processes' in Ed Darby and MacGinty, *Contemporary Peacemaking: Conflict, Violence And Peace Processes*, Palgrave Macmillan:UK, 2003.

13. OCHA.

14. As General Sir Gerald Templer famously said of the Malayan campaign—only 25% of the problem was military. *Templer.* John Cloake, *Tiger Of Malaya: The Life Of Field Marshal Sir Gerald Templer*, London: Harrap, 1985.

15. According to the author's conversations with Generals Mike Jackson and David Richards, British Army commanders had in the 1990s contingencies accepted that at street level the soldier was following tactics and procedures that were closer to countering insurgency than the strictly limited actions of a peacekeeper. In Whitehall, ministers and their respective civil service advisory staff publicly acknowledged this situation later

and in particular in 2003 when insurgents in Iraq attacked British troops and UN and ICRC headquarters.

16. See, for example, the list of merchant shipping owned by the LTTE in John Mackinlay, *Globalisation and Insurgency*, p. 71, table 1.

17. Keen, David, 'The Economic Functions of Violence in Civil Wars'.

18. The UN's observer teams organised from UNTSO were also ubiquitously deployed to all the major trouble spots and maintained their own lines of communications and command structures.

19. For a recent example of multiple donors see the *Afghan National Development Strategy* at www.ands.gov.af.

20. During the 1980s the Commonwealth response to the settlement of the Zimbabwe/Rhodesia insurgency involved contingents whose borders ran contiguously to Zimbabwe. See 'Operation AGILA/Operation Midford: The British Empire's Last Sunset', *Digger History*, 2000, http://www. diggerhistory.info/pages-conflicts-periods/other/rhodesia.htm Rhodesia. htm.

21. In 1993 I interviewed some NCOs of 1st Battalion Cheshire Regiment as they were waiting to embark at the end of their Bosnia tour. They confirmed that when they were required to take action against adversaries, in doctrinal terms they fell back on what they had learned in Northern Ireland. The British approach to counter-insurgency however was not embodied in UN procedures; see also Bob Stewart, *Broken Lives*, Harper Collins; London, 1994.

22. George Orwell, *Homage To Catalonia*, Penguin: London, 1962.

23. Nik Gowing, Main Presenter BBC World, presentations during the RUSI conference series 'Transformation of Military Operations on the Cusp'. See *Conference Synopsis: Transformation of Operations on the Cusp*, Royal United Services Institute and US Joint Forces Command, 14-16 March 2005.

24. Ibid.

25. Castells.

26. "Strategic narrative"—a compelling story line that can explain events convincingly to a particular audience, not necessarily analytical or grounded in evidence it may rely more on appeals to emotion and dubious historical analogies. A strategic narrative plays an useful role in how organisations and nations define themselves. See Lawrence Freedman, 'The Transformation of Strategic Affairs', *Adelphi Paper* 379, Routledge: Oxford, p. 22.

27. Bruce Hoffman, 'Insurgency and Counter-insurgency in Iraq', *Occasional Papers*, RAND, 2004.

28. Faisal Devji, *Landscapes of the Jihad: Militancy, Morality, Modernity*, Hurst; London, 2005.

29. In Madrid 2004 and London 2005 attacks on the commuter population caused Spain to withdraw its forces from the Iraq Coalition and foment-

ed public scrutiny of "Blair's wars" and their connection to Islamic radicalisation. Meanwhile, on the ground, groups that relied on a high degree of local consent to their presence found themselves completely unprotected, as was the case in Iraq and Afghanistan for members of the UN, ICRC and some NGOs.

## 6. THE MIGRATION FACTOR

1. "After the Vietnam War, we purged ourselves of everything that had to do with irregular war or insurgency, because it had to do with how we lost that war". General Jack Keene on the *Jim Lehrer News Hour*, 18 April 2006. Cited by John Nagl in the Introduction to *The US Army Marine Corps Counter Insurgency Field Manual*, University of Chicago Press, July 2007.
2. 'Countering Insurgency—A Handbook for Commanders', *UK Army draft—Army Code 71749*, May 2008, (Un-published draft).
3. From John Sutherland and Faisal Devji, 'The Ideas Interview: Faisal Devji', *Guardian Unlimited*, 08 July 2007.
4. Teece (2003) cited in HW Fowler, *A Dictionary Of Modern English Usage*, revised by Ernest Gowers, Oxford, 1965.
5. 'European Muslim Population', *Muslim Population Worldwide*, as of 20 August 2007, www.islamicpopulation.com/europe_general.html.
6. An assessment based on UNHCR and IOM figures made by Leila Talani in *Out of Egypt: Globalisation, Marginalisation and Illegal Migration to the EU*, UCLA Centre for European and Eurasian Studies, 2005.
7. The concept that Northern European countries would de facto in due course become the lifeboats of the populations that would be dispossessed by climate change was discussed in James Lovelock, *The Vanishing Face Of Gaia*, London: Penguin Books, 2009.
8. According sources interviewed in East London the Asian communities call forward migrants from their villages and families on the availability of jobs and for marriage purposes with greater authority than the British Home Office (From the author's research, August 2007).
9. It was disclosed to a Home Affairs Select Committee in 2006 that officials had no idea how illegal immigrants remained in the United Kingdom because tracking their movements was not "an effective enforcement strategy". It was revealed that between 200,000 and 300,000 national insurance numbers were being issued annually to foreigners but that immigration checks were being carried out on only around two per cent of them. 'Officials "haven't the faintest idea" of immigrant count', *The Times* (London), 16 May 2006, http://www.timesonline.co.uk/tol/news/uk/article719671.ece.
10. The failure to monitor these developments in Britain is described in a strident polemic by Melanie Phillips, *Londonistan: How Britain Is Creating A Terror State Within*, Gibson Square: London, 2006.

11. Or, in Iraq, the *perceived* presence of this global element.
12. By 2006-7 this monolithic approach had become more nuanced and there was a more manoeuvrist concept of operations which successfully exploited the tensions between the incoming al-Qaeda cadres (post-Maoist) and local insurgents (traditional) whose ambitions were territorially and culturally defined. See David Kilcullen, 'Anatomy of a Tribal Revolt', *Small Wars Journal blog*, 29 August 2007, http://smallwarsjournal.com/blog/2007/08/anatomy-of-a-tribal-revolt/.
13. Marc Sageman, 'The Next Generation of Terror', *Foreign Policy*, March /April 2008.
14. Late 1990s Rowntree studies on isolation of migrant communities.
15. 'Oldham Riots: Two Perspectives', *BBC*, reported on 20 August 2007, http://news.bbc.co.uk.
16. Community Pride not Prejudice, *Bradford Race Review*, 2020 Vision, 2001. http://www.bradford2020.com/pride/report.pdf.
17. Muhammad Anwar, 'Muslims In Britain: Issues, Policy and Practice' in Tahir Abbas (ed), *Muslim Britain, Communities Under Pressure*, UK: Zed Books, 2005.
18. See Muhammad Anwar and Bakhsh Qadir, *British Muslims and State Policies*, Warwick Centre for Research in Ethnic Relations in EU Commission, 2003.
19. Muhammad Anwar, 'Muslims in Britain: Issues, Policy and Practice', p. 26.
20. Letter from John Geive PS Home Office to Sir Andrew Turnbull at Cabinet Office, 10 May 2004, www.globalsecurity.org/security/library/report/2004/muslimext-uk.htm.
21. Michael Howard, 'Mistake to Declare this a War', *RUSI Journal*, Vol 146, No 6, December 2001.
22. A significant percentage were reluctant to condemn the 9/11 bombings, in 'The Great Divide: How Westerners And Muslims View Each Other', *PEW Global Attitudes Project*, 22 June 2006.
23. "200 groupings or networks, totaling over 1,600 identified individuals (and there will be many we don't know) who are actively engaged in plotting, or facilitating, terrorist acts here and overseas." This was the assessment by former head of MI5, Eliza Manningham Buller, speaking at Queen Mary College, University of London, 9 November 2006.
24. From 'Understanding Suicide Terrorism: A Homeland Security And Resilience Department Workshop', *RUSI*, London, 3 November 2006.
25. Gilles Kepel, *The War For Muslim Minds*, Harvard: Belknap, 2004, pp. 243-286.
26. This syndrome was explained by Ed Husain who, as a young, radicalised British Muslim, moved to Syria and noticed that, in contrast to the Muslims in Damascus, he dressed and behaved in a very old-fashioned and

orthodox manner. Ed Husain, *The Islamist*, London: Penguin Books, 2007, p. 225.

27. This account is compiled from the author's interviews in the Manchester area in 2006.

28. This information is from discussions with officials in the Community Cohesion Department of the British Home Office in February and June 2007.

29. Alison Pargeter provides this interview from her similar account of cultural separation: "the majority of the first wave of Muslim immigrants to Britain originated among the peasantry of South Asia and Africa …the effects on their children can be imagined: children of a Mirpuri textile worker had to muddle through homework without any assistance or supervision from illiterate parents, who in turn were more concerned to indoctrinate their kids with the only thing they knew—the rudiments of their religion as taught to them be the village mullah." An account by Maruf Kwaja, 'Muslims in Britain: Generations, experiences, futures', *Open Democracy*, 2 August 2005, in Alison Pargeter, *The New Frontiers Of Jihad*, London: I.B. Tauris, 2008.

30. The sensation of being between two cultures is also described by a terrorism suspect as like supporting England at football and Pakistan at cricket. "It is in that tension that everything is played out. Its about how the global plugs into the local, about the interaction of what happens personally to an individual and the world geopolitical trends to which they are exposed." From Jason Burke, 'The Britons Who Became Bombers', *Observer Magazine*, 20 January 2008.

31. Shiv Malik, 'My Brother the Bomber', *Prospect*, June 2007, pp. 30-41.

32. This account is from Ed Husain, *The Islamist*.

33. As cited in Shiv Malik, 'My Brother the Bomber'.

34. Ed Husain, *The Islamist*, p. 122.

35. Shiv Malik, 'My Brother the Bomber', p. 36.

36. Ibid., p. 37.

37. The concept of a bottom up process which is organic and individually sustained is also described by Jason Burke's interviews in Jason Burke, 'The Britons Who Became Bombers'. See also Fraser Nelson's interviews to the effect that the largest group of AQ supporters comprises "the self-starting groups which have bought into the AQ franchise". Fraser Nelson, 'Al Qa'eda's Secret UK Gangs', *Spectator*, 22 March 2008.

38. This particular list was collected by the author during his research in a Muslim community near Manchester in 2006.

39. Referring to the British usage of the word and its various shortened forms (kuf) to impolitely categorise the white, non-Muslim, infidel population.

## 7. THE VIRTUAL BATTLEFIELD

1. Intercepted web chat conversion with Al-Qaeda web propagandist Younis Tsouli, (aka Irhabi 007), in 'Internet Jihad', *The Economist*, 14 July 2007.
2. Sergei Nechaev in John Gray, 'A Trail of Terror Stretching 200 Years', *The Times* (London), 30 June 2007.
3. From Rick Coolsaet "Anarchist Outrages", *Le Monde Diplomatique*, September 2004, in Neville Bolt, 'Propaganda of the Deed and the Irish Republican Brotherhood', *RUSI Journal*, Vol 153, No 1, (2008).
4. Krotopkin was the founder of Anarcho-Communism.
5. Neville Bolt, 'Propaganda of the deed'.
6. Ibid.
7. Piaras F Mac Lochlainn, *Last Words: Letters and Statements of the Leaders Executed after the Rising at Easter 1916*, Kilmainham Jail Restoration Society Dublin, 1971 in Neville Bolt, 'Propaganda of the deed'.
8. Ibid., p. 56 (citing Thomas MacDonagh: Address to the Court Martial, 2 May 1916).
9. Ibid., pp. 28-9 (citing Patrick Pearse: Address to the Court Martial, Kilmainham Jail, 2 May 1916).
10. Maurice Tugwell, *Revolutionary Propaganda and Possible Counter Measures*.
11. Ibid., p. 112.
12. The IRA were swifter than the British in reaching communities beyond Ulster; Neville Bolt points out that the IRA's Bobby Sands death by hunger strike in 1981 was marked by anti-British demonstrations in Athens, Antwerp, Milan, Oslo, Brisbane and Chicago, and over 110,000 longshoremen boycotted all British ships entering US ports for 24 hours. Neville Bolt, 'Propaganda of the deed'.
13. The drama of a hotel being bombed would make the headline spot but not the capture of the perpetrators. Maurice Tugwell, *Revolutionary Propaganda*, p. 225.
14. At the time of writing this is still the case. In 2008-09 my efforts to introduce propaganda of the deed to the British military headquarters staff preparing for active duty in Iraq and Afghanistan met with disbelief.
15. O'Shaughnessy cites a study in which a selected audience willingly ate fudge when it looked like fudge but not when it was made to look like animal droppings, even though they knew for certain it was fudge. Nicholas Jackson O'Shaughnessy, *Politics And Propaganda—Weapons Of Mass Seduction*, Ann Arbor: University of Michigan Press, 2004, p. 41. The study referred to is from page 41 in which he refers to Paul Rosin, Linda Millman and Carol Nemerhoff, 'Operations of the laws of sympathetic magic in disgust and their domains', *Journal of Personality and Social Psychology*, No 50, 1986, pp. 58-71.

16. Ibid., p. 110.

17. Ibid.

18. *US Army Field Manual* 3-24, p. A-7.

19. Lawrence Freedman, *Transformation of Strategic Affairs*, p. 23.

20. The political dimension represents 80% of the action (the military dimension only 20%) in any successful insurgency according to Galula's concept of insurgency.

21. 'Taliban Propaganda: Winning The War Of Words?', *ICG Asia Report No 158*, International Crisis Group, 24 July 2008. Steve Tatham, 'Hearts and Minds. Time To Think Differently?', *The Naval Review*, Vol 26, No 4, 2008.

22. Lawrence Freedman, 'Transformation of Strategic Affairs', pp. 23-4.

23. *Control Room*, Directed by Jehane Noujaim, 2004.

24. *US Army Field Manual* 3-24 and UK Army, *Countering Insurgency—A Guide for Commanders—Army Code 71779 (Draft 1)*, September 2007 (not yet published).

25. *US Army Field Manual* 3-24 (chapter 3 and also at Appendix B).

26. *US Army Field Manual* 3-24 (chapter 8 and Appendix A).

27. Daniel Bell, *The Coming Of Post-Industrial Society: A Venture In Social Forecasting*, Hammondsworth: Penguin, 1976.

28. John Sutherland and Faisal Devji, 'The Ideas Interview: Faisal Devji'.

29. See an excellent description of the relationship between Bell and Castells in Frank Webster, 'Making Sense of the Information Age', *Information, Communication and Society*, Vol 8, No 4, December 2005.

30. Research by Manuel Castells, cited by him during his lecture at the *London School of Economics and Political Science*, November 2008.

31. Simon Marginson and Erlenawati Sawir, 'Interrogating Global Flows in Higher Education', *Globalisation Society and Education*, Vol 3, No 3, November 2005, pp. 285-309.

32. Manuel Castells, 'Internet Beyond Myths: the Record of Scholarly Research', a lecture at *London School of Economics and Political Science* on 24 October 2008.

33. Ibid., Governments and their individual ministries and departments communicate internally but less successfully with their respective publics. Doctors, schoolteachers and local civil servants communicate by Internet far more within their respective institutions than to their patients, pupils and ratepayers.

34. For example, Timothy Thomas, 'Cyber Silhouettes', *Foreign Military Studies Office*, Leavenworth 2006.

35. This paper having been circulated as a draft in 2005 disappeared from public sight which might be construed as a sign that it was either highly valuable or highly objectionable to the US DoD. Rick Brennan, Adam Grissom, Sara Daly, Peter Chalk, William Rosenau, Kalev Sepp, Steve Dalzell, *Future Insurgent Threats*, RAND, February 2005.

36. Lawrence Freedman, 'Transformation of Strategic Affairs', p. 23.
37. The sense of this "netwar" fixated debate is conveyed in Bruce Hoffman, et al, *The Implications of Network-Centric Insurgencies on US Army Operations*. RAND, DRR-3847-A, (Prepared for Department of the Army), January 2006.
38. Bruce Sterling's account of the cyber manipulation of a crowd of unrelated strangers so that they brought their different functions together to overrun a bank was fictitious and futuristic but it pointed out a trend.
39. As one expert put it: "It's like the old game of space invaders. When you clear the screen of potential attackers, another formation appears in its place." 'Internet Jihad—a world wide web of terror', *The Economist* (Print Edition), 14 July 2007.
40. In the case of Guantanamo Bay and Abu Ghraib the single icon frames were taken by the government and the involved soldiers respectively.
41. 'The Britons who become bombers', *Observer Magazine*, 20 January 2008.

## 8. POST-MAOISM

1. This refers principally to the 1990s UN interventions in Bosnia, Somalia, Rwanda, Liberia and Angola
2. After each intervention some military contingents, particularly the US, the United Kingdom, the UN and NATO would have their own institutional "lessons learned" process in which the tactical and procedural lessons were incorporated into reports. The more spectacular events took place as internationally organised multidisciplinary conferences often hosted by Nordic countries with the support of concerned NGOs and UN agencies.
3. *Saving Lives Together: A Framework for improving Security Arrangements Among IGOs, NGOs and UN in the Field*, Inter-Agency Standing Committee, 66ᵗʰ. Working Group Meeting, 15-17 November, 2006.
4. To some the forces who resisted the international intervention were merely spoilers and to some they were armed adversaries. For a military view see William Reno, *Warlord Politics And African States*, Boulder: Lynne Reinner, 1998. For an idealistic view, see Marie-Joelle Zahar, 'Reframing the 'Spoiler Debate in Peace Processes' in Darby and MacGinty (eds), *Contemporary Peacemaking: Conflict, Violence, And Peace Processes*, Palgrave Macmillian, 2003.
5. As mentioned above, the only shared definition was the loose description of complex emergencies from *Working Paper on the Definition of Complex Emergency*, Inter-Agency Standing Committee, December 1994.
6. The Americans in Vietnam, the French in Algeria, the Spanish in Iraq—campaigns that fell foul of the electorate back home, who pressured their governments into withdrawal.
7. For example, the Shia, Sunni, and Kurds in Iraq.

8. For example, the importance of Pakistan's Federally Administered Tribal Areas to the coalition campaign in Afghansitan.

9. As in Iran's influence over the Iraq insurgency, and its harbouring of Afghan refugees.

10. Such as the UAE contingent of Special Forces in Helmand province, Afghanistan.

11. The International Security Assistance Force (ISAF) in Afghanistan consists of 41 nations: Albania, Austria, Australia, Azerbaijan, Belgium, Bulgaria, Canada, Croatia, Czech Republic, Denmark, Estonia, Finland, France, Georgia, Germany, Greece, Hungary, Iceland, Ireland, Italy, Jordan, Latvia, Lithuania, Luxembourg, Macedonia, Netherlands, New Zealand, Norway, Poland, Portugal, Romania, Singapore, Slovakia, Slovenia, Spain, Sweden, Turkey, Ukraine, the United Arab Emirates, the United Kingdom, and the US.

12. Such as the nations which headed up regarding Afghanistan reconstruction plan as a result of the Bonn Accord.

13. Ricks suggests that faced with an operation which had no apparent centre of gravity, General Franks developed an operational plan that addressed nine centres of gravity in Iraq. Thomas Ricks, *Fiasco: The American Military Adventure In Iraq*.

14. "Centre of gravity" is a Clausvitzian term that has exercised a great deal of debate about its true meaning. Loosely understood, it is the factor or set of factors that provides the strongest moral or physical impetus to successful action.

15. In Jason Burke's sample "…More than a third had a university degree or similar qualification and a high proportion were studying when they became involved in radicalism, usually in technical and science faculties, particularly engineering or IT. But 10% had left school at sixteen, another 15% had dropped out of further education." Jason Burke, 'The Britons who become bombers', *Observer Magazine*, 20 January 2008.

16. For an excellent example of the continuing obsession with territory gained and bodies counted read Charles M Sennott, 'The General's Knowledge', *The Times* (London), 29 June 2008, http://www.timesonline.co.uk/tol/news/world/us_and_americas/article4212055.ece.

17. Al Qaeda also use the BBC news footage to illustrate their propaganda mainly because it is the usually the best imagery available.

18. The idea that activists are radicalised in extremist mosques appears exaggerated. British government analysis shows that less than 10 per cent of radicalising activity takes place in places of worship. Jason Burke, 'The Britons who became bombers'.

19. 'A world wide web of terror', *The Economist*, 14 July 2007.

20. Omar Nasiri's account of travelling to Pakistan and being swept up by successive jihadi organisations without having previous instructions or introductions illustrates the concept of a social current that catches the disaffected in its flow. Omar Nasiri, *Inside The Global Jihad*, Hurst: UK. 2006.

21. For example of a traditional training camp see Dalrymple's description of an LTTE training camp the size of a university campus built like a heavily camouflaged jungle town with conference theatres, lecture rooms and dormitories. William Dalrymple, *The Age Of Kali: Indian Travels And Encounters*, London: Flamingo, 1999.

22. Kevin McDonald, *Global Movements: Action And Culture*, Malden: Blackwell, 2006.

23. Yuezhi Zhao, 'Falun Gong, Identity, and the Struggle over Meaning Inside and Outside China' in Nick Couldry and James Curran (eds), *Contesting Media Power: Alternative Media In A Networked World*, Lanham: Rowman & Littlefield, 2003, pp. 209-223.

24. He shares this conviction with Urry ...

25. Faisal Devji, *Landscapes of the Jihad*, pp. xi–xvi.

26. During the author's visits to commanders of international forces during the 1990s in sub-Saharan Africa, South Asia, Eastern Europe and the Balkans, and to the British training teams responsible for the preparation of the British contingents, the adversary was always depicted as a monolithic idea.

27. From the author's interviews with battalion officers during his visit to 1st. Battalion Green Howards and to the Norwegian contingent in 2004.

28. David Gompert and John Gordon IV., (et al.), *War By Other Means*, RAND, (California), (2008).

29. In my view his measurement was largely kinetic, Gompert was using the same tools to assess Type 4 as he had for Types 1-3. His assessment implies that Type 4 was just another form of physical insurgency whose potency could be measured in bodies counted, regimes overthrown and territory held. Gompert is a colleague and I respect his view, however we are destined to disagree on this point.

30. Written Evidence Submitted by Professor Robert Springborg to the Select Committee on Foreign Affiars, House of Commons, February 2006.

31. Rick Brennan, Adam Grissom, Sara Daly, Peter Chalk, William Rosenau, Kalev Sepp and Steve Dalzell, *Future Insurgency Threats*, RAND, February 2005. This appeared in the form of a draft that was circulated as part of the RAND insurgency study for the US DoD RAND draft for the OSD.

32. Rick Brennan, et al, *Future Insurgency Threats*, pp. xiii-xiv.

33. As well as Brennan and Springbord, see Kilcullen, 'Anatomy of a Tribal Revolt'.

34. Angel Rabassa, Peter Chalk, Kim Cragin, Sara A Daly, Heather S Gregg, Theodore W Krasik, Kevin A O'Brien, William Rosenau, *Beyond al-Qaeda: Part 1, The Global jihadist Movement*, RAND (California), (2006).
35. Donald D., *Local beats Global*, Submission to BISA, Cambridge December 2007.

## PART III:  RESPONDING TO POST-MAOISM

1. I argue in Chapter 8 that the US FM 3-24 is essentially expeditionary in its approach. During the same period in which it was being written British Army Staff prepared 3 successive drafts for a counter-insurgency manual which were also expeditionary, territorial and therefore essentially Maoist addressing a previous rather than the prevailing era of insurgency.
2. For example from the individual activist groups hidden in the attic rooms of British midland towns and their connection to the insurgent forces in Afghanistan. See Brigadier Ed Butler's assertions that intercepted conversations between Taliban fighters revealed individuals with Yorkshire and Midland accents. Con Coughlin, Duncan Gardham, and Thomas Harding, 'British Muslims fighting with "Taliban in Afghanistan"', *Telegraph*, 2 August 2008, http://www.telegraph.co.uk/news/worldnews/asia/afghanistan/2485750/British-Muslims-fighting-with-Taliban-in-Afghanistan.html.
3. *Final Report of the National Commission on Terrorist Attacks Upon the United States London*, Norton: London, p. 365.
4. Ibid., p. 366.
5. *Muslim American, Middle Class and Mostly Mainstream*, Pew Research Center, 2007. *Muslims in the American Public Square*, Zogby International, October 2004.
6. Jonathan Eyal, *War in Iraq: Combat and Consequence*, Whitehall Paper 59, RUSI, 2003.

## 9.  THE EXPEDITIONARY APPROACH

1. Ricks, *Fiasco: The American Military Adventure In Iraq*.
2. Ibid., p. 79.
3. For example see this announcement from the Whitehouse which revises the status of Taliban not long after the intervention in Afghanistan: 'Taliban Executive Order', Office of the Press Secretary, 3 July 2002, http://georgewbush-whitehouse.archives.gov/news/releases/2002/07/20020703-1.html.
4. In both Afghanistan and Iraq they encountered a Federated Insurgent Complex which comprised a jihadist element as well a nationalist element. In both cases the latter was much stronger than the foreign insurgents who

it could be argued were now attracted to these placed because of the presence of Coalition troops.

5. *National Strategy for Combating Terrorism*, US Government, 2003. Found in http://www.fas.org/irp/threat/nsct2006.pdf.

6. This altered emphasis was demonstrated by a greater enthusiasm for understanding counter-insurgency in the US. Also the tacit acceptance in the British government that the "Global War On Terror" was probably a misleading title. Jason Burke, 'Britain Stops Talk of "War on Terror"', *The Observer*, 10 December 2006. According to General Barno in 2003 "unit commanders were forbidden from using the word COIN in describing their missions". Correspondence with US advisor Daniel Marston June 2009.

7. 'Quadrennial Defense Review Report', *US Department of Defense*, 6 February 2006, http://www.globalsecurity.org/military/library/policy/dod/qdr-2006-report.htm.

8. *National Strategy for Combating Terrorism*, US Government, 2003, p. 6

9. Ibid., p. 7.

10. Ibid., p. 11.

11. Ibid., p. 22.

12. Individual government advisers were using the term insurgency to describe what was happening in Operation Enduring Freedom and Iraqi Freedom.

13. *Quadrenniel Review Report*, US Department of Defence.

14. Ibid., p. 11.

15. British Military Assistance Training Teams (BMATT) were established in Eastern European and Baltic states with similar US teams to prepare former Warsaw Pact armies for NATO Membership. The more recent manifestation of British Defence Diplomacy is explained in *Ministry of Defence Policy Paper number 1; Defence Diplomacy*, Director General Corporate Communication, Ministry of Defence, London

16. State Department and USAID's commitments to the Global War On Terror are alluded to in "FY 2007-2012 Department of State and USAID Strategic Plan: Transformational Diplomacy", US Department of State, 7 May 2007, http://www.state.gov/s/d/rm/rls/dosstrat/2007/.

17. To implement this strategy, U.S. Ambassadors, as the President's personal representatives abroad, lead interagency Country Teams that recommend strategies using all instruments of U.S. statecraft to help host nations understand the threat, and strengthen their political will and capacity to counter it. Assessment by Ambassador Henry A. Crumpton, Coordinator for Counterterrorism Testimony, 'The Changing Face of Terror: A Post-9/11 Assessment', 13 June 2006, http://www.senate.gov/Senate404.html.

18. Bartosz Stanislawski has coined an excellent piece on so-called "global black spots". Bartosz Stanislawski, 'Para-States, Quasi-States, and Black

Spots: Perhaps Not States, But Not "Ungoverned Territories", Either',
*International Studies Review*, No 10, (2008).

19. The International Institute for Strategic Studies, *The Military Balance*,
London: Routledge, 2008.

20. The principle of self-defence is set out in Article 51 of the United Nations
Charter.

21. This is a proposition of Andrew Bacevich, *The New American Militarism:
How Americans Are Seduced By War*, Oxford: OUP, 2005.

22. In David Kilcullen's experience the weaker partner is always dominant
because the intervener is always in a position of trying to prevent them
from collapsing, while the growing security of the weaker partner allows
it to behave more freely. Thomas Ricks, *The Gamble*, London: Penguin,
2009, p. 142.

23. The UN's interpretation of the composition of a multinational force is
that in the UN case the force is traditionally structured as far as possible
in such a way that it cannot be accused of favouring any particular contributing nation's interest, with each national contingent is represented
in the key staff jobs in the controlling HQ. Some US analysts articulate
a division of labour whereby the US do the intervention and the practicalities of regime change, leaving the soft side of peace support to a second line of lesser partners who will also be the long-term occupiers.

24. Mary Kaldor, *New And Old Wars: Organised Violence In A Global Era*,
Cambridge: Polity Press, 1999, Chapter 3. See also Ignatieff's description
of the 'narcissism of minor differences' in Michael Ignatieff, *The Warriors
Honor: Ethnic War And The Modern Conscience*, London: Vintage, 1998,
p. 34.

25. In Iraq the US Army transition from force protection or self-protection
to protecting the population, Ricks 2009.

26. Steve Tatham, *Losing Arab Hearts And Minds: The Coalition, Al Jazeera
And Muslim Public Opinion*, London: Hurst and Co., 2006.

27. CNN International Com/World, 'US and Coalition Casualties'; CRS
Report for Congress, *US Military Casualty Statistics*, (Code R522452),
18 March 2008; Global Security Organisation. *US Casualties in Iraq*,
August 2008; *Operations in Iraq: British Casualties*, UK MoD, http://
www mod.uk/DefenceInternet/FactSheets/OperationsFactsheets/Op-
erationsInIraqBritishCasualties.htm; *Operations in Afghanistan: British Casualties*, UK MoD, http://www.mod.uk/DefenceInternet/Fact-
Sheets/OperationsFactsheets/OperationsInAfghanistanBritishCasualties.
htm.

28. Matthew Hickley and James Chapman, 'Fury as injured soldiers are denied aid as defence chiefs refuse to reveal casualty lists', *Mail Online*,
22 September 2006. Accessed on 18 August 2008 from http://www.
dailymail.co.uk/news/article-406558/Fury-injured-soldiers-denied-aid-
defence-chiefs-refuse-reveal-casualty-list.html.

29. Ned Temko and Mark Townshend, 'Scandal of treatment for wounded Iraq veterans', *The Observer*, 18 March 2007.

30. Richard Greene, UK troops face trauma after Iraq, *BBC News*, 12 August 2005.

31. Linda Bilmes and Joseph Stiglitz, 'The Economic Costs of the Iraq War: An appraisal three years after the beginning of the conflict', *NBER Working Paper* 12054, (February 2006). In 2003 Rumsfeld had rejected his appointee's estimate of $200 billion see Guardian report above.

32. Joseph Stiglitz and Linda Bilmes, *The Three Trillion Dollar War: The True Cost Of The Iraq War*, New York: W W Norton and Co., 2008.

33. Frank Furedi, *Invitation To Terror: The Expanding Empire Of The Unknown*, United Kingdom: Continuum, 2007.

34. According to John Meuller the population in US had the same likelihood of drowning in the bath as being blown up by terrorists. John Mueller, *How Politicians And The Terrorism Industry Inflate National Security Threats And Why We Believe Them*, Routledge: United Kingdom, 2007.

35. See, for example, Ambassador Henry A. Crumpton, Coordinator for Counterterrorism 'Testimony Before the Senate Committee on Foreign Relations', 13 June 2006, http://www.senate.gov/Senate404.html.

36. Hambali or Riduan Isamuddin was seen as bin Ladens's campaign manager in Southeast Asia. From Ambassador Crumpton, "Testimony Before the Senate Committee on Foreign Relations".

37. Allegedly Mustafa al-Usayti, a Libyan who was an al Qaeda planner who moved and acted between Pakistan and North Africa. Ibid.

38. A dossier of material dispatched to diplomatic posts worldwide cites condemnation of al Qaida from Dr Fadi, a former leader of Egyptian Islamic Jihad, and Salman Abu-Awdah, a leading Saudi scholar who has published an open letter to Osama bin Laden calling al Qaida's aims illegitimate and immoral. Alan Travis, 'Revealed: Britain's Secret Propaganda War Against al Qaida', *The Guardian*, 26 August 2008, http://www.guardian.co.uk/world/2008/aug/26/alqaida.uksecurity?ref=opinion.

39. Frank Gardner, Radio 4 Current Affairs, 'Analysis; al Qaeda's Enemy Within', Transcript of a Recorded Documentary, *BBC*, White City, London, 7 August 2008.

40. Qadir's importance and authority at this crucial moment of the interview was that he represented one of many local NGOs working with Muslim youth in urban areas of the United Kingdom and could be expected to see some improvement in the numbers of radicalised young people passing through his hands.

41. It could be argued that the US megabases may send the required message of a long-term interest although it is not clear yet how visible they are to the wider public.

42. *Foreign Policy Aspects of the War on Terrorism*, House Commons Foreign Affairs Committee, paragraph 9, 15 October 2003, http://www.publications.parliament.uk/pa/cm200203/cmselect/cmfaff/cmfaff.htm.
43. Jonathan Eyal, *War in Iraq: Combat and Consequence*.
44. The best example of the failure of the concept of anti-personnel barriers was on the British Hong Kong border at the New Territories where a state-of-the-art barrier fence guarded by infantry battalions, ships at sea and helicopters failed to keep out large numbers of illegal immigrants from the Chinese mainland. (The author commanded sectors of that obstacle in 1970s).
45. *Muslim Americans*, PEW Research Center, 22 May 2007. As we have seen from another PEW study, *The Great Divide: How Westerners and Muslims View Each Other*, a significant percentage was reluctant to condemn the 9/11 bombings. *The Great Divide: How Westerners and Muslims View Each Other*, PEW Global Attitudes Project, 22 June 2006.

## 10. THE DOMESTIC APPROACH

1. This is referring, first of all, to a body of work emanating from Manuel Castells and his research associates. See Castells' webpage, http://www.manuelcastells.info/en/index.htm. And also to the fact that in addition to the military analysts anthropologists, communications experts, market analysts and political scientists were by now being included in the doctrine writing process in Britain and the US
2. In Northern Ireland the British military doctrines during the 1970s including several revisions, were: 'Counter-Revolutionary Operations' in *Land Operations*, Volume III, Parts 1, 2 and 3, MoD UK. Printed for HMSO by Bemrose, Derby, 1977.
3. At the operational level of the expedition they tended to be colonial police, the national intelligence services, the British military contingent, the host government or the rump of a colonial administration and the array of concerned government departments.
4. According to Kevin O'Brien there was also a loss of counter-subversion expertise as a result of the post-Cold War reductions. Interview and correspondence, March 2009.
5. The US arc of hostility put into effect by the Global War on Terror strategy even included movements such as the Nepalese Maoists, a nationalist movement struggling to overthrow a despotic Himalayan monarchy that had no ambitions beyond the Nepalese borders and at the time of writing constitute the elected government of Nepal.
6. A contemporary expression used by British counter-terrorist officials. Interview with Dr Kevin O'Brien, Kings College London, October 2008.
7. Ibid.
8. This pattern of moving in a succession of network flows had already been described in an insurgent context by Brennan in his 2005 paper and before

that in a purely sociological context by Manuel Castells. See particularly
the descriptions in Chapter 8.

9. *Community Pride not Prejudice*, Bradford Race Review, *2020 Vision*, 2001,
http://www.bradford2020.com/pride/report.pdf.

10. Interview with former Home Office official, Kings College London,
November 2008.

11. Sir David Omand has presented the motivations of extremism as:

- humiliation, revenge and honour, resentment
- personal identity crisis and/or alienation
- Lure of conspiracies, feeling special, in-group loyalties
- escapism, adventurism, aggression,
  all overlaid by strongly felt sense of injustice and grievance
  but, given meaning by a persuasive ideology.

(Interview with author op cit.)

12. Faisal Devji, *Landscapes Of The Jihad*, chapter 4.

13. Alan Travis, 'MI5 Report Challenges Views on Terrorism in Britain',
*The Guardian*, 21 August 2008, http://www.guardian.co.uk/uk/2008/
aug/20/uksecurity.terrorism1. Note in contrast to the military briefing
system established during the Northern Ireland campaign in which the
operators, in some case very junior commanders, were the authentic communicators, the Home Office Security Services tended leaked this information in a secretive and un-attributable manner.

14. Ibid.

15. Ibid.

16. 'Behavioural Science Unit Operational briefing note: Understanding
Radicalisation and Violent Extremism in the UK', MI5 Report No
BSU/02/2008, *The Guardian*, 12 June 2008, http://image.guardian.co.uk/
sys-files/Guardian/documents/2008/08/20/mi5.pdf. Cited in Ibid.
Lecture by David Omand, 'Nature of War Conference', delivered at
Christchurch College, University of Oxford, 13 September 2007.
Huda Jawad, *Forward Thinking: Forgotten Voices*, Forward Thinking:
London, 2008.
"The Great Divide: How Westerners and Muslims View Each Other."

Interviews:
Executive officials of Forward Thinking, London, August 2008;
Dr Kevin O' Brien, at Kings College London, October 2008;
Garry Hindle at the Royal United Services Institute London (Depart-
ment of Homeland Security and Resilience), 28 October 2008;
Official of Department of Communities and Local Government, Home
Office, London, August 2007.
Former officials of Home Office (OSCT), at Kings College London,
October 2008;
Staff Officers from the London Metropolitan Police (Communities
Together team), London, October 2008.

17. 'Muslims and the West', PEW 2006, Part 1.

18. The 2008/9 bombing of Gaza caused large numbers of previously uncommitted British Muslims to take to the streets, attend meetings and actively demonstrate against the British government's failure to make a convincing condemnation. From local NGO interviewed in Manchester, 17 February 2009.

19. Simon De Bruxelles and Adam Fresco, 'Cafe blast suspect "was sent a text message of support"', *The Times* (London), 24 May 2008; Mark Sappenfield and Mark Rice-Oxley, 'Global terror's India connection', *Christian Science Monitor*, No 10 July 2007; Anand Giridharadas and Jane Perlez, 'Severe Personality Shift Seen in Bomb Suspect', *The New York Times*, 9 July 2007.

20. This conclusion is made from comparing the periodic statements by MI5 as summarised by V Chandrashekhar, 'New MI5 chief says terror suspects in Britain have doubled last year', *Christian Science Monitor*, No 7, November 2007.

21. *Final Report of the National Commission on Terrorist Attacks Upon the United States London*, Norton: London, 2002, chapter 12.

22. 'Counter-Terrorist Strategy', UK Home Office.

23. The United Kingdom, since 2000, had been developing systems for the multi-agency management of the many complex challenges facing the country, both at home and overseas. These are exemplified by the National Security Strategy, the Civil Contingencies Act 2004 and the terrorism specific 'Contest' strategy. The implementation requirements of these systems fall on all levels of governance from the Prime Minister's Office to the Town Hall and the local Police Authority. Correspondence with Professor Frank Gregory, 19 April 2009.

24. The conduct of operations and the instructions for interdepartmental co-operation was guided by a series of letters and instructions that were signed jointly by the OSCT and ACPO (TAM). Interviews at GMP Regional Headquarters Old Trafford Manchester, 18 February 2009.

25. At every level of the operation there was a feeling of being involved in a developing process that was brand new in many respects. Interviews at GMP.

26. 'The Prevent Strategy, A Guide for Local Partners in England', HM Government, HMG undated pamphlet, p. 9.

27. Interview with John Dunstan, Regional Prevent Delivery Manager for Government Offices North West (Manchester), 18 Feb 2009.

28. Reports of Home Office security services' reluctance to participate in a wholehearted fashion with local and local authorities and police forces were volunteered by concerned individuals at regional level.

## 11. THE INSURGENT ARCHIPELAGO

1. The Nepalese Maoist attacks in 2002 /3 period could involve up to a total of 1000 including local levies, logistic load carriers in addition to the military cadres. Ashkok K Mehta, *The Royal Nepalese Army: Meeting the Maoist Challenge*, Rupa, New Delhi, 2005.
2. Email correspondence with General Alastair Irwin, April 2009.
3. This is how it seemed from the Muslim perspective. Huda Jawad, *Forgotten Voices: Developing more effective Engagement with Muslim Youth and Communities*, Forward Thinking, 2009.
4. The intervening swarm could be divided into several main categories of activity, Countering Terrorism and Radicalisation (CTR) overseas, which was funded by the FCO, the Channel Project to intervene in the case of vulnerable individuals implemented by the police, the Community Leadership Fund (CLF) for supporting individuals and organisations to tackle the factors influencing violent extremism, and Faith Communities Capacity Building and Preventing Violent Extremism.

    These initiatives were deployed overseas through the Strategic Programme Fund. *See Strategic Programme Fund—Countering Terrorism & Radicalisation (CTR) Programme*. Foreign and Commonwealth Office, http://www.fco.gov.uk/en/about-the-fco/what-we-do/funding-programmes/strat-progr-fund/strat-pro-fund-terrorism.
5. Shiraz Maher and Martyn Frampton, *Choosing Our Friends Wisely, Criteria For Engagement With Muslim Groups*, Policy Exchange London, 2009
6. See account of Richard Watson's investigation for *BBC 2 Newsnight* film, 14 December 2007, which made grave allegations about Policy Exchange's evidence for asserting that some reputable Muslim organisations were responsible for distributing hate literature.
7. Anthony Giddens, *The Politics Of Climate Change*, London: Polity, 2009.
8. James Lovelock, *The Vanishing Face Of Gaia: A Final Warning*.
9. *Pursue Prevent Protect Prepare—The United Kingdom's Strategy for Countering International Terrorism*, HM Government, March 2009.
10. In Malaya they also referred to focusing on the swamp rather than the mosquitoes and more recently General Petraeus's energetic advocacy for protecting the population before going after the obvious military wing of the insurgency. Thomas Ricks, *The Gamble*.

# BIBLIOGRAPHY

## BOOKS

Anwar, Muhammad, 'Muslims In Britain: Issues, Policy and Practice' in Abbas, Tahir (ed), *Muslim Britain, Communities Under Pressure*, United Kingdom: Zed Books, 2005.

Bacevich, Andrew, *The New American Militarism: How Americans Are Seduced By War*, Oxford: OUP, 2005.

Barnett, Correlli, *Britain And Her Army*, London: Penguin Press, 1972.

Bell, Daniel, *The Coming Of Post-Industrial Society: A Venture In Social Forecasting*, Hammondsworth: Penguin, 1976.

British Army Staff College, *Counter Revolutionary Warfare Handbook*, Camberley, 1989.

Cairncross, Frances, *The Death Of Distance 2.0: How The Communications Revolution Will Change Our Lives*, London: TEXERE Publishing Limited, 2001.

Chandrasekaran, Rajiv, *Imperial Life In The Emerald City*, London: Vintage, 2006.

Clapham, Anthony, *African Guerrillas*, Bloomington: Indiana University Press, 1998.

Cloake, John, *Templer, Tiger of Malaya: The Life Of Field Marshal Sir Gerald Templer*, London: Harrap, 1985.

Dallaire, Romeo, *Shake Hands With The Devil*, Canada: Knopf, 2003.

Dalrymple, William, *The Age Of Kali: Indian Travels And Encounters*, London: Flamingo, 2000.

Devji, Faisal, *Landscapes Of The Jihad*, London: Hurst, 2005.

Dobson, Christopher and Payne, Robert, *War Without End*, London: Harrap, 1986.

Duffield, Mark, *Global Governance And The New Wars*, London: Zed Books, 2001.

Etherington, Mark, *Revolt On The Tigris*, London: Hurst, 2005.

Forrest, Joshua, 'State Inversion and Non-state Politics' in Villalon, Leonardo and Huxtable, Phillip (eds.), *The African State At A Critical Juncture*, Boulder, CO: Lynne Reinner, 1998.

Furedi, Frank, *Invitation To Terror: The Expanding Empire Of The Unknown*, United Kingdom: Continuum, 2007.

Gerbner, George., 'Symbolic Functions of Violence and Terror' in Alexander, Yonah and Picard, R. G., *The Camera's Eye: News Coverage Of Terrorist Events*, Washington: Brassey's, 1990.

Giddens Anthony, *The Politics Of Climate Change*, London: Polity, 2009.

Griffith, Sam, *Mao Tse-Tung On Guerrilla Warfare*, New York: Praeger, 1961.

Guevara, Che, *Guerrilla Warfare*, Harmondsworth: Penguin, 1969.

Harvey, David, *Conditions Of Post Modernity*, Oxford: Blackwell, 1989, cited in Ed Hoogvelt., *Globalisation And The Post Colonial World 2nd Edition*, Basingstoke: Palgrave, 2001.

Held, David and McGrew, Anthony, et al., *Global Governance 5*, 1999.

Husain, Ed, *The Islamist*, London: Penguin Books, 2007.

Ignatieff, Michael, *The Warriors Honor: Ethnic War And The Modern Conscience*, London: Vintage, 1998.

Jawad, Huda, *Forgotten Voices: Developing more effective Engagement with Muslim Youth and Communities*, London: Forward Thinking, 2008.

Keen, David, *The Economic Functions Of Violence In Civil Wars*. Adelphi Papers, Routledge, 14 February 2005.

Kepel, Gilles, *The War For Muslim Minds*, Harvard: Belknap, 2004.

Kramer, Martin, 'The Moral Logic of Hizbullah' in Reich, W (ed.), *Origins Of Terrorism: Psychologies, Ideologies, Theologies, States Of Mind*, Cambridge: Cambridge University Press, 1990.

Kaldor, Mary, *New And Old Wars: Organised Violence In A Global Era*, Cambridge: Polity Press, 1999.

Kennedy, Paul 'Preparing for the 21st Century: Winners and Losers', *The New York Review Of Books*, 11 Feb 1993. Cited in O'Meara, Patrick, Mehlinger, Howard, and Krain, Matthew (eds), *Globalization And The Challenges Of A New Century: A Reader*, Bloomington: Indiana University Press, 2000.

Kwaja, Maruf, 'Muslims in Britain: Generations, Experiences, Futures', *Open Democracy*, 2 August 2005 in Pargeter, Alison, *The New Frontiers Of Jihad*, London: I.B. Tauris. 2008.

Lovelock, James, *The Vanishing Face Of Gaia: A Final Warning*. London: Penguin Books, 2009.

Mac Lochlainn, Piaras F., *Last Words: Letters And Statements Of The Leaders Executed After The Rising At Easter 1916.*

Maher, Shiraz and Frampton, Martyn, *Choosing Our Friends Wisely, Criteria For Engagement With Muslim Groups*, London: Policy Exchange, 2009.

Marchal, Roland, 'Forms of violence and ways to control it in an urban war zone: The *Mooryan* In Mogadishu' in Adam, Hussein and Clark, Richard (eds), *Mending Rips In The Sky: Options For Somali Communities In The 21st Century*, New Jersey: Red Sea Press.

Marcuse, Peter and van Kempen, Ronals, *Globalising Cities, A New Spatial Order*, Blackwell: Oxford, 2000.

Mehta, Ashkok K., *The Royal Nepalese Army: Meeting The Maoist Challenge*, Rupa, New Delhi, 2005.

Marks, Thomas, *Maoist Insurgency Since Vietnam*, London: Cass, 1996.

McDonald, Kevin, *Global Movements: Action And Culture*, Malden: Blackwell, 2006.

McKenzie, Lewis, *Peacekeeper, The Road to Sarajevo*, Douglas and McIntyre Ltd., 1993.

Meisner, Maurice, *Mao Zedong*, Cambridge: Polity Press, 2007.

Mueller, John, *How Politicians and the Terrorism Industry Inflate National Security Threats and Why We Believe Them*, Routledge: United Kingdom, 2007.

Nagl, John, *Counter Insurgency Lessons from Malaya and Vietnam*, London: Praeger 2002.

Nasiri, Omar, *Inside The Global Jihad: How I Infiltrated Al Qaeda And Was Abandoned By Western Intelligence*, Hurst: London, 2006.

O'Meara, Patrick, Mehliinger, Howard, and Krain, Matthew (eds), *Globalization And The Challenges Of A New Century: A Reader*, Bloomington: Indiana University Press, 2000.

O'Neill, Bard, *Insurgency And Terrorism: Inside Modern Revolutionary Warfare*, Washington: Brassey's, 1990.

O'Shaughnessy, Nicholas Jackson, *Politics And Propaganda: Weapons Of Mass Seduction*, Ann Arbor: University of Michigan Press, 2004.

Oppenheimer, Martin, *Urban Guerrilla*, Chicago: Quadrangle Books, 1969.

Orwell, George, *Homage To Catalonia*, Penguin: London, 1962.

Phillips, Melanie, *Londonistan: How Britain Is Creating A Terror State Within*, London: Gibson Square, 2006.

Reno, William, *Warlord Politics And African States*, Boulder: Lynne Reinner, 1998.

Ricks, Thomas, *The Gamble*, Penguin Press: USA, 2009.

——, *Fiasco: The American Military Adventure In Iraq*, Washington: Penguin, 2006.

Rubin, Barry, 'The origins of the PLO's terrorism' in Rubin, Barry (ed.), *Terrorism And Politics*, London: Macmillan, 1991.

Sampson, Anthony, *The Midas Touch: Money People And Power From The East To The West*, London: Hodder and Stoughton, 1989.

Schram, Stuart, *Mao Tse-Tung Basic Tactics*, New York: Praeger, 1961.

Sewall, Sarah, 'Introduction' in *US Army/Marine Corps Counterinsurgency Field Manual*, Chicago: University of Chicago Press, 2007.

Shaw, George Bernard, *Saint Joan*, London: Penguin, 1960.

Stewart, Bob, *Broken Lives*, Harper Collins; London. 1994.

Stewart, Rory, *Occupational Hazards: My Time Governing In Iraq*. London: Picador, 2006.

Stiglitz, Joseph and Bilmes Linda, *The Three Trillion Dollar War: The True Cost Of The Iraq War*, New York: W W Norton and Co., 2008.

Tatham, Steve, *Losing Arab Hearts And Minds: The Coalition, Al Jazeera And Muslim Public Opinion*, London: Hurst and Co., 2006.

Teece, (2003) in Fowler, HW., *A Dictionary Of Modern English Usage*, revised by Gowers, Ernest, Oxford, 1965.

The International Institute for Strategic Studies, *The Military Balance*, London: Routledge. 2008.

*The 9/11 Commission Report: The Full Final Report of the National Commission on Terrorist Attacks Upon the United States*, W.W. Norton & Co., 26 July 2004.

Thomas, Timothy, *Cyber Silhouettes*, Foreign Military Studies Office, Leavenworth (2006).

Tse-Tung, Mao, *Selected Works*, London: Lawrence and Wishart, 1958.

Tugwell, Maurice, 'Terrorism and Propaganda' in Wilkinson Paul and Stewart Alasdair, (eds), *Contemporary Research On Terrorism*, Aberdeen: Aberdeen University Press, 1989.

Wilkinson, Paul, *Terrorism Versus Democracy: The Liberal State Response*, London: Routledge, 2006.

Zarrow, Peter, *China In War And Revolution—1895-1949*, London: Routledge, 2005.

Zahar, Marie-Joelle, 'Reframing the Spoiler Debate in Peace Processes' in Darby, Ed and MacGinty, Roger, *Contemporary Peacemaking—Conflict, Violence And Peace Processes*. United Kingdom: Palgrave Macmillan, 2003.

Zhao, Yuezhi, 'Falun Gong, Identity, and the Struggle over Meaning Inside and Outside China' in Couldry, Nick and Curran, James (eds), *Contesting Media Power: Alternative Media In A Networked World*, Lanham: Rowman & Littlefield, 2003.

## INTERVIEWS

Author's research visit to Freetown, Sierra Leone, September 2001.
Correspondence with General Alastair Irwin, 16 April 2009.
Correspondence with General Alastair Irwin, 17 April 2009.
Correspondence with Professor Frank Gregory, 19 April 2009.
Correspondence with Doctor Daniel Marston June 2009.
Correspondence with Doctor David Betz December 2008.
Interview and correspondence with Dr Kevin O'Brien, March 2009.
Interviews at GMP Regional Headquarters, Old Trafford Manchester, 18 February 2009.
Interviews with battalion officers, 1st Battalion Green Howards and Norwegian contingent, 2004.
Interview with Dennis Bright, Commission for Conciliation and Peace, (Freetown, Sierra Leone), September 2001.

Interview with Dr Kevin O'Brien at Kings College London, October 2008.

Interview with executive officials of *Forward Thinking*, London, August 2008.

Interview with former Home Office official at Kings College London, November 2008.

Interview with former Home Office officials of (OSCT), at Kings College London, October 2008.

Interview with John Dunstan, Regional Prevent Delivery Manager for Government Offices North West (Manchester), 18 Feb 2009.

Interview with Garry Hindle at the Royal United Services Institute London (Department of Homeland Security and Resilience), 28 October 2008.

Interview with General Richards for *RUSI*, April 2007.

Interview with General Sir Mike Jackson, 1996.

Interview with local NGO in Manchester, 17 February 2009.

Interviews, Manchester, 2006.

Interview of NCOs of 1st Battalion Cheshire Regiment, 1993.

Interview with official of Department of Communities and Local Government, Home Office London, August 2007.

Interviews with officials in United Kingdom Home Office, Community Cohesion Department, in February and June 2007.

Interview with Paul Molinaro, Department of Defence Management and Security Analysis, Cranfield University, 6 August 2001.

Interview with Staff Officers—Metropolitan Police (Communities Together team), London, October 2008.

Interview with sources in East London, 2007.

Supervising the MA theses of British officers at the United Kingdom Joint Services Command and Staff College 2005/6 who had recently served in Iraq.

## JOURNALS

Barber, Benjamin R, 'Jihad vs. McWorld', *Atlantic Monthly*, (March 1992).

Bhupendra Jasani, 'Orbiting Spies: Opportunities and Challenges', *Space Policy*, No 18 (2002).

Brennan, Rick, Grissom, Adam, Daly, Sara, Chalk, Peter, Rosenau, William, Sepp, Kalev, and Dalzell, Steve, *Future Insurgent Threats*, RAND (California), (February 2005).

Coolsaet, Rick 'Anarchist Outrages', *Le Monde Diplomatique*, September 2004, cited in Bolt, Neville, 'Propaganda of the Deed and the Irish Republican Brotherhood' *RUSI Journal*, Vol 153, No 1, (2008).

Crystal Procyshen, 'Islam, Institutions and Insurgency', in *Conflict, Security, and Development*, Vol 1, No 3, (2001).

Donald D., 'Local beats Global' Submission to BISA, Cambridge, December 2007.

Freedman, Lawrence, 'The Transformation of Strategic Affairs', *Adelphi Paper 379*, (Oxford: Routledge), International Institute for Strategic Studies, (2006).

Gompert, David C., and Gordon, John IV., (et al.), *War By Other Means*, RAND, (California), (2008).

Hoffman Bruce, 'Insurgency and Counter-insurgency in Iraq', *Occasional Papers*, 127, RAND (California), (2004).

Howard, Michael, 'Mistake to Declare this a War', *RUSI Journal*, 146, 6 (2001).

Keen, David, 'The Economic Functions of Violence in Civil Wars'. *Adelphi Paper 320*, (New York: Oxford University Press), International Institute for Strategic Studies, (1998).

Linden, Eugene, 'Exploding Cities of the Developing World', *Foreign Affairs*, Vol 75, No 1, (1996).

Mackinlay, John, 'Globalisation and Insurgency', *Adelphi Paper 352*, (Oxford), International Institute for Strategic Studies, (2002).

Mackinlay, John and Al-Baddawy, Alison, *Re-thinking Counterinsurgency*, RAND, 5 (California), (2006).

Malik, Shiv, 'My Brother the Bomber', *Prospect Magazine*, 135, (June 2007).

Marginson, Simon and Sawir, Erlenawati, 'Interrogating Global Flows in Higher Education', *Globalisation Society and Education*, Vol 3, No 3 (2005).

Rabassa, Angel, Chalk, Peter, Cragin, Kim, Daly, Sara, Gregg, Heather, Krasik, Theodore W, O'Brein, Kevin, Rosenau, William, *Beyond al-Qaeda: Part 1, The Global jihadist Movement*, RAND (California), (2006).

Rosin, Paul, Millman, Linda and Nemerhoff, Carol, 'Operations of the laws of sympathetic magic in disgust and their domains', *Journal of Personality and Social Psychology*, No 50, (1986).

Sageman, Marc, 'The Next Generation of Terror', *Foreign Policy*, (March / April 2008).

Webster, Frank, 'Making Sense of the Information Age', *Information, Communication and Society*, 8, 4, (December 2005).

## WEB SOURCES

Afghan National Development Strategy, www.ands.gov.af.

Ambassador Henry A. Crumpton, 'The Changing Face of Terror: A Post-9/11 Assessment', 13 June 2006, http://www.senate.gov/Senate404.html.

Ambassador Henry A Crumpton, 'Testimony Before the Senate Committee on Foreign Relations', 13 June 2006, http://www.senate.gov/Senate404.html.

Bakunin, Mikhail, *Letters to a Frenchman on the Present Crisis*, 1870, www.marxists.org/reference/archive/bakunin/works/1870/letter-frenchman.htm.

'Behavioural Science Unit Operational briefing note: Understanding Radicalisation and Violent Extremism in the UK', Report No BSU/02/2008, *The Guardian*, 12 June 2008, http://image.guardian.co.uk/sys-files/Guardian/documents/2008/08/20/mi5.pdf.

Burke, Jason, 'Britain Stops Talk of "War on Terror"', *The Observer*, 10 December 2006.

Castells, Manuel, et al., www.manuelcastells.info/en/index.htm.

'Civil-Military Relationship in Complex Emergencies', *Inter-Agency Standing Committee*, IASC Reference Paper, 28 June 2004, http://www.humanitarianinfo.org/iasc/pageloader.aspx?page=content-products-products&sel=8.

'Community Pride not Prejudice', Bradford Race Review, *2020 Vision*, 2001, http://www.bradford2020.com/pride/report.pdf.

Coughlin, Con Gardham, Duncan, and Harding, Thomas, 'British Muslims fighting with "Taliban in Afghanistan"', *The Daily Telegraph*, 2 August 2008, http://www.telegraph.co.uk/news/worldnews/asia/afghanistan/2485750/British-Muslims-fighting-with-Taliban-in-Afghanistan.html.

CRS Report for Congress, *US Military Casualty Statistics*, (Code R522452), 18, March 2008.

De Bruxelles, Simon and Fresco, Adam, 'Suspected suicide bomber in Exeter, Nicky Reilly, "was sent a message of support"', *The Times* (London), 24 May 2008, http://www.timesonline.co.uk/tol/news/uk/crime/article3994866.ece.

'European Muslim Population', *Muslim Population Worldwide*, www.islamicpopulation.com/europe_general.html.

*Foreign Policy Aspects of the War on Terrorism*, House Commons Foreign Affairs Committee, 15 October 2003, http://www.publications.parliament.uk/pa/cm200203/cmselect/cmfaff/cmfaff.htm.

*FY 2007-2012 Department of State and USAID Strategic Plan: Transformational Diplomacy*, US Department of State, 7 May 2007, http://www.state.gov/s/d/rm/rls/dosstrat/2007/.

Giridharadas, Anand and Perlez, Jane. 'Severe Personality Shift Seen in Bomb Suspect', *The New York Times*, 9 July 2007. http://www.nytimes.com/2007/07/09/world/asia/09britain.html.

Gray, John, 'A Trail of Terror Stretching 200 Years', *The Times* (London), June 30 2007. http://www.timesonline.co.uk/tol/comment/columnists/guest_contributors/article2007476.ece.

Greene, Richard, 'UK troops face trauma after Iraq', *BBC*, 12 August 2005, http://news.bbc.co.uk/1/hi/uk/4632263.stm.

Hickley, Matthew and Chapman, James. 'Fury as injured soldiers are denied aid as defence chiefs refuse to reveal casualty lists', *Mail Online*, 22 September 2006, Accessed from http://www.dailymail.co.uk/news/article-406558/Fury-injured-soldiers-denied-aid-defence-chiefs-refuse-reveal-casualty-list.html on 18 August 2008.

International Crisis Group, 'Taliban Propaganda: Winning the War of Words?', *ICG Asia Report*, 158, 24 July 2008, http://www.crisisgroup.org/home/index.cfm?id=5589.

'Karzai survives attempt on his life', *BBC*, 5 September 2002, http://news.bbc.co.uk/2/hi/south_asia/2238428.stm.

Kilcullen, David, 'Anatomy of a Tribal Revolt', *Small Wars Journal blog*, 29 August 2007, http://smallwarsjournal.com/blog/2007/08/anatomy-of-a-tribal-revolt/.

John Gieve, Home Secretary to Sir Andrew Turnbull, Secretary of the Cabinet, 10 May 2004, www.globalsecurity.org/security/library/report/2004/muslimext-uk.htm.

Maher, Shiraz, and Frampton Martyn, *Choosing Our Friends Wisely, Criteria for Engagement with Muslim Groups*, Policy Exchange London, 2009, http://www.policyexchange.org.uk/images/publications/pdfs/Choosing_Our_Friends_Wisely.pdf.

*National Strategy for Combating Terrorism*, 2003, US Government, 2003. Found in http://www.fas.org/irp/threat/nsct2006.pdf.

Nelson Fraser. 'Al Qa'eda's secret UK Gangs: Terror As A "Playground Dare"', *The Spectator*, 18 March 2008, http://www.spectator.co.uk/the-magazine/features/564271/alqaedas-secret-uk-gangs-terror-as-a-playground-dare.thtml.

*The Observer*, Editorial, 2 Jan 2000.

*OCHA Orientation Handbook on Complex Emergencies*, Office for the Coordination of Humanitarian Affairs, August 1999, http://www.reliefweb.int/library/documents/ocha__orientation__handbook_on__.htm.

'Officials "haven't the faintest idea" of immigrant count', *The Times* (London), 17 May 2006, http://www.timesonline.co.uk/tol/news/uk/article719671.ece.

'Oldham Riots, Two Perspectives', *BBC*, Information reported on 20 August 2007, http://news.bbc.co.uk.

'Operation AGILA/Operation Midford: The British Empire's Last Sunset', *Digger History*, 2000, http://www.diggerhistory.info/pages-conflicts-periods/other/rhodesia.htm Rhodesia.htm.

'Operations in Afghanistan: British Casualties', UK Ministry of Defence, http://www.mod.uk/DefenceInternet/FactSheets/OperationsFactsheets/OperationsInAfghanistanBritishCasualties.htm.

'Operations in Iraq: British Casualties', UK Ministry of Defence, http://www.mod.uk/DefenceInternet/FactSheets/OperationsFactsheets/OperationsInIraqBritishCasualties.htm.

'Quadrennial Defense Review Report', US Department of Defense, 6 February 2006, http://www.globalsecurity.org/military/library/policy/dod/qdr-2006-report.htm.

Sappenfield, Mark and Rice-Oxley, Mark, 'Global terror's India connection', *Christian Science Monitor*, 10 July 2007, http://www.csmonitor.com/2007/0710/p01s02-wosc.html.

'Select Committee on Foreign Affairs, Third Report', House of Commons, February 2006, http://www.publications.parliament.uk/pa/cm200607/cmselect/cmfaff/269/26905.htm.

Sennott, Charles, 'The General's Knowledge', *The Times* (London), 29 June 2008, http://www.timesonline.co.uk/tol/news/world/us_and_americas/article4212055.ece.

'Strategic Programme Fund—Countering Terrorism & Radicalisation (CTR) Programme', Foreign and Commonwealth Office, http://www.fco.gov.uk/en/about-the-fco/what-we-do/funding-programmes/strat-progr-fund/strat-pro-fund-terrorism.

Sutherland, John and Devji, Faisal, 'The Ideas Interview: Faisal Devji', *The Guardian*, 17 October 2005, http://www.guardian.co.uk/world/2005/oct/17/alqaida.academicexperts.

'Taliban Executive Order', Office of the Press Secretary, 3 July 2002, http://georgewbush-whitehouse.archives.gov/news/releases/2002/07/20020703-1.html.

Tatham, Steve, 'Hearts and Minds: Time to Think Differently', *Naval Review*, http://da.academia.edu/SteveTATHAM/Papers/90066/Hearts-and-Minds—Time-to-think-differently-.

Temko, Ned and Townshend, Mark, 'Scandal of treatment for wounded Iraq veterans', *The Observer*, 11 March 2007, http://www.guardian.co.uk/uk/2007/mar/11/military.health.

Travis, Alan, 'MI5 Report Challenges Views on Terrorism in Britain', *The Guardian*, 21 August 2008, http://www.guardian.co.uk/uk/2008/aug/20/uksecurity.terrorism1.

*US Casualties in Iraq*, Global Security Organisation, 31 July 2008.

## DOCUMENTS

*Army Code 71779 (Draft 1)*, *UK Ministry of Defence*, September 2007, (not yet published).

'Counter-insurgency Operations', *UK Ministry of Defence Army Field Manual*, 2001.

'Counter-insurgency Operations', *UK Army Field Manual*, Vol 1, Part 10.

'Countering Insurgency—A Guide for Commanders', *US Army Field Manual*, 3-24 and *British Army Field Manual*.

'Countering Insurgency—A Handbook for Commanders', United Kingdom Army draft—Army Code 71749.

'Counter-Revolutionary Operations', in *Land Operations* Volume III, Part 1, 2 and 3. Printed for HMSO by Bemrose, Derby, United Kingdom Ministry of Defence, 1977.

*Counter-Revolutionary Operations Part I: General Principles*, United Kingdom Ministry of Defence, 1977.

'Defence Diplomacy', *The Ministry of Defence Policy Papers, Number 1*, United Kingdom Ministry of Defence, (Produced by) the Director General Corporate Communication, London.

*Director General Doctrine and Development Tactical Handbook for Operations other than War*, United Kingdom Ministry of Defence, 1998.

HMSO, 'Wider Peacekeeping', *Army Field Manual*, Vol 5, Part 2, (interim version), 1994.

HMSO, *Peace Support Operations*, (JWP 3-50), 1996.

HMSO, *The Military Contribution to Peace Support Operations*, (JWP 3-50, Second Edition), 2004.

*Land Operations Vol III Counter Revolutionary Operations*, UK Ministry of Defence, Part I, 1977.

'Operations Other Than War—Counter-insurgency Operations', *UK Ministry of Defence Army Field Manual*, Vol 5, 1995.

*Pursue Prevent Protect Prepare—The United Kingdom's Strategy for Countering International Terrorism*, HM Government, March 2009.

Rufin, Jean-Christophe, 'The Economics of War: A New Theory for Armed Conflicts', *Forum: International Committee of the Red Cross* (Geneva), Series 2, 2000.

Talani, Leila in *Out of Egypt; Globalisation, Marginalisation and illegal Migration to the EU*, UCLA Centre for European and Eurasian Studies, 2005.

*The United Kingdom's Strategy for Countering International Terrorism*, British Government publication, 24 March 2009.

Tugwell, Maurice, *Revolutionary Propaganda and Possible Counter Measures*, PhD Thesis, King's College London—Department of War Studies, Submitted March 1979.

*UK Army (Directorate General Development and Doctrine) Land Operations*, UK Ministry of Defence, May 2005.

*UK Keeping the Peace*, published in 1957, revised in 1963.

'British Doctrine of the Cold War Period', *UK Ministry of Defence, Counter-Revolutionary Operations*, Land Operations, Vol 3, part 1, 1977.

RESEARCH CENTRES

Anwar, Muhammad and Qadir, Bakhsh, *British Muslims and State Policies*, Warwick Centre for Research in Ethnic Relations in EU Commission, 2003.

Eyal, J., '*War in Iraq: Combat and Consequence*', Whitehall Paper 59, *RUSI*, 2003.

*Muslim Americans*, PEW Research Center, 22 May 2007.

*The Great Divide: How Westerners and Muslims View Each Other*, PEW Global Attitudes Project, 22 June 2006.

*The Military Contribution to Peace Support Operations*, Joint Warfare Publication—Joint Doctrine and Concepts Centre, Swindon, 2004.

## CONFERENCES/LECTURES

Bilmes, Linda and Stiglitz, Joseph, *The Economic Costs of the Iraq War: An appraisal three years after the beginning of the conflict*, ASSA Meetings, Boston, January 2006, National Bureau of Economic Research, Working Paper 12054, issued in February 2006.

Buller, Eliza Manningham, Lecture at Queen Mary's College, University of London, 9 November 2006.

Castells Manuel, 'Internet Beyond Myths: the Record of Scholarly Research', Lecture—London School of Economics and Political Science, 24 October 2008.

Inter-Agency Standing Committee, 10th Meeting, (IASC), December 1994.

Inter-Agency Standing Committee, *Saving Lives Together: A Framework for improving Security Arrangements Among IGOs, NGOs and UN in the Field*, 66th Working Group Meeting, 15-17 November, 2006.

Inter-Agency Standing Committee, *Working Paper on the Definition of Complex Emergency*, December 1994.

Omand, David, 'Nature of War Conference', Lecture—Christchurch, University of Oxford, 13 September 2007.

Royal United Services Institute, 'Understanding Suicide Terrorism: A Homeland Security and Resilience Department Workshop', London, 3 November 2006.

RUSI conference series 'Transformation of Military Operations on the Cusp', in *Royal United Services Institute for Defence and Security Studies In Partnership with United States Joint Forces Command Transformation*, 14-16 March 2005.

## MAGAZINES

Burke, Jason, 'The Britons Who Became Bombers', *Observer Magazine*, 20 January 2008.

'Internet Jihad—a world wide web of terror', *The Economist* (Print Edition), 14 July 2007.

## TV and RADIO

*BBC Radio 4 News*, 27 May 2001.

Gardner, Frank, 'Analysis: al Qaeda's Enemy Within', Radio 4 Current Affairs, (Transcript of a recorded documentary), BBC—White City, London, 7 August 2008.

'General Jack Keene on the Jim Lehrer News Hour', *Jim Lehrer News Hour*, 18 April 2006.

Watson, Richard, BBC *Newsnight*, 14 December 2007.


FILMS

*Apocalypse Now*, Dir. Francis F Coppola, Paramount, 1979.

*Control Room*, Dir. Jehane Noujaim, Noujaim Films, 2004.

# INDEX

Note: Bold page numbers refer to Tables; those in italics refer to Figures.

Abu Baseer al Tartisi, 189
activism
  local community focus (UK),
    215–16
  promoted by mass communication,
    95, 101
  propaganda and, 129–30
  radical Islamist, 4, 106, 107, 207–9
actors, multiple, 89–92, 95, 96
Afghanistan, 47
  attack on National Day parade
    (2008), 133–4
  casualties, **184**
  co-existing insurgencies, 157, 160,
    166, 172–3
  and global jihad, 107–8
  International Security Assistance
    Force (IASF), 157
  post-Maoist insurgency, 95, 105
  role of population, 81–2
  Soviet occupation, 107
  US-led coalition in, 3, 4, 6–7, 99,
    169
  weak national leadership, 191
  *see also* expeditionary response to
    insurgency
Africa, 32, 240*n*
  civil wars, 36
  Horn of, 175, 188
  insurgents, 37

migrants from, 85, 103
NATO interventions, 52, 62
sub-Saharan, 2, 240*n*
aid agencies, international, interventions by, 86–7, 89, 90
AKP (Islamist party), Turkey, 106
Al-Jazeera news station, 134, 184–5
al-Qaeda, 3, 106, 197, 201
  and 11 September attacks, 69, 167
  Muslim condemnation of, 189,
    190, 261*n*
  "nebula", 160
  US interpretation of, 167, 168,
    173, 188
  weakening of, 188–9
Algeria, Islamic Salvation Front, 106
Anarchists, Russian empire, 126–7
anti-globalisation movements, 153–4
Anwar, Muhammad, 110
armed forces, public isolation from,
  185
art, narrative and propaganda, 132–3
aspiration, to define insurgents, 36–7

Bahrain, Shi'a activists in, 106
Balkans, 52, 178
BBC World Service, 34
Beeston, Notts, Mullah boys (gang
  culture), 115–16, 117, 118, 119,
  202

Bell, Daniel 136
Berlin Wall, dismantling (1989) 77
"black hole" areas, weak states 177
Blair, Tony, Prime Minister 212, 228
Bolt, Neville 126, 127, 253n
Borneo, North 1, 49
Bosnia 47, 68
Bradford, Muslim communities 108
Brennan, Rick 158–60
British Army Staff College
    1989 handbook 63–4, 65–6
    counter-insurgency scenario 63–4
    and peace support operations 67,
        69, 246n, 248n
British doctrine
    2001 counter-insurgency doctrine
        76, 88
    battalion-level operations 48, 243n
    colonial version of counter-insur-
        gency 62–6
    Defence Diplomacy 176
    failure to recognise post-Maoist
        insurgency 165
    limitations of 47–54
    misapprehension about "global war
        on terror" 74
    "Operations Other than War"
        handbook 69
    and propaganda of the deed 57, 59
    "Wider Peacekeeping" 88
British Empire 83–4, 191
    colonial administration 51–2, 89
    insurgencies 15, 86
    see also decolonisation
Brown, Gordon, Chancellor of the
    Exchequer 186
Bush, George W., US President 172,
    187, 188, 202
Butt, Hassan 118

Cambodia 67, 82
Cantle, Professor Ted 108–9, 202
Castells, Manuel 137, 156
casualties, Iraq and Afghanistan
    184–5, **184**

Central America, civil wars 36
centre of gravity, concept of 82–3, 94,
    97, 144, 147–8, 256n
Charles I, and Common Prayer Book
    125
Children's Trusts, 216
China
    to early 19th century 15–16
    Falun Gong movement 154
    Mao Tse-Tung's campaign 15–19
    People's Republic 19
    rural areas 35–6
    see also Maoist Insurgency
Christian Aid 104
"citizen journalists" 93
civil agencies, role in interventions
    179, 183–4
civil wars, post-Cold War 36
clans, insurgent type 39–40
Clapham, Anthony 37
climate change, and migration 104,
    232–3
co-existing insurgencies 157–60
Cold War 12, 27
    and counter-insurgency 23–4,
        84–5
    end of 28–9, 36, 77, 136
communications
    between individuals 92–3
    digital 93
    revolution in 5, 31–2, 43, 92–5,
        198, 224
    state surveillance of 41
    see also mass communications
"complex emergencies" 62, 87–8, 156,
    245n
    IASC definition 88–9, 248n
concerned populations 145–6, 148
containerisation, effect on illegal
    trade 30
CONTEST strategy (UK Home
    Office counter-terrorism) 8,
    212–14, 219, 227–8, 34–6
    architecture 212–13, 228

defects of 235–6
Prevent strategy 214, 216–18, *216*
Pursue programme 216, *216*
regional operations 214–18
counter-insurgency 10, 12, 46
    colonial version of 1–2, 49–50,
        62–6
    disadvantages of 43–7, 223
    evolution of 227–31
    failure to adapt 12–13, 43–60,
        61–2
    failures of interventions (1990s)
        53, 86–7, 88, 143
    future for 231–3
    international coalitions 41, 53–4,
        91
    lack of coherence 91–2, 96–7,
        227–8, 244*n*
    local operations 228–30, 231
    and mass communication 31–2,
        94–5
    and model of radicalisation 208–9
    multiple actors 89–90
    and multiple populations 147–8
    and networks 138–9
    and post-Maoist military context
        155–6
    relationship to peacekeeping op-
        erations 2–3, 66–72, 87–8
    and response to propaganda of the
        deed 130, 135
    and social structure 6
    and use of narrative 134
    and war on terror 6, 169–70
    *see also* domestic response; expedi-
        tionary response; "Global War
        on Terror"; interventions
counter-terrorism
    British plans 209–12
    concentration on 70, 71–2, 135
    officials' lack of experience 91,
        199–200, 235–6
Crime and Disorder Reduction
    Partnerships (CDRP) 216–17

crime, organised 73, *73*, 247*n*
Crumpton, Ambassador Henry A.
    189
Cuban revolution 36
cultural change 33–5
culture
    alternative offered by Islamism 124
    and differing response to insur-
        gency 46
    in migrant communities 113–14
    rejection of British (among mi-
        grants) 114–17
currency markets 32–3

Dayton Agreement (1996) 2
decision-making
    in post-Maoist counter-insurgency
        98
    in state reconstruction 183–4
decolonisation 48–9, 86
    and Maoist insurgency 36
    and nationalist insurgencies 12,
        19–20, 84–5
deeds, effect of 124–5
democracy
    establishment of 181–2
    and restraints on state action 46,
        191, 234
developing countries *see* weak states
development agencies 33
diasporas
    influence of 147–8
    and insurgency 12, 73–4, 82–3
    and mass communication 94, 96,
        123, 142
    and PLO campaign 59–60, 94
"disembodied terrorist" 74
Dobbie, Lt Colonel Charles 246*n*
doctrine
    capacity for evolution 232
    changed concept of "the enemy"
        136
    failure of 42, 91, 164–5
    humanitarian interventions 87–8

and propaganda of the deed 130
reappraisal after 11 September
    attacks 100
and significance of networks 138–9
domestic response to insurgency 169,
    197–218
    UK counter-terrorist campaign
        198–200

economic deregulation, effect on
    insurgency 32–3, 35
Edinburgh, 17th-century riots 125
education, migrants and 103, 114–15
Egypt
    Islamic Jihad 106
    Muslim Brotherhood 106
emotion
    and propaganda 131
    in US response to 9/11 attacks
        171–2, 195
environment
    to define insurgent 37–8
    urban 21–2
European states
    complexity of political response
        195–6
    domestic threat 168–9, 194–5
    and fall of Berlin Wall 77
    Muslim migrants in 102, 103–4,
        150, 168
    open borders 194
    perspective on Afghanistan and
        Iraq 192–6
    response to post-Maoist insur-
        gency 136, 227–31
    view of US war on terror 7, 167–9,
        194–5
    view of warfare 192
expeditionary response to insurgency
    169, 171–96
    casualty costs 184–5
    characteristics 179–80
    concept of 173–6, 234
    European perspective 192–6

financial costs 186
motives for intervention 176–8
status of occupier 180
training and assistance missions
    175, 176
US objectives 178
US perspective 187–91
utility of 186–7
and withdrawal strategies 191
see also interventions
Eyal, Jonathan 169, 192

Falun Gong movement, China 154
Faraj-al-Liki, Abu, capture of 188
fear, of terrorism 187–8
federated insurgency complex (FIC)
    159, 160, 162
feral militias 38–40, 42
    clans 39–40
    links with other insurgencies
        156–7
    resistance to peace support opera-
        tions 68
Foreign Office (UK)
    and counter-terrorism 111, 211
    and peace support operations 67
France 103
    counter-insurgency doctrine 76
Franks, General 171
Freedman, Lawrence 134
funding
    by superpowers 28
    from trade 28–9
Furedi, Frank 187–8

Gama'a al Islamiyya 106
gang culture, among young Muslims
    115–16, 117, 118, 119
Gapon, Georgi 126
Gardner, Frank, Radio 4 broadcast
    (2008) 190
Gaza Strip 55
    Israeli bombing (2008/9) 214–15,
        264n

Geddes, Jenny 125
Geneva Conventions 180
Germany 28, 76, 103
Giddens, Anthony 233
global insurgency 41–2, 47, 73–4, *73*, 78, 223
    centrality of virtual networks 139–40
    compared with national insurgency 104–8
    evolution of 47
    as generic instrument 231–3
    international actors 85
    operational nature 224
    *see also* networks; post-Maoist insurgency
global jihad 48, 97, 106, 158
    as cultural alternative 124
    and globalisation 101
    Maoist operational concept 78
    structure and organisation 107–8
    Western surprise at 75, 227
global movements 153–4
"Global War on Terror" 4, 6–7, 76, 99, 227
    and campaign in Afghanistan 172
    and definition of insurgency 10
    effect of doctrine failures on 166
    effect on Muslim migrant communities 168, 189–90, 194–5, 198, 210
    European view of 7, 167–9, 194–5
    fallacy of 74
    and fear 188
    and motives for interventions 176–8
globalisation
and cultural change 34–5
effect on insurgency 27–8, 77–8, 101
Gompert, David 157
Gowing, Nik 93
Great Britain
    anti-war public opinion 185

Civil Contingencies Act (2004) 264*n*
Community Cohesion Review Team 108
CONTEST strategy 212–18, *219*, 227–8
counter-insurgency tradition 11, 48, 198, 199, 230–1, 242–3*n*
counter-terrorism plans 209–12
"insurgency" in 200–9
internal security campaign 7–8, 198–218
isolation of armed forces 185
limitations of counter-insurgency doctrine 47–54
migrants in 103, 233, 250*n*
Muslim immigrants 108–13
    MI5 research into 203–9
Office of Security Counter Terrorism (OSCT) 213
policy towards refugees 201
role of Home Office 199–200, 212–14, 230, 235–6
role of police forces 199–200, 214, 216–18
    *see also* British doctrine; British Empire
grievance
    and disaffection 206–7, 228
    manipulation of 22, 125
Guantanamo Bay 194
*Guardian, The* 203
guerrilla warfare, compared to insurgency 23
Guevara, Che 36
Guomindang (GMD) forces 16
Gurkha Rifles, 6th 1–2

Hamas 106, 158
Hambali, capture of 188
Hizb ut-Tahrir 106, 117, 118
Hizbollah, Lebanon 106, 158
Home Office (UK), role in counter-terrorism 199–200, 212–14, 230, 235–6

Horn of Africa 175, 188
host-state populations 145
    influence on interventions 181–2
    reaction to interventions 84–5, 88,
        173, 179, 180, 191
Howard, Michael 111–12
"human terrain" 22
humanitarian disasters, and public
    opinion 86
humanitarian interventions 87–8, 143
Husain, Ed 116–17, 118

ideology
    in global insurgency 42
    Mao's use of 18–19
    power of 21
    spread by new communications 31
IISS Asian Security Summit (2007)
    104
image, use of 133–4, 141, 142
India, and Sri Lanka 82
Indonesia 32
industrialisation, and changing
    environment 21
"information asymmetry" 93–4, 95
insurgency 197
    concept of 2–3, 9–10
    definitions 4–5, 9–10, 223
    as evolutionary 5–6, 10, 42, 61,
        72–6, 223–4
    monolithic nature of 35, 42
    as political process 4–5, 223, 231
    proliferation of 35–42
    relationship with terrorism 70–2
    social origins 5–6, 12
    see also global insurgency; Mao-
        ist insurgency; post-Maoist
        insurgency
insurgency, types of 72, 73, 156, 223
    feral militias 38–40, 42, 68, 72
    global insurgents 41–2
    popular insurgents 40
insurgent archipelago 221–36
insurgents

celebrity (notoriety) 56, 57, 58, 59
    in collapsing states 68
    typology of British Muslims 205–9
intelligence
    and end of Cold War 77
    role in counter-terrorism 202, 213,
        218
Inter Agency Standing Committee
    (IASC), definition of complex
    emergencies 88–9
Intergovernmental Panel on Climate
    Change (IPCC) 104
International Security Assistance
    Force (IASF), Afghanistan 157
Internet 31, 93, 222
    anonymity 139–40
    networks 137, 138
    and radicalisation 119, 152
    state monitoring 41
interventions
    casualty costs 184–5
    complexity of 89, 173
    doctrine 87–8
    four functions of 90
    lack of coherence 91–2, 96–7, 179
    multinational (UN) 53, 86–7, 88,
        143, 180–1, 187
    multiple actors in 89–90
    NATO 52–4, 62
    ownership of reconstruction pro-
        cesses 183–4
    political intentions 177–8
    reactions of populations to 84–5,
        88, 173, 179, 180
    responsibilities of intervening
        forces 182–3
    status of occupier 180
    US-led (unilateral) 181
    see also expeditionary response;
        peacekeeping; weak states
Iraq
    casualties 184–5, **184**
    co-existing insurgencies 105, 160,
        166

Coalition's lack of authority 52
invasion (2003) 3, 99
role of population 81–2
Sadrist movement 158
Sunni insurrectionists 106
weak national leadership 191
*see also* expeditionary response to
   insurgency
Ireland 15
Easter Rising 127–8
*see also* Northern Ireland
Irish Republican Army (IRA) 12, 55
and diaspora 94
government engagement with
   230–1
and propaganda of the deed
   129–30, 253*n*
use of media 123, 131
Irish Republican Brotherhood 54,
   127–8
Irwin, General Alastair 66, 246*n*
Islam
and concept of Ummah (Islamic
   world state) 106, 158
deterritorialisation 97, 106,
   149–50, 190
and Islamist revival 103
and national liberation movements
   106, 158
Sufism 116
*see also* Islamism
Islamic Action Front, Jordan 106
Islamic Jihad 106
Islamism 103, 200–1
British military doctrine and 59
forms of 105–6, 158
and globalised insurgency 78,
   100–1, 154
media interest in 75, 99
propaganda of the deed 154
radical activism 4, 101, 106, 107
and radicalisation 113–14, 115–17
recruitment 119, 204
*see also* global jihad

isolation
of armed forces from public 185
as factor in Muslim radicalisation
   113–14
of Maoist insurgencies 92
Israel, and PLO 55–60

Jackson, General Mike 53, 248*n*
Jamat-e-Islami 116
Jinggangshan (mountains), China
   16–17
Jordan 55
Islamic Action Front 106

Karzai, Hamid, Afghan prime
   minister 133
Kelly, Ruth, Secretary for Communi-
   ties 228, 230
Kimmit, Brigadier, US Army 174–5
Kosovo 47, 67
Kropotkin, Peter 126
Kuwait, Salafi activists 106

Laden, Osama bin 75, 107, 154
Laos 82
Latin America 47
Lawrence, T.E. 15, 174
leadership, effect of virtual networks
   on 139–40, 141
Lebanon, Palestinian militants in
   55–6
Lee Hsein Loong, Prime Minister of
   Singapore 104
Liberia 86
local authorities, counter-terrorism
   partnerships 216–18
Local Strategic Partnerships 216
London, 7 July 2005 attacks 117, 197

MacDonagh, Thomas 127–8
McDonald, Kevin, global movements
   153–4
Malaya Emergency 1–2
principles derived from 49–50

Malaysia 32
Malik, Shiv 115
Mallinson, Colonel Alan 246*n*
Mao Tse-tung 15–19
    early campaign 16–17
    operational concept 17–19
Maoist insurgency 9–13, 20
    dissemination 19–23
    end state 153
    and environment 21–2
    as evolutionary milestone 25–6, 27
    and globalised insurgency 26,
        27–8, 78
    ideology 21
    manipulation of grievance 22
    military dimension 223
    as model 35–6
    people's war theory 4, 11, 25–6,
        72, 239*n*
    and popular support 23–4, 28
    populations 17–18, 20–1, 25–6, 28,
        36, 81, 144–5
    response of adversary 22–3
    rivalries 225
    structure 225–6, *225*
    territorial dimension 17, 19, 37
    Western interpretations of 12, 23–5
    *see also* global insurgency; post-
        Maoist insurgency
mass communications 79, 80, 81, 222
    centrality of 96, 231
    and connectedness 92, 93–4
    and diasporas 83, 94, 96, 123, 142
    networks 137–40
    and post-Maoist insurgency 93,
        95, 101
    *see also* communications; media;
        networks
media 32, 34, 93
    fascination with terrorism and
        Islamism 75, 99
    and propaganda of the deed 56,
        79–80, 130, 131, 151, 224, 226
    random news stories 141–2

    state and 92, 93–4, 97, 141,
        249–50*n*
    United States 184
    use of narrative 134
    *see also* mass communications;
        propaganda; virtual dimension
MI5, research document 203–4
Middle East 188
    migrants from 85
migrant communities 78, 79, 223
    Great Britain 108–13
    identity in 119–21, 203, 252*n*
    influence on campaigns 147–8
    isolation in 113–14
    lack of integration 109, 113
    and mass communication 94, 142
    poverty 110, 150
    racial prejudice 109–10, 120
    second and third generations in
        114–17, 120, 202, 252*n*
    *see also* Muslim migrant communi-
        ties
migration 85, 89–90, 99–121, 223
    and climate change 104, 232–3
    and displacement 104, 112
    illegal 194
    Muslim 102–4
    and radical Islam 101
Mohammed, Bakri 117
monopoly of violence 2–3, 180,
    182–3
Morocco 106
multiple populations 83–8, 89–90,
    91–2, 96
    and campaign centre of gravity
        147–8, 256*n*
    in post-Maoist insurgencies 97–8,
        144–8, *146*, 161
    and propaganda of the deed 150–1
Muqtada al Sadr 106
Muslim Brotherhood 106, 158
Muslim Council of Britain 230
Muslim migrant communities 101,
    102, 201

actively disaffected 206–7, 228
effect of Gaza bombing on
214–15, 264n
effect of migration on 108–13
effect of "War on Terror" on 168,
189–90, 194–5, 198, 210
European view of 167, 168
groomed and mentored 207
and Islamism 78, 107, 201
life-changing experience 207
local Muslim organisations
228–30, 265n
Midlands gang culture 115–16,
117, 118, 119
operationally ready 207–8
passively disaffected 206
riots 108, 202
self-radicalised 107, 119
uncommitted 206
see also radicalisation; subversion

narrative
concept of 132–5
strategic 94, 249n
nationalism
and Islamism 106–7, 158
and migrants 103
post-war insurgencies 19–20, 104–5
NATO
failure to recognise post-Maoist
insurgency 164
in Iraq and Afghanistan 3, 6, 48,
167–8
military configuration 66
peacekeeping missions 2, 54
post-Cold War operations 47,
52–4, 62
natural resources 32, 38
exploitation of 90
and globalisation 35
Nepal 38
Maoist insurgency in 95, 262n,
265n
networks 137–40, 141, 163–4, 222

"flows" 137–8, 139–40
hub-core structure 159
and leadership 139–40, 141
and post-Maoist insurgency 156
and power 138
self-starting 224
and self-subversion 152–3
see also vertical structures
non-governmental organisations
(NGOs) 32, 90
Muslim 8, 228–9
Northern Ireland 2, 49, 55
and British military doctrine 65–6,
68, 242n
and Irish diaspora 83
narrative 132–3
peace process 230
and propaganda of the deed
128–30
Northern Ireland Training and
Advisory Team (NITAT) 69
Noujaim, Jehane, Control Room
(documentary) 134

Official Secrets Act 200
Oldham, interracial violence 108
Oman 49
Omand, Sir David 210–12, 263n
O'Neill, Bard 37
Operation CONTEST see
CONTEST
Operation Enduring Freedom 176,
186, 189, 234
Operation Iraqi Freedom 176
Organisation of the Islamic Confer-
ence 102
Orwell, George 92
O'Shaughnessy, Nicholas 131
Othman, Nuiman bin 189
Overseas Development, Department
of (UK) 67
Owsley, Lord, Community Pride not
Prejudice 108

Pakistan, al-Qaeda in 188
Palestine Liberation Organisation
    (PLO) 12, 55–60, 94
    media recognition of 57
    methodology 58
    use of media 123, 131
Palestinians
    diaspora 83, 94
    refugees 55–6
peacekeeping
    in collapsing states 66, 67, 86–7
    dominance of policy 61, 62
    UN forces' role 2
Pearse, Patrick, Irish Republican
    Brotherhood 54, 127–8
Petraeus, General David 223
Policy Exchange 230–1
political leadership 170, 191
politics
    and conduct of wars in Iraq and
        Afghanistan 185–6
    and motives for interventions
        177–8
    and reaction to insurgency 44–5
    and secrecy of CONTEST opera-
        tion 235
popular insurgency 40, 158
population(s)
    categories 145–7
    colonial 83–4
    and conduct of intervening forces
        84–5, 179
    frontline states 82, 145
    intervening states 146–7, 148
    in Maoist insurgency 17–18, 20–1,
        25–6, 28, 36, 81, 144–5
    and mass communications 93–4
    popular support 23–4, 28, 50, 222,
        243n
    and post-modern society 140–1
    reaction to peacekeeping interven-
        tions 88, 173, 179, 180
    role in counter-insurgency 50, 51,
        145

    traumatised 181–2
    see also diasporas; host-state popu-
        lations; multiple populations;
        public opinion
post-Maoist insurgency 59, 78, 79,
    85, 91–2, 143–62
    characteristics 160–2
    co-existing types 157–60
    end state 153–5, 161
    evolution of 190
    and mass communications 93, 95,
        101
    military dimension 155–6
    and multiple populations 97–8,
        144–8, 146, 161
    organisation and structure 159
    as political violence 226
    recognition in doctrine 100
    responses to 135–6, 163–70
    structure 226–7, 226
    see also global insurgency
power
    of ideology 21
    and networks 138
propaganda 24, 130–2
    "multiple exaggerations" 131
propaganda of the deed 124–5,
    126–8, 140, 224, 226
    11 September 2001 attacks as 75
    growing significance 54–60, 231
    and media 56, 58–9, 79–80, 130,
        131
    and multiple populations 150–1
    as operational concept 128–30, 162
    responses to 135–6, 140, 163–70
    used by global insurgents 41, 135,
        162
public opinion, international
    and collapsing states 86
    and costs of wars in Iraq and
        Afghanistan 185–6
    and "global terrorism" 99
    in multiple populations 91
    and propaganda of the deed 58–9

Qadir, Hanif 190, 261

Rabassa, Angel 160
radicalisation, Muslim 113–14,
    115–17, 142, 155
    and activism 4, 107, 207–9
    categories of 205–9
    effect of Global War on Terror on
        189–90, 202
    grooming 205, *205*, 207
    in local communities 215–16
    role of religion in 203–4
rebellion, historical 29, 35, 46
refugees 85–6, 104, 200–1
Reid, John, Home Secretary 228,
    246*n*
religion, factor in radicalisation
    203–4, 256*n*
Rhodesian insurgency 91
Richards, General David 237*n*, 248*n*
Richie, David 108
Ricks, Thomas 171
road bandits 73, *73*
Roman Empire 191
Rufin, Jean-Christophe 28
Rumsfeld, Donald 171–2, 186
rural areas, changes 33
Russian Revolution 15, 126–7

Sadrist movement, Iraq 158
safe havens
    concept of 167, 168, 177
    US view al-Qaeda's 188–9
Sageman, Marc 107, 108
Said Iman (Dr Fadl) 189
Salafi activists 106
    and global jihad 107
September 11 attacks (9/11) *see*
    World Trade Center
shanty towns 33, 34
Shi'a activists 106
Short, Clare, Secretary for Interna-
    tional Development 67, 246*n*
Sidique Khan, Mohammad 117–18

Sierra Leone 68, 86
slogans 132
Smith, General Rupert 242*n*
social change
    and nature of insurgency 10
    pace of 5, 223
society
    post-modern 197
    steps from pre-modern to post-
        modern 136–7
    and virtual networks 136–40
Somalia 38
South Asia 188
    migrant communities from 113–14
Southeast Asia 2, 85
    civil wars 36
Soviet Union, former 30, 36
    *see also* Cold War
Spain, migrants in 103
Spanish civil war 92
Springborg, Robert 105–7, 157–8
Sri Lanka 82
state(s)
    control over media 92, 93–4, 97,
        249–50*n*
    counter-terrorism policies 70, 71–2
    democratic restraints on 46, 191,
        234
    need to adapt to global insurgency
        170
    negative media 141
    over-reaction to insurgency 44
    security organisations 126
    use of propaganda 131
    *see also* collapsing states; Great
        Britain; population(s); United
        States; weak states
Stewart, Rory 52
Stiglitz, Joseph 186
Straw, Jack, Foreign Secretary 228
subversion
    among young Muslim immigrants
        117–21, 202, *205*
    of diasporas 74

Maoist use of 22–3, 26, 239$n$
of multiple populations 149, 150
self- (radicalisation) 151–3
*see also* radicalisation
suicide bombing, psychology of 112
Sun Tzu 25
Sunni insurrectionists 106
superpowers
funding by 28
use of proxies 27
symbolism 132
iconic images 133–4
Syria 55, 82
Islamists in 106

Taliban, attack on Afghan National
Day parade (2008) 133–4
telephones
mobile usage 137, 138, 222
technical revolution 92–3
territory
in British doctrine 50, 57, 58, 59, 64
constraint on US-led interventions
166
and international terrorism 64–5
and limits of rebellion 46
in Maoist insurgency 17, 19, 37
and post-Maoist insurgency 97
and post-modern society 137
terrorism
in British military doctrine 64
globalised 3–4, 6, 26, 64–5, 69–70
as option for insurgent 24–5, 26
policy 66–7, 70–1
popular support for 71, 173
psychology of 112
relationship to insurgency 70–2
risks of 187–8
use of term 198–9
trade
illegal 30, 177
by militias in failing states 28–9, 35
training and assistance missions 175,
176

transnational corporations (TNCs)
32, 103
transport
containers 30, 240$n$
effect of changes 29–30, 85–6
Tugwell, Brigadier Maurice 61, 63,
128–9
Turkey, Islamists in 106

*UK Army Field Manual*
1977 edition 24, 50
1995 edition 24, 50
1996 edition 68
Ummah (Islamic world state),
concept of 106, 158
unemployment, Muslim migrants 110
United Nations
failure of interventions 53, 86–7
and multinational interventions
180–1, 260$n$
peacekeeping framework 67–8,
87, 91
Populations and Climate data 104
rules on interventions 178
Security Council, deployment of
international forces 2
United Nations Training Assistant
Groups (UNTAG) 69
United States
costs of Afghanistan campaign 186
emphasis on national security
187–8, 194
"Global War on Terror" 4, 6–7, 76
international view of 189, 194
Muslims in 168, 194
national interests 192
need for retribution 178
perspective on Afghanistan and
Iraq 6–7, 187–91
relationship with Europe 169
response to 11 September 2001
attacks 75–6, 167–9
response to post-Maoist insurgency 135–6

view of Islamism 105–6
*see also* United States doctrine;
World Trade Center attacks
(9/11)
United States doctrine
2006 counter-insurgency (COIN)
78, 88, 100, 193–4
CENTCOM (2006) 175
counter-insurgency 76
"Federated Insurgency Complex"
139
FM 3–24: 165, 258*n*
National Strategy for Combat-
ing Terrorism 167, 173–5, 187,
189–90, 193
RAND studies 139
urban areas 21–2, 33–4
effectiveness of deeds in 125
Muslim immigrants in 110–11
popular insurgents in 40
urbanisation, in post-colonial states
86
Urry, John 137
US Combined Joint Task Force in
the Horn of Africa (CJTF HOA)
175
US Department of Defense,
Quadrennial Review 174
US–European Command, Counter-
Terrorism Initiative in Trans-
Saharan region 175–6
USAID 176

vertical structures 163
assumed for terrorist organisations
6, 107, 119, 121, 173–4
compared with post-Maoist networks 141, 150, 156, 224
in media 93, 95
in state organisations 97, 138, 166,
170, 227–8
*see also* networks
Vietnam 82, 133, 244*n*
violence

expectation of 125
vmonopoly of 2–3, 180, 182–3
and propaganda of the deed 54
virtual dimension 12, 59, 97, 123–42
and concept of narrative 132–5
insurgent campaign in 149–50
networks 137–40
propaganda 124–32
social context 136–40
*see also* Internet; media
Voice of America 34

Warsaw Pact 66
dissolution (1991) 28, 50
weak states 32, 35, 86
"black hole" areas 177
complexity of interventions 89
feral militias in 72–3
international aid in 29–30
militias in 28–9, 35
peacekeeping in 66, 67, 86–7
*see also* interventions
wealth gap 5, 103
weapons, supply of 29, 38
West Bank (Palestine) 55
West, the
failure to evolve counter-insurgency strategy 42, 74
interpretation of Maoist insurgency 20, 24
surprised by 11 September 2001
attacks 12, 75
*see also* European states; Great
Britain; NATO; United Na-
tions; United States
wilderness, military significance of
21, 29
Wilkinson, Paul 25, 73, 238–9*n*
World Trade Center attacks 11
September 2001 (9/11) 3, 75
recognition as insurgency 100
seen as terrorism 69, 99
US and European priorities 167–9

Western response to 12, 75–6
World Trade Organisation (WTO),
   protests 153–4

Young Muslim Organisation 116
Yugoslavia, former 36

peacekeeping missions 2, 62

al-Zarqawi, Abu Musad, death of
   188
Zarqawiyyin jihadists 106
Al-Zawahiri 96